FICTION IN THE AGE OF PHOTOGRAPHY

∽ NANCY ARMSTRONG ∾

FICTION IN THE
AGE OF PHOTOGRAPHY

The Legacy of British Realism

HARVARD UNIVERSITY PRESS

Cambridge, Massachusetts

London, England

1999

Library of Congress Cataloging-in-Publication Data
Armstrong, Nancy.
Fiction in the age of photography : the legacy of British realism
/ Nancy Armstrong.
p. cm.
Includes bibliographical references (p.) and index.
ISBN 0-674-29930-2 (alk. paper)
1. English fiction—19th century—History and criticism.
2. Realism in literature. 3. Literature and photography—Great
Britain—History—19th century. 4. Literature and photography—
Great Britain—History—20th century. 5. English fiction—20th
century—History and criticism. I. Title.
PR878.R4A76 1999
823'.80912—dc21   99-35660

FOR MY PACK,
LEN AND MAUDE

✑ ACKNOWLEDGMENTS ✑

Sections of Chapters 3, 4, 5, and 6 have appeared in different form in the journals *differences: A journal of feminism and Cultural Studies, Novel: A Forum on Fiction, Narrative,* and *Modernism/Modernity,* respectively. I am grateful to the editors of those journals for permission to include some of this material. Part of Chapter 2 began as a paper for the English Institute in 1995 and appeared as a chapter in *Human, All Too Human* (New York: Routledge, 1996) before assuming its present form. Lindsay Waters and Mary Ellen Geer took excellent care of the manuscript during its review and production, and Bill Rice expertly reproduced many of the prints appearing in the book.

Over the years, a number of colleagues have shared their knowledge of Victorian photography with me. Margaret Homans, Richard Stein, and Andrew Szegedy-Maszek were especially generous in this respect. I must also thank Richard Ohmann and Marie Irene Ramalho de Sousa Santos for their unfaltering support of this project over the years. It took me quite a while to realize that this project was about realism, an old bone I had to pick with Lukács, and for letting me test this insight I am particularly indebted to my graduate students at Brown University. To Rey Chow's coaxing I owe my first clear statement of what became an enabling conviction: that contrary to modernism's view of the Victorians as simple-minded imperialists, the great novelists of the nineteenth century knew exactly what they were doing when they presumed to show a mass readership what was real. Ivan Kreilkamp helped me sift through nineteenth-century journals for the material substantiating this aspect of my argument. My colleagues at Brown—especially Ellen Rooney, Pierre Saint-Amand, and Elizabeth Weed—provided the standard to which I consistently held my imaginary reader, while Len Tennenhouse gave internal coherence and continuity in time to the various fragments of this book and its author.

Oak Bluffs, 1999

≈ CONTENTS ≈

❧ ILLUSTRATIONS ❧

FIGURE 1.1   View from Mr. Repton's cottage, at Harrestreet, before it was improved. Humphry Repton, *Fragments on the Theory and Practice of Landscape Gardening* (London, 1816). Reprinted in J. C. Loudon, *The Landscape Gardening and Landscape Architecture of the Late Humphry Repton, Esq.* (London, 1840). / 64

FIGURE 1.2   View from Mr. Repton's cottage, at Harrestreet, as improved by him. Humphry Repton, *Fragments on the Theory and Practice of Landscape Gardening* (London, 1816). Reprinted in J. C. Loudon, *The Landscape Gardening and Landscape Architecture of the Late Humphry Repton, Esq.* (London, 1840). / 65

FIGURE 2.1   East Hill, Colchester (c. 1860). Gernsheim Collection, Harry Ransom Humanities Research Center, The University of Texas at Austin. / 88

FIGURE 2.2   *Close No. 193, High Street.* Thomas Annan, *The Old Closes and Streets of Glasgow* (1868). / 92

FIGURE 2.3   *Bluegate Fields.* Gustave Doré, *A Pilgrimage* (London, 1872). / 93

FIGURE 2.4   A butcher's shop (c. 1900). National Museum of Photography, Film, and Television. / 97

FIGURE 2.5   *The Temperance Sweep* (c. 1876). John Thomson. Courtesy of George Eastman House. / 99

FIGURE 2.6   *The Crawlers* (1876). John Thomson. Courtesy of George Eastman House. / 100

FIGURE 2.7   *Loading up at Billingsgate Market, Cutout Figure* (c. 1894). Paul Martin. Gernsheim Collection, Harry Ransom Humanities Research Center, The University of Texas at Austin. / 101

Illustrations

Illustrations

Illustrations

xiii

Introduction:
What Is Real in Realism?

THIS BOOK CONSIDERS HOW THE TECHNIQUES WE NOW IDEN-
tify with realism came to dominate Victorian fiction, why we regard
them as the most self-evident of literary techniques, and how, as a
result, we tend to misread realism. To address this literary problem,
I had to confront two well-established arguments hostile to visual
representation. One argument can be traced back to Karl Marx's
famous description of the commodity fetish, which considers mass-
reproduced images deleterious because they keep us from seeing an
object in its original wholeness and specificity. The Frankfurt School
modified this theory of what went wrong with production to explain
what went wrong with cultural reproduction, and from there this
iconophobia subtly but surely found its way into poststructuralist
theory.[1] A second major argument has coalesced over the past three
decades around identity politics—the holy trinity of race, class, and
gender—in England, the United States, and Australia. Proponents of
this argument insist that visual representations of "the body" are
deleterious because they operate as stereotypes to occlude the subjects inhabiting specific bodies.

At the end of the twentieth century, perhaps as never before, we inhabit a reality overdetermined by images, or so most critics of visual culture maintain. Digital technology and electronic communication have collaborated to present today's observer with a flow of images detached from any history of usage and the technical supports that gave rise to them. Their usage may well be so commonplace as to appear only natural, and the technology that originally produced these visual representations is now indeed becoming obsolete. Cultural objects tend to lose contact with the material conditions of their production, undergo transformations resembling the commodification process, and assume a form which is disparagingly called "the image" or "free-floating images."[2] I would agree that cultural objects tend to acquire the appearance of universality as they pass into mass-mediating culture. But, I would also insist, this tendency on the part of modern cultures to convert medium-specific objects into freely circulating images is hardly a new development. Beginning with cheap lithography, followed by the development of the English calotype process and the further refinements of that process that came to be known as photography, people throughout Europe and the United States were confronted with an unprecedented number of images of the world and its peoples. There are clear indications that the literate public greeted each technological advance in this new art of portraiture with at least as much interest as they found in the subject matter. New expressive conventions developed with the technology of the calotype as opposed to the daguerreotype, with fast as opposed to slow exposure time, and with studio as opposed to amateur work, but I will not be dwelling on these. For my purposes as a literary historian, what I will henceforth call "the image" is far more important.

In using this term, I realize full well that I am creating a source of possible confusion, which I will now try to nip in the bud. During the 1970s, literary criticism began to encourage what might be called "images of" studies, a genre of American criticism that is enjoying an undeserved afterlife under the title of "images of women in literature," or some ethnic, racial, gender, or class-based permutation thereof. In defiance of the specifics of the historical moments and mode of cultural production, these studies tend to further the decon-textualizing work of "the image" itself. As a result, the term "image" has an imprecision in English studies that needs correcting. I am interested in identifying the moment when modern cultures gave their literate populations an ample supply of images and unstated rules for using them for purposes of thinking about themselves and their world. These images were produced by individuals of different backgrounds and varying degrees of talent, with their own purposes in mind and with variant materials and methods for achieving these diverse objectives. To do justice to the range of formal distinctions among just the major nineteenth-century photographers would re-quire at least a book; I will deal with such distinctions in passing.

This is a book about Victorian fiction and how "the image"—or, more accurately, a differential system thereof—supplanted writing as the grounding of fiction. Visual culture supplied the social classifica-tions that novelists had to confirm, adjust, criticize, or update if they wished to hold the readership's attention. In my study of the English domestic novel, I explained how novelists defined a certain kind of woman as the only one capable of producing and maintaining a modern, middle-class household.[3] Domestic fiction accomplished this major historical change not by way of reference to a class of women who already ran such a household, but by authorizing the kind of women described in the conduct books of the period. Simi-larly, in establishing a relationship between fiction and photography, I will insist that the kind of visual description we associate with liter-ary realism refers not to things, but to visual representations of things, representations that fiction helped to establish as identical to real things and people before readers actually began to look that way to one another and live within such stereotypes. It is the referent common to both Victorian fiction and photography that I mean by the term "image."

Counter to the argument that mass-reproduced images created an artificial barrier between observers and a reality that antedated and even now lingers behind those images, I will argue that *such images are and have told us what is real for more than a century now.* Our remarkable ability as modern individuals to move in the world and carry the categories we inhabit with us hinges, I believe, on our ability to understand almost anyone and anything in terms of just those categories. By suggesting how they came into being as the components of a comprehensive visual map of a vast and heterogeneous population, I have tried to combat the assumption that we can get rid of harmful stereotypes simply by refusing to think in terms of mass-produced images. If it is by differentiating ourselves from one or more of these stereotypes that one acquires individuality, then without them we would have no identity, or at least no modern identity. And if, as I am assuming, getting rid of stereotypes is virtually impossible, then in order to deal with the stubborn divisions we rightly feel these images produce within and among groups of human beings, it is imperative for us to acquire a more sophisticated understanding of what they are, where they came from, and how they acquired so much power. To this end, I examine nineteenth-century British culture as the time when and the place where image and object began to interact according to the rules and procedures commonly called "realism." In thinking of literary realism as fiction's anticipation of and reaction to the sudden proliferation of transparent and reproducible images that marks the mid-Victorian period, I will also suggest how a differential system of such images became basic psychological equipment for that readership and their definitive way of classifying both things and people.

From time to time, literary scholarship has floated the question of what if anything is real about Victorian realism, but I believe that investigation should be pushed significantly further than scholars have been willing to go. From the importance that visual evidence assumes in Victorian literature of all kinds, the fact that images can serve iconically for whatever they represent, one can infer that Victorians willingly participated in a change of reading practices that eventually turned conventional mimesis on its ear. Beginning in the late 1850s, new literary techniques and new technologies of seeing promised to bring the reader ever closer to the material world. In order to do so, however, these same techniques and technologies reversed the traditional relationship between image and object observed. The so-called material world to which Victorians were apparently so committed was one they knew chiefly through transparent images, images which in turn seemed to bring them conceptual and even physical control over that world. It was to cash in on the giddy expansion of referential possibilities afforded by the reversal of the mimetic priority of original over copy that fiction developed the repertoire of techniques most commonly associated with realism. When a novel such as *Bleak House* refers to the street people and dilapidated tenements of nineteenth-century London, that novel is actually referring to what either was or would become a photographic commonplace. But if this mutually authorizing relationship between fiction and photography was so obvious to Victorian readers as I am suggesting, then why did it not become a commonplace of literary history?

The Pictorial Turn

In fact, whenever some critic addresses the question of realism and what makes it real or not, we will find the impact of popular images registering in literary criticism, provided we know how to recognize it. In his preface to *Studies in European Realism,* Georg Lukács charges realism with the sacred duty of maintaining "the organic, indissoluble connection between man as a private individual and man as a social being, a member of a community."[4] His study of the historical novel identifies 1848 as the year when the novel abandoned this mission. Lukács blames this failure on a sudden infusion of "ornamental detail," "immobile background," "pictorialism," "picturesque atmosphere," and "photographic authenticity" which fiction slipped in between readers and the social world around them.[5] More recent studies of the novel describe realism much as Lukács did—as exposing the brutal social order sometimes obscured by an increasingly complex and fluctuating economy. Yet, despite this common ground, those who write on the novel today generally assume that realism was just coming into its own in 1848, the very moment when Lukács claimed it had begun its downward spiral. Whether one sees the second half of the nineteenth century as the age in which realism flowered rather than as the period of its decline depends entirely on the literary historian's attitude toward images and whether visual description prevents or provides access to the realities of modern urban existence. Critics from Ian Watt and Harry Levin to George Levine, Elizabeth Ermarth, D. A. Miller, Naomi Schor, and Michael Fried understand the Victorian novel as the culmination of a tradition that was part and parcel of the modernization process itself.[6] Each acknowledges that the novel's use of painterly technique, perspective, detail, spectacle, or simply an abundance of visual description served to create, enlarge, revise, or update the reality shared by Victorian readers. Indeed, today many of us would hold the very kind of description we associate with realism at least partly responsible for changing the terms in which readers imagined their relation to the real.

But what do we make of the fact that the novel's turn to pictorialism coincided with the sudden ubiquity of photographic images in the culture at large? Why did *pictures* begin to speak louder than words? Even our most sophisticated explanations of realism continue to beg this question. In his well-known discussion of reification, Fredric Jameson argues that "the ultimate form of commodity reification in contemporary consumer society is precisely the image itself."[7] In his view, we will never grasp what he calls "an increasing, tendential, all-persuasive visuality as such" so long as we simply rail against mass culture and yearn for the relation to objects we imagine to have existed prior to commodification.[8] Whenever we define the objects worthy of analysis in opposition to reproducible images, we simply enhance the allure of commodity culture. To resist that allure, Jameson urges us to subject "the image" itself to historical analysis. I accept the proposition that to understand the power of visuality and to discover how it emerged and gained authority in modern culture are essentially the same task. But I do not think this can be done in quite the way Jameson proposes, namely, by examining the emergence and development of popular cinema.

As I have already suggested, what might be called the rise of the photograph was under way a good half-century before the motion picture was even on the drawing board. Until that moment, European fiction may actually have stuck to the task that Lukács assigned it and told the story of class struggle out of which both a modern middle class and an imperial nation state were going to emerge. But by the late 1840s, about the time Dickens was becoming England's favorite author, fiction had begun to turn in another direction and was devising a new set of formal procedures for just this purpose. One's family and religion and manner of speaking no longer proved sufficient bases for assigning that individual a place within the new social order. Written in 1852–1853, a novel like *Bleak House* demonstrates the conceptual muddiness of social identities once they had mingled in the streets of London, only to offer a finite number of visual fields in which virtually everyone could be placed. The same demand that encouraged fiction to turn to certain kinds of visual description during the 1850s was also responsible for the rapid production and wide dissemination of photographic images. Victorian fiction was the first English fiction, I am suggesting, to convert a particular kind of visual information—infinitely reproducible and capable of rapid and wide dissemination—into what was both a way of seeing and a picture of the world that a mass readership could share. The following propositions attempt to reconceptualize literary realism in relation to the new medium of photography, whose privileged relationship to the modern city that fiction simultaneously foresaw and emulated.

> *Proposition 1:* By the mid-1850s, fiction was already promising to put readers in touch with the world itself by supplying them with certain kinds of visual information.
> *Proposition 2:* In so doing, fiction equated seeing with knowing and made visual information the basis for the intelligibility of a verbal narrative.
> *Proposition 3:* In order to be realistic, literary realism referenced a world of objects that either had been or could be photographed.

Proposition 4: Photography in turn offered up portions of this world to be seen by the same group of people whom novelists imagined as their readership.

I have taken care not to suggest that England was awash with photographs of every important genre during the 1850s, when Lukács pinpoints the onset of an encroaching pictorialism. Indeed, the images distributed during the 1840s and 1850s were mostly daguerreotypes, and these were generally portraits of respectable people rather than denizens of the busy city streets and sordid tenements. Thus the sequence of my propositions is meant to indicate that, when it came to portraying disreputable places and people, fiction often came first and referred to things and people in a way that would only later materialize as a familiar genre of photography.

Fiction could not have taken the pictorial turn to the extent or in the way it did, were its readership not already hungry for certain kinds of visual information. This fact is not in dispute. There are, however, at least two different explanations for evidence of photographic desire before the fact. One traces the origins of photography back from Louis Daguerre and William Henry Fox Talbot to the lithography and line drawings that had become a burgeoning business in the decades before the discovery of modern photographic technology.[9] This account observes the one visual medium ceding naturally to the other as the two existed side by side and interchangeably with each other until the 1870s, when photography became substantially cheaper and more accessible. This explanation is troubled, however, by the fact that various men and women of science, art, and manufacturing were known to have been experimenting with methods of taking images directly from objects well before 1802, when Thomas Wedgwood was reported to have copied images onto glass. Geoffrey Batchen argues compellingly that the discovery of the photographic process was not a cause but an effect of more than a century of extremely ingenious individuals wishing to capture and produce absolutely unmediated images, a wish that could at first perhaps be attributed to a few quirky intellectuals but which quickly became what Batchen calls "a universal imperative" once the technology was available.[10] There are indeed ample indications to suggest that the nineteenth-century readership saw it Batchen's way. That is to say, they understood the advent of mass visuality as something that had been in the works for over a century by the time photographic studios opened up in all the major towns and photographs began to bring the world to readers on pieces of paper the size of playing cards.

An 1867 essay entitled "Photography: Its History and Applications" begins by describing photography as "a fact of the day" whose "origin, growth, and variety of application have had no parallel in the history of the graphic and pictorial arts." This history credits Thomas Wedgwood, "the celebrated potter," and Sir Humphry Davy, who "had assisted in the experiments," with having "discovered but half the spell; the pictures could not be fixed."[11] At the same time, this account sees even Wedgwood and Davy's experiments with visual reproduction as the expression of an attempt to fix the image that begins "as early as the sixteenth century."[12] Another essay from the same period, entitled "A Suppressed Art," represents the prehistory of photography as something of a scandal. The estate of one Matthew Boulton, regular host to the infamous Lunar Society which boasted Thomas Wedgwood among its members, contained "two curious pictures, which bore a strong resemblance to photographs; and two other pictures on copper plated with silver, that were undoubtedly of a class precisely the same as those commonly known as daguerreotypes."[13] Lady Elizabeth Eastlake, something of an expert on the new art of photography, observes that although the images of Daguerre and Talbot have made the English readership feel "the existence of a power, availing itself of the eye of the sun both to discern and to execute," that same readership has yet to acknowledge "the unclaimed and unnamed legacy of our own Sir Humphry Davy."[14] Coming at the history of photography with quite different purposes in mind, these various critics nevertheless assume that history extends back well before Daguerre's and Talbot's discoveries.[15] Such accounts assume, further, that the desire to fix an unmediated image of an object has a purely English origin.

The history of literary realism is no less hypothetical than the history of photography. In describing the production of a new visual order, my argument assumes there is no work of Victorian realism pure and simple about which we now care all that much. The novels of Mrs. Gaskell, Benjamin Disraeli, and Mrs. Humphry Ward are the first that come to mind of a second tier of fiction that more than occasionally strives for a documentary effect. A study of realism might very well read Charles Dickens, George Eliot, and Thomas Hardy in relation to these lesser figures in order to show that they all have a similar purpose in mind. My own study pursues another tack, however, on the assumption that conventional historicism significantly misrepresents what realism actually accomplished. I believe that Lukács is indeed partly right in claiming that realism began to disappear at almost the same moment it came into being. As a result, any novel that sought to offer an accurate representation of social conditions in the manner of Disraeli or Ward holds relatively little interest for all but a handful of specialized scholars today. At the same time, it is also true that such authors as Dickens and Gaskell did usher in a moment in literary history that extended well into the twentieth century. During this period, everyone knew what realism was; authors wrote in relation to it, and readers read with a standard in mind based on the fidelity of language to visual evidence. Indeed, we still recognize this kind of writing as realism today.

This book will consider several genres of fiction, most of which are usually discussed in opposition to realism. My point is to show that it is precisely their violation of the visual standard that prompts us to classify *Wuthering Heights, Alice's Adventures in Wonderland, The Picture of Dorian Gray,* or *King Solomon's Mines* as romance and fantasy. There is no doubt in my mind that these novels, as emphatically as any scene from Dickens, defined what was real in terms of what could and would eventually be depicted by a photographic image. As I use the term, then, realism does not indicate a genre or mode of writing that strives to document actual social conditions by means of visual description. On the contrary, the documentary effect is only one result of the collaboration between fiction and photography. By "realism," I mean the entire problematic in which a shared set of visual codes operated as an abstract standard by which to measure one verbal representation against another. I believe it is accurate to situate not only works of romance and fantasy within this problematic, but literary modernism as well. No less dependent on a visual definition of the real than Victorian realism, modernism nevertheless located whatever it considered authentic in nature or culture within an invisible domain on the other side of the surfaces one ordinarily sees. Indeed, it was in order to lay claim to this greater realism beyond the conventional that modernism reduced the category of realism to a caricature of its former self—a futile attempt at documentary fidelity to the object world. By thus reducing realism to a genre, modernism did not situate itself historically beyond the limits of realism but squarely within the same problematic with the very writing it deemed superficial.

While the works of realism I will be discussing do not attempt to "reflect" an extratextual reality, this is certainly not to say they had no relation to that reality. In collaboration not only with photography but with many other cultural products of their moment as well, these novels made the world intelligible to a mass readership in an entirely new yet seemingly mimetic way. Although I focus on kinds of fiction that emerged between the late 1840s and the 1920s in apparent violation of visual norms, I have no intention of trotting out these novels and reading them in a historical sequence. What is important about the kinds of fiction I have chosen are the territories of mind and world geography they render legible in visual terms—the city, the Celtic fringe, the colonies, territories attractive to the camera as well. In mapping out a historical paradigm, in other words, this book will in some respects mirror the very spatial structure I want to elaborate. This story cannot be told as a linear narrative; it was neither in a day nor by an orderly sequence spanning Victoria's reign that this spatial structure made the world intelligible to readers. Various fields of vision formed by a process of accumulation that thickened what were merely images into tangible spaces. At the same time, this same process differentiated any one such space from all others in the system. The visual order that resulted began to determine such basic principles of modern life as how a city or countryside or colony should look, where and how it felt right to live, and who could not possibly belong to one's kin group.

Photography's Object

Although Louis Daguerre clearly won the race for a process that could chemically reproduce the light traces of objects on photosensitive material, I am somewhat arbitrarily identifying the invention of photographic technology with William Henry Fox Talbot's publication of *The Pencil of Nature* in 1844. For the purposes of a project on literary realism, I am less interested in the technological competition between the two men and their ability to eclipse what may well have been a host of predecessors than in the fact that Talbot and those few who purchased rights to use his method established the format, the kind of subject matter, and the aesthetic issues that would be popularized by the new medium. Larry J. Schaaf writes that by the 1860s, when photographic images had thoroughly saturated the cultural scene,

> Henry Talbot and Louis Daguerre had unwittingly traded places. Each eventually met his rival's goal. Daguerre was the public communicator and it would be fair to assume that his pursuit of the daguerreotype was initially motivated by a desire to bring ever more realistic images to his audiences. Ironically, what he created was the most intimate of all photographic representations, a precious and shiny little plate under glass. Henry Talbot, on the other hand, started with the goal of making an amateur sketch for his own use. He eventually achieved something far greater—one of the most powerful mass communication mediums ever devised.[16]

On a trip to Italy in 1833, by his own account, Talbot tried sketching the landscape on a piece of paper mounted within a camera obscura, a popular drawing device that projected a reverse image on a piece of paper within a darkened box so that someone with a modicum of talent could sketch it in. To improve on the murky image projected in the darkened box, Talbot's friend John Herschel had begun drawing prolifically and well with the aid of a camera lucida. This device was little more than a small prism set atop a brass stem that one adjusted until the view before him struck his eye. To copy that image, the sketcher had only to move his eye until he could also see the paper on the drawing board before him. Upon trying out this instrument, Talbot found that the camera lucida only compounded the effects of his poor draftsmanship with those of his failing eyesight, and this sense of deficiency gave rise to a wish to eliminate the inept sketcher's hand and eye completely, a fantasy that perfectly observes the logic of the camera obscura: "how charming it would be if it were possible to cause these natural images to imprint themselves durably, and remain fixed upon the paper." In imagining this possibility, Talbot figured out the physics of photography:

> The picture, divested of the ideas which accompany it, and considered only in its ultimate nature, is but a succession or variety of stronger lights thrown upon one part of the paper, and of deeper shadows on another. Now Light, where it exists, can exert an action, and, in certain circumstances, does exert one sufficient to cause changes in material bodies. Suppose, then, such an action could be exerted on the paper; and suppose the paper could be visibly changed by it. In that case surely some effect must result having a general resemblance to the cause which produced it: so that the variegated scene of light and shade might leave its image or impression behind.[17]

On returning to England, Talbot began a protracted set of experiments with paper laid on glass plates and brushed with a solution of silver salts in varying strengths, until he finally discovered what solution would give the paper enough light sensitivity to record the light rays bouncing off the object and yet not enough to blacken the entire paper. The result was an image with the tonalities of light and dark reversed. Early in 1839, he developed the technique for "photogenic drawing" when he placed light-sensitive paper beneath the negative and re-exposed that image to sunlight. By 1841, he had perfected the "calotype" method which shortened exposure time, applied solutions that allowed the image to "develop" on its own, and then permanently fixed both negatives and the images printed from them. Despite this remarkable sequence of personally motivated and seemingly accidental discoveries, by the time Talbot relinquished his patent on the calotype in 1852, another Englishman had already developed the more efficient collodion glass-plate negative. Although this process rendered Talbot's virtually obsolete at the moment it went public, the collodion glass-plate process incorporated and immortalized the fantasy driving Talbot's discovery of the calotype—a "natural image" that could imprint itself directly and durably on paper.

To the success of this fantasy for making apparently unmediated copies from a negative image, we owe our assumption that visibility and invisibility come to us in relative degrees of light and shadow that are technically interchangeable rather than in the variegated metallic sheen of the daguerreotype. To the triumph of the technology that fulfilled the wish for unmediated mediation, we also owe the tremendous variety of subsequent technical and aesthetic experiments that flourished in the second half of the nineteenth century. As Abigail Solomon-Godeau points out, "the calotype was not a rigidly codified technology, but, on the contrary, encompassed a broad range of variation and individual experimentation in the preparation of the negative, the papers used, the chemistry, the development, and the printing."[18] The medium that granted the wish for unmediated mediation would therefore prove a highly mediating one.

The process Talbot bequeathed to posterity allowed Victorian photographers to visualize chunks of the world that a person was not likely to see were he or she simply to look at the world in all its radical diversity. Such refinements as the panoramic lens and rapid exposure allowed the camera to focus on certain details in ways that immediately came to be seen as so many properties of its subject matter. At the same time, Talbot's process yielded a picture that seemed capable, through repetition, of representing the visible world as it actually was, whole and entire.

By extending our field of vision and yet presenting consumers with something already seen, the calotype simultaneously incited and thwarted a historically new desire to make contact with the world itself—a desire for documentary evidence of some person, place, or event—or what might be called archival desire. Amassing visual information invariably called attention to bad information which the archive failed to exclude as well as to good information for which the archive had no place within its classificatory system. I will try to explain the epistemological conundrum of realism by considering what happened when two Victorian scientists turned to photography to provide each with a method of reading the social world that would pass the test of reality. This comparison will, I hope, shed some light on the entire problematic of visuality that includes not only Victorian fiction but literary modernism and, ultimately, contemporary cultural studies as well.

What Derrida calls "archive fever" begins as a wish to locate some originary and patriarchal form of authority, at once to preserve and to make it public.[19] We make a home for this authority through a gathering of signs that aims at consolidating a single corpus whose elements are bound together as by an ideal unity. In order for the archive so constituted to authorize those who reproduce the materials it contains, the authenticity and unity of the archive must be unimpeachable. For a historical instance of such a fantasy, one can go almost anywhere in Victorian culture. With England's expansion into Asia and Africa, literate people apparently found it irresistible to imagine the Empire itself as an archive. It must have struck them as far easier to unify an archive made of texts than an empire made of diverse territories and disparate peoples. The archive so conceived "was not a building, nor even a collection of texts," according to

Thomas Richards, "but the collectively imagined junction of all that was known or knowable, a fantastic representation of an epistemological master pattern."[20] Here, then, we encounter a mutually defining relationship between "realism" and "reality" as the structure of the archive. If the archive is a house within the empire, and the empire is an archive contained within a house, then realism is at once a text that reproduces its context and a context that reproduces its text. In both cases, we confront a system of representation that observes the paradoxical logic of the Möbius strip, striving at once to put its inside on the outside and to contain its outside within itself.

Taken at face value, the photograph is the purest of archival documents, in that it maintains a special closeness to whatever original it happens to copy.[21] Indeed, the photograph's incontestable frame, the legitimacy deriving from the bond it establishes with its subject matter, its seeming frankness and internal unity identify it as an ekphrasis for the archive itself. But there is a corrosive side to archival desire, and photography pictures this for us as well. As Derrida explains, the archive contains the theory of its own institutionalization, essential to which are the rules determining what the archive must contain in order to be complete and what must be kept out in order for it to seem unified.[22] The wish to contain the outside on the inside cuts a paradoxical figure through every medium and discipline that feels the need to ground itself in a reality outside itself. That tautology compels us both to house the authentic origins of knowledge and to expose that housing to the public in a way that ultimately admits its retrospective construction. Early attempts to create photographic archives ran aground on just this internal contradiction.

In "The Body and the Archive," Allan Sekula compares two well-known, concerted efforts to create a system of photographs capable of identifying those members of urban society prone to crime: one by the Parisian police officer Alphonse Bertillon, the other by the English statistician and eugenicist Francis Galton.[23] Sekula's research is instructive, first, because it demonstrates how quickly the heterogeneous populations congealing around certain metropolitan centers were overcome with an intense desire for visual mastery. This desire extended well beyond criminology to the surveying of the Asian subcontinent and the statistical mapping of England's metropolitan and rural subgroups.[24] Most important to this project, however, were the production and circulation of hundreds of millions of *cartes de visite* familiarizing consumers not only with the more inaccessible pockets of empire but with respectable Europe and North America as well. Between 300 and 400 million of these photographic portraits were sold in England from 1861 to 1867 alone.[25] These images presumed to offer such an accurate reading of the human body that just on the basis of that reading, one could assign any body to its proper category. People came to visualize themselves and others not only in terms of gender, class, race, and nation, but in terms of intelligence, morality, and emotional stability as well. The new sciences of identity—by which I mean all the human sciences, as well as physiognomy, phrenology, and criminology—invariably used photographic technology to make the body legible.

Both Bertillon and Galton proceeded from the positivist assumptions that truth is in the body to be read, that all bodies are equivalent, and that the features distinguishing one from the other can therefore be statistically determined. Bertillon imagined the body novelistically. He thought that history—in the form of work, war, accidents, and habitat—inscribed itself indelibly on the body and could be detected amidst the mutable features, assumed positions, and false stories which the criminal used to conceal his or her true identity. Assuming that a good many crimes were committed by repeat offenders, Bertillon constructed a filing system for photographic portraits to catch each criminal the second time around. Intent on extracting the individual from the species, he created categories based on the exact proportions of various body parts. He developed the deadpan frontal and profile poses now known as mug shots to capture those features free of the variables of facial expression, clothes, angle, or lighting. Upon apprehending a suspect, the police took his or her photograph and then tried to match it to a portrait within the archive. Given his reliance on matching one photograph with another, Bertillon's method might strike us as a rigorously anti-essentialist identification system. As the cards in the police files swelled to tens of thousands, however, the police could hardly survey each and every portrait on file in search of a possible match. Thus Bertillon took to measuring certain body parts and facial features in terms of their distance from abstract images that provided the categories for a filing system that could quickly be consulted for a match. Enter modern essentialism. The police no longer matched photograph to photograph; instead, they matched photograph to an idealized image which began to seem more primary than either individuals or their portraits.

Galton began with a contrastingly poetic notion of what made bodies legible.[26] According to the eugenicist, inborn tendencies and hereditary traits within the body determined the kind of life an individual was destined to live. To read for this inborn and transindividual kernel of identity, Galton rejected the kind of nominalism embraced by Bertillon. As he explained, any method that relies on particular photographs is bound to be "swayed by exceptional and grotesque features more than by ordinary ones, and the portraits supposed to be typical are likely to be caricatures."[27] To subdue the inessential features made visible in mug shots, he constructed a camera that could take twelve different portraits on the same plate, giving each one-half the normal exposure time. By means of these composite portraits, he reasoned, only the features that each individual shared with his type would dominate the image. Galton soon discovered, however, that real people invariably differed from all of the images he had produced, so that establishing the identity of actual individuals was likely to run aground on the problem of genre, or what type we should read an individual body as a variation on.

Where Bertillon attempted to place each photo within an infinitely expandable differential system, Galton tried to contain that system within the frame of a single photograph.[28] As they sought to reduce visual information to those traces of the body that would produce their respective readings, however, both fulfilled the paradox of the archive. Although the traces they sought in photographs were indeed traces of what might be called actual bodies, and even though both methods were granted considerable credibility in their day, no actual body could validate the visual information of the photograph. Thus any attempt to read actual bodies as if they were photographs was doomed to fail, whether because there were too many bodies, as in Bertillon's filing system, or because there were too few or none at all that clearly conformed to one of Galton's multilayered portraits. In both cases, photography, as a method of reading, reversed the priorities of object over image, so that the image usurped the position of the individual body as the basis for legibility.

Given its repeated failure to offer an empirically valid picture of the world beyond itself, why, we must ask, was photography so successful? It can be argued that photography allowed literate Europeans not only to share a notion of the real, but also to feel they were in touch with and could negotiate a world undergoing modernization at an ever-increasing pace. From 1850 on, photographs themselves indicate that the rapid proliferation of new and exotic faces and figures fueled a compensatory need to receive new information in utterly familiar ways. Thus as the subject matter for these little portraits increased in scope and variety, the kind of shot grew more predictable.[29] The difference between a family portrait and a mug shot became as clear as that distinguishing a celebrity from a native or a sentimental figure from the target of lampoon, as photographs offered either normative or distinctively disfigured images of European respectability. The constant influx of visual material thus reproduced, revised, and revitalized a multitude of subdivisions within both respectable culture and its criminal underworld to create what operated as an immense shadow archive, or visual order of things. Despite their repeated failure to receive validation from bodies themselves, the generic images marking various positions within the visual order acquired the rhetorical force of nature and common sense at once.

The structure of a device called a stereoscope or stereopticon allows me to suggest, by way of analogy, how the visual order of things acquired the status of the order of things themselves. Like the *carte de visite,* the stereograph is a two and a half by four-inch photograph mounted on cardboard backing. The stereograph differs from the *carte* only in that stereographs come in pairs, each of which reproduces exactly the same object at just about the same time, but from two slightly different angles. The viewer positions these photographs at the end of a stereoscope whose lens superimposes the two, just as the brain superimposes the two images of a single object produced when we look at that object with both eyes. The result is depth, roundness, solidity. Seen through the lens of a stereoscope, two flat stereographs converge to form what appears to be a three-dimensional object. What if these photographs repeated certain features of a type in the manner of Galton's mechanism for superimposing multiple exposures, but with all their individual peculiarities still intact? Could these *cartes* have achieved something like the stereoscopic effect, even though they didn't come in pairs precisely calibrated to produce a three-dimensional object?

True, the sheer repetition of shots, say, of a cityscape or a group of aborigines, made seeing a very different activity from the experience of looking through a stereoscope, whose object emerged from images designed so as to reproduce their referent for the viewer by means of a contraption appropriate for parlor use and private entertainment. This apparatus distinguished the viewing of stereoscopic photographs from viewing either ordinary photographs or objects in the world, and it defined the objects it produced as marvelous artifices, parlor tricks, or experiments as opposed to ordinary objects. By way of contrast, consuming *cartes* and other brands of popular photography appeared to be a rather haphazard process more in keeping with the way we ordinarily look at the world. But through the photograph's uncanny ability to make its subject matter seem both unique and utterly predictable, the consumer of this visual information would nevertheless have recognized a given category of subject matter simply by recognizing the pose, a few background details, and a constellation of physical features. What first caught the viewer's eye was not the unique object of each photograph. Instead, each example conjured up for the consumer a type or category, one of a system of such categories capable of classifying virtually everything that could be seen and on this basis considered real. Thus an entire epistemology of knowing imperceptibly installed itself in readers' imaginations along with the images that allowed them to identify virtually anything that either had been or could be rendered as a photograph. On the assumption that a natural predisposition toward certain forms of behavior would be apparent on the surface of the body so disposed, Victorian social scientists took to photographing the faces and bodies of criminals, whores, the indigent, the homeless, and mentally disturbed individuals, hoping to identify the visual signature of their social pathologies. While few of these efforts proved empirically reliable, I am convinced that as members of a culture immersed in such photographs saw one shot after another of a given kind, all shot in approximately the same way, yet each capturing a unique moment and specific subject, a finite number of visual categories acquired the power to identify almost every person, place, or thing.

As the subject matter of empire grew more diverse, the generic protocols for classifying, posing, shooting, and naming that subject matter grew increasingly predictable. At the point where what consumers looked for was the category itself, any particular photograph would serve as just so much more material evidence. Each new photograph not only repeated a composite or prototypical image of families, celebrities, criminals, street people, natives of the world, and so forth, but each photograph also made that image seem capable of accounting for new and variant details. Such accumulation created sets of objects embodying the categories that organized the visual world. As Bertillon discovered, particular photographs become meaningful only in relation to a generic image. When one has observed a sufficient number of similar mug shots, that observer will perform synthesizing procedures resembling those Galton developed to produce his combination portraits and grant the image itself the thickness, the very body, of a criminal. But the ordinary process of consuming photographs had certain advantages over Galton's method. Where he strove to rid the image of the details that kept it faithful to a particular object, the ordinary viewer took pleasure in that very kind of visual information, so long as it was contained within a familiar framework.[30] Indeed, any such image acquires substance and vitality from the individual differences necessarily incorporated within the mug shot or, for that matter, within any photographic genre. If not reproduced with a difference, a category tends to die.

This is precisely what popular photography did for the visual spaces constituting the modern world and the varieties of human beings who could occupy them. To say that somebody has a female body, a black body, or any culturally marked body at all, is at once to acknowledge and to substantiate an image resembling the stereoscopic image-object. To put it yet another way, *cartes de visite* operated within an entirely different symbolic economy from the one that scientists and social scientists sought to establish. These little portraits acquired their meaning, not in relation to the body and by virtue of their resemblance to actual persons, places, and things, but strictly within a system of images and by virtue of their difference from all other images in that system.

Realism's Subject

This extensive and systematic reversal of original and copy never could have occurred across the entire range of modern cultural production, were it not for the fact that this same set of images also provided modern middle-class men and women with a means of recognizing themselves as such. The iconography of the period clearly shows that individuals were "hailed" into various social categories, more by recognizing themselves in an image than, as Althusser assumes, by recognizing themselves as the target of "a verbal call or whistle."[31] Similarly, I would argue, Lacan's allegory of the mirror phase subtly avoids the problem posed when his struggle for and against a coherent and autonomous identity is kicked into gear by the child's identification of himself with a mirror image toward which he staggers instinctively: "Unable as yet to walk, or even to stand up, and held tightly as he is by some support . . . he neverthe-less overcomes, in a flutter of jubilant activity, the obstructions of his support and, fixing his attitude in a slightly leaning-forward position, in order to hold it in his gaze, brings back an instantaneous aspect of the image."[32] All of us must quite literally *see* ourselves as separate, fully integrated and entire objects, Lacan contends, before we can begin to develop relations as such with a world of people and things outside and other than ourselves. The image in the mirror provides, in this respect, the foundation for both the individual's interiority and the position he or she will actually occupy within the symbolic order. The image Lacan has in mind in this early essay is the image of a child which belongs to a specific child simply because it reflects his natural body. Only by so positioning his exemplary child before a mirror can Lacan avoid the very questions raised when he places so much theoretical weight on the existence of such a self-image: what image? whose image? from whence did it come? why does the child embrace it as himself? Were we, however, to substitute the photo-graph for the mirror in Lacan's account of how the individual ac-quires an identity, we would suddenly improve the chances of under-standing our unique ability as modern individuals to locate and maintain ourselves in an increasingly fluid and heterogeneous social order.

The photograph I have in mind is not any particular photograph but something much more like the generic images on which both Galton and Bertillon depended for identifying individual portraits. Even if a particular photograph were to provide a mirror for certain individuals, that photograph can hail us only insofar as it reproduces with canny accuracy an image in terms of which we have already been seen. Moreover, even though we wear one image or another, no image ever fits exactly; the product of misrecognition, this image is something we have, or wear, or perform, or disavow, rather than what we are. Driven to close the gap between themselves and some original state of full being, modern individuals layer variant reproductions between themselves as they are at a given moment and the founda-tional image they imagine themselves once to have been. The greater the gap, Lacan would argue, the more urgently one wants to close it. Since all our attempts to do so are destined not only to fail, but therefore also to repeat themselves, we will always have plenty of bad and simply irrelevant material to slough off in the retroactive process by which we endeavor to remain consistent with ourselves. Throughout Victorian culture, but especially in its fiction and photography, we find evidence to suggest that, with the advent of mass visuality, a member of this culture would have been forced to negotiate a rapid shift from an identity based on identification ("that's me") to an identity based on difference ("that's not me").

In his later work, Lacan himself makes something like this move, according to Kaja Silverman, when he "refers to [the representation on which the subject relies for visual identity] as a 'screen' rather than a mirror reflection. Rather than simply misrecognizing him- or herself within the screen, the subject is now assumed to rely for his or her structuring access to it on an . . . unlocalizable gaze, which for over 150 years now has found its most influential metaphor in the camera."[33] Rereading Lacan's early version of "the mirror phase" in terms of this later refinement, Silverman identifies the mother's gaze as the power that connects the child's look with the image in the mirror producing the misrecognition that founds his identity. Where Silverman would stress the transhistorical form of the dynamic whereby the individual takes up this self-defining relation to an image, my own analysis leans heavily in the other direction—toward the history of the process by means of which late nineteenth-century culture became saturated with certain kinds of images. Only then, in my opinion, would it seem plausible to link the mother's gaze not only with the specific technology of the camera but also with the ubiquitous surveillance characterizing modern institutions. Indeed, for all we know, it took the advent of mass visual culture along with the invigilating structure Michel Foucault describes in *Discipline and Punish* to produce subjects whose formation begins with an identification with an image and involves them in a lifelong attempt to maintain that relationship. When Jeremy Bentham envisioned the criminal captured in a hive of individuated cells and illuminated by the light from a window behind him, where he could be seen at any moment by a nameless, faceless observer at the center of this model institution, Foucault contends, he was imagining both a new method of subject formation and the means of enforcing it. Bentham's panopticon at once conceptualizes the subject photographically and makes sure the subject will conceptualize himself that way. In so doing, the panopticon suggests why it took the reconception of the nation as a population that included not only the most abject of city dwellers but the peoples of Africa and Asia as well to make the identities formed in modern institutions—home and schoolroom, as well as prison and workhouse—depend on another, debased and racially marked version of themselves.

The early Lacan allows us to imagine just how culturally disseminated images might have entered into that individual's development by providing a self-image he could either replicate or violate, but with which he had to struggle for a lifetime either way. His later work suggests what might have happened to modern individuals with the shift from identification to difference as the principle on which they depended for membership in the new visual order. Assuming they begin as a mix of categorical possibilities—neither male nor female, black nor white, of high social status or of low, and so forth—individuals become complex and reasonably coherent bearers of certain of these attributes as they abject, or cast out of themselves, many of the features of race, class, and gender their culture had made available for this purpose, some of which are the basis of past identifications. We may display only those attributes that feel consistent with our respective identities. But giving up such bits and pieces of ourselves is not a negation strictly speaking so much as an internalization of the outcast image, thus its preservation as a part we must continue to disavow.[34] By means of the repeated act of disavowal that maintains the integrity of one's self-image, we constitute another body and an opposing set of practices that must remain external to ourselves, lest the negated attributes destroy our hard-won sense of a stable position within the visual order. What Lacan means by the symptom embodies this negative self-definition. Rather than threaten the individual's integrity and durability, it maintains whatever difference the culture has decreed most fundamental to that individual over time. Were the symptom to dissolve, the individual itself would necessarily disintegrate. Thus to say that woman is the symptom of man, as Lacan does, or that the native is the symptom of the Westerner, as Rey Chow does, is to acknowledge that men and Westerners cannot exist as such without women and natives.[35] As Victorian photography established the categories of identity—race, class, gender, nation, and so forth—in terms of which virtually all other peoples of the world could be classified, literary realism showed readers how to play the game of modern identity from the position of observers.[36] Maintaining their difference from those who did not occupy this position was paramount. Maintaining that difference transformed their images of other people into the secret core of Western individuality.

The critical tradition may ask us to think of photographic realism as one of many subvarieties of Victorian realism, but I am convinced it is more accurate to think of realism and photography as partners in the same cultural project. Writing that aims to be taken as realistic is "photographic" in that it promised to give readers access to a world on the other side of mediation and sought to do so by offering certain kinds of visual information. What is more, the writing we now call realism provided this information in such a way that the reader would recognize it as indeed belonging to the objects and people of the world themselves. The same equation held true even when a novel did not offer much in the way of visual description; before long, it was enough to invoke the stereotype and give it a few new details. A Victorian author could write about almost any situation and—so long as that author acknowledged the visual stereotypes of race, class, gender, and nation—assume that a diverse readership could "see" that situation in approximately the same way he or she did. Moreover, whenever Victorian fiction presumed to enlighten the reader by stripping away some euphemizing image so as to reveal the social reality beneath, that fiction was referring not to some object behind the image, but to another, somehow more adequate image.

Realism exploited the gap within Victorian culture between competing assumptions about visual representation. Proceeding on one assumption, readers derived the meaning of any such representation from its resemblance to objects out there in the world (as did nineteenth-century phrenologists, physiognomists, and criminologists). But proceeding on the other assumption, readers found meaning in the difference between that representation and all others within a system of images. In referring to the real world, I am suggesting, realism necessarily referred to something like a composite photograph, especially when a photograph of that person, place, or thing had not yet been taken. No matter: such an image would soon exist in numerous versions, because popular photography reproduced what people thought they had agreed something was supposed to look like. In thus referring to images, realism was therefore referring to something very real.

Coming at the situation from this perspective, we can expect the relation between fiction and photography to be a complicated one. Nor could it have worked in one direction only. To show how photography authorized fiction as a truth telling medium, I will try to demonstrate that the reverse was true as well, that in order to convince readers fiction was indeed offering them mastery of the world of objects, fiction had to authorize the transparent, reproducible image. Any novel that wanted to qualify as a reliable guide for selecting those peculiarities belonging to the reality at hand offered up a number of visual descriptions, as if to a person selecting the correct mug shot, before revealing which description correctly fixed the category of the thing or person. Through this process of trial and error, "realism" not only taught readers how to make such a match between image and object, it also filled them with a sense that it was imperative to do so. I have explained how the repetition of photographic images produced a shadow archive composed of what might be described as image-objects, neither image nor object, yet the ultimate source of meaning for both. This effect was greatly compounded by the fact that in some cases fiction referred to components of the visual order for more than a decade before those components materialized in countless photographs, and photography endowed fiction's rendering of certain characters, settings, and objects with a truth-telling capability resembling the transparency attributed to the photograph.

Together fiction and photography produced a spatial classification system specific to their mutual moment and class of consumers. This classification system contained the bodies, possessions, and practices of these consumers, and it arranged their bodies, possessions, and practices in relation to those whom the Victorian readership considered outside the boundaries of self, home, class, and nation. As suggested by the first of the four propositions offered at the opening of this introduction, fiction authorized photography to mark out these visual-spatial boundaries. Pointing to certain images as if they were chunks of the world itself, however, fiction authorized only those images that met the visual expectations of its readership, expectations that fiction itself had delineated. If the process by which fiction and photography authorized each other in the name of realism appears to be a circular one, that is because realism could not have achieved its power to tell the truth in any other way. I find it difficult to imagine how such a thoroughgoing change as the one for which I am arguing could occur on both sides of the Cartesian equation, as a radical restructuring of the difference between "inside" and "outside," the domains of subject and object, respectively, unless it occurred in both domains at once and through a process of continuous circulation.

Realism Today

If we think of the cultural logic of the archive as that of the photograph, must we then conclude that a century and a half of photographic realism has indeed condemned us to perform acts of simulation in a world of vampiric image-objects or fetishes? Precisely this iconophobia energizes critiques of modernization from Marx's essay on the commodity fetish, through Lukács's condemnation of encroaching pictorialism in the novel, to Baudrillard's diatribe against "the murderous capacity of images" that he calls simulation. All find indications that real things and authentic feelings have, for some time now, been receding behind successive veils of images, until even the traces of such an unmediated reality are on the verge of extinction. I find these critiques useful only to a point.

It is well worth considering that they might chronicle a sudden and massive infusion of the kind of images I have been describing into Western culture at some point after 1848, an infusion of images that did in fact, as Marx predicted, proceed at an ever-increasing pace to displace earlier ways of producing and exchanging objects. In addition, these accounts offer valuable insight into the whole notion of "authenticity" that came to stand for the world as it was before these images usurped the place of objects in mediating human relationships. In each case, such critiques persuade us to accept the world of "good" mediation, or mediation by objects, as if it were more real than the present regime of "bad" mediation, or mediation by apparently free-floating images. Each represents the new visual order as a world upside down, whether in terms of a dancing table,[37] the obliteration of narration by description,[38] or a "map that precedes the territory."[39] Each thereby identifies what is real as the way things were before the regime of images. In doing so, however, Marx, Lukács, and Baudrillard seem to abandon history, giving us gothic descriptions of history's demise. Where Marx saw participation in commodity culture as tantamount to "flight in the misty realm of religion," Lukács glimpsed "the general decline of the epoch" in "the decadence of the banal degeneracy," and Baudrillard still more recently proclaimed the modern world a gothic Disneyland in which "everything is already dead and resurrected in advance."[40] With the onset of mass visuality, in other words, these ardent antagonists of late modern culture insist that reality, history, and humanity as we know it have receded into spaces as yet untouched by mass-reproducible images—the past, art, and the third world.[41]

I have argued that whenever it refers to the world beyond itself, a photograph refers only to images rather than to things as they were before they were reduced to visual information. Thus, as Lukács might have predicted, studying the proliferation of photographic genres in relation to literary realism does not give us access to social history. What we observe instead is the slow but certain inversion of the classic relation between image and object represented and how that inversion endowed certain images with the power, if not to produce their referents, then certainly to determine how people saw them. At the same time, as I have also argued, the photograph does indeed refer beyond itself to a shadow archive composed of images in some respects resembling Galton's combination prints. These types have through time and the sheer repetition and accumulation of photographs achieved something like the status of objects. If photographs testify to anything besides themselves, then, it is to the existence of a coherent system of such image-objects. It is the story of how that system formed in collaboration with fiction, a collaboration from which realism has yet to disengage, to which I hope to give shape and substance in this book. Critiques of modernization—and such critiques are overwhelmingly iconophobic—have convinced me that the onset of mass visuality was a major event. They have convinced me as well that the domain of good mediation is not and was never the domain of history proper so much as a fantasy of pre-visuality constructed retrospectively from a post-visuality perspective—thus one more overvaluation of a truth obstructed by mass mediation. From these convictions there is only one conclusion to be drawn: the need for a history of mediation. Did the onset of mass visuality really invert mimetic priorities so that mediation began to constitute the very subject and object it presumed to mediate? What does this mean for a class and nation so mediated? How can the history of this transformation of the very ground for history be told?

Too much of what goes by the name of cultural studies avoids precisely these questions. Too often such analyses—often sensationally descriptive and marbled with photographs—present us with what I regard as unsatisfactory options. I am referring to our tendency to call some cultural categories good and real when they seem to be grounded in the reality of the body, especially a body racially inscribed and marked by class. I will use abundant reprints of photographic images in much the same way I use passages from parliamentary reports or medical journals to suggest what fiction was picturing as real. I am not interested in proving that any of these representations are false or bad, even though many of them eradicate individual differences for purposes of exalting or degrading an entire group. Rather, my purpose is to explain how a representation does this and to what effect on its consumers. I have also tried very hard not to contribute directly to the essentialism-nominalism debate which tends to become the main topic of cultural studies no matter what kind of subject matter has been put under the lens of critical analysis. I regard both sides of this debate as deficient for the same reasons the archives of Galton and Bertillon were found to be so.[42] As inheritors of what I have called the shadow archive, we do not have a single body image to call our own, but live for others and ourselves in relation to a concatenation of such images that more or less approaches and avoids shadowy prototypes that rarely if ever reveal themselves for what they are, even in our dreams. Cultural stereotypes are real, not because they refer to real bodies, but because they allow us to identify and classify bodies, including our own, as image-objects with a place and name within a still-expanding visual order.

⤚ CHAPTER ONE ⤙

The Prehistory of Realism

DURING THE PERIOD FROM 1790 TO 1810, MANY OF ENGLAND'S more prominent authors, artists, and intellectuals took part in a politically charged discussion of landscaping.[1] There was hardly a novel, poem, or aesthetic treatise that did not take a position on such questions as how a landscape should look, what it said about its owner, how much of its beauty should be made available to those who sought amusement by traveling through the countryside, and whether human intervention could improve on nature's plan. These questions found expression in the theory of the picturesque. Although the debate that swirled around this theory flourished during the decades following the French Revolution, the consequences of that debate reverberated through the nineteenth century. Indeed, I plan to hold the picturesque aesthetic in part responsible not only for changing the landscape of rural England, but for setting the terms of Victorian realism as well.

Those who first ventured into the countryside during the late eighteenth century in search of picturesque vistas understood the nation as virtually the same as the countryside they saw unfolding before them.[2] But to those early Victorians who first turned to the literature of the picturesque for a style of home and garden that would properly reflect their newly won prosperity, the countryside provided a model that could be reproduced in part and on a smaller scale to serve as a refuge from one's business in the city.[3] In the hands of photographers who at mid-century sought out picturesque scenes and rustic people, the substitution of the visual representation for the object represented was complete, and the countryside served as raw material for photographs that consumers could enjoy at exhibitions, in galleries, and even in the comfort of their homes.[4] The consumers of these photographs were the first, I believe, to imagine their nation as a system of images with an urban observer situated at its core. This chapter will follow the picturesque from late eighteenth-century aesthetic treatises to the lawns and parlors of Victorian England. In pursuing this concept, I will be describing a transformation in the ontology of "the image" that gave certain images the power to change both the lay of the English landscape and what it represented. In this respect, the theory of the picturesque can be considered our most important legacy from eighteenth-century aesthetics.

One Species More

William Gilpin's 1792 essays on picturesque beauty begin with the modest claim that he wished "merely [to] illustrate, and recommend one species [of beauty] more."[5] In so deferring to the notion of beauty that Edmund Burke had infused with significance for late eighteenth and early nineteenth-century men and women of letters, Gilpin appears to build on the definition of beauty Burke had already established. But in adding this one species more, Gilpin's theory of the picturesque in fact performs less as a complement to Burke's theory of aesthetic pleasure and more as a supplement to revise the theory of seeing that had dominated the eighteenth century. To argue for the central importance of the picturesque in nineteenth-century British culture, let me offer a brief summary of the eighteenth-century theory of seeing which the picturesque permanently modified, despite all appearances to the contrary.

Foremost among the principles that Gilpin uses to define the category of picturesque beauty was Burke's restatement of the Lockean argument that all sensory information can be thought of in terms of images that present themselves to the whole spectrum of humanity in approximately the same way. "As there will be very little doubt that bodies present similar images" to virtually everyone, Burke had contended, "it must necessarily be allowed, that the pleasure and the pains which every object excites in one man, it must raise in all mankind."[6] By virtue of the fact that we are human, we all see in approximately the same way. Burke proceeds on this assumption to argue that, much like our preference for certain foods, some aspects of visual taste are natural. "Light is more pleasing than darkness," for example, as a swan is in comparison with a goose, or a peacock with a Friezland hen (15). Just as culture comes along and tinkers with nature to produce different nations who have their own cuisines, so culture also inculcates visual preferences specific to a nation. Nevertheless, Burke insists, our reaction to visual stimuli will always be more closely tied to human nature than our responses to information received through the other senses, since sight is "not so often altered by considerations which are independent" of natural sensation, or "sight itself" (15).

In Burke's estimation, even the imagination can do little to change this natural relation between the perceiving subject and the object seen; "it can only vary the disposition of those ideas which [imagination] has received from the senses" (16–17). Our reaction to imaginary images is so securely bound by "the same principle on which the sense is pleased or displeased with the [corresponding] realities," because, he contends, "the imagination is only the representative of the senses" (17). Thus, for Burke, the imagination is "incapable of producing anything new" (16). Before embarking on an argument that attempts to differentiate between the sublime and the beautiful, then, he sees fit to anchor those differences in the different natures of the objects eliciting each response. At the same time and in apparent contradiction to his claim that art depends on a world already given, he attributes aesthetic pleasure to art's capacity to create "*new images*" (17). Art both can and cannot produce something new, according to Burke's theory, because the pleasure we take in art comes from a source that logically opposes the notion of judgment put forth by "Mr. Locke." As the faculty that makes and ranks differences, judgment governs the way modern, civilized people experience life on a daily basis. For this reason, "when two distinct objects are unlike to each other, it is only what we expect; things are in their common way; and therefore they make no impression on the imagination" (17).

Thus far, the object is indistinguishable from the image we see; any aesthetic response depends primarily on "resemblances, which the imitation has to the original," and only secondarily on differences (17): "By making resemblances we produce *new images*, we unite, we create, we enlarge our stock, but in making distinctions we offer no food at all to the imagination; the task itself is more severe and irksome, and what pleasure we derive from it is something of a negative and indirect nature" (17–18). Despite the gratification they afford us, however, "new images" are not "anything new," because they add to the store of culture without changing the world of real, or natural, phenomena.

It is through "taste" that our ability to perceive categorical differences comes back into play, placing limits on resemblances and setting good representations apart from bad ones. Burke does distinguish between two kinds of observers, one who comes to nature with only the natural preferences common to his species, and another who possesses the critical judgment required for discriminating taste. Thus taste not only distinguishes good from bad representations, it also marks differences between various sectors of an audience or readership. Everyone takes much the same pleasure in the resemblances created by a work of music, according to Burke: "the rude hearer is affected by the principles which operate in these arts even in their rudest condition; and he is not skilful enough to perceive the defects" (25). Education changes this situation. As if in anticipation of the principle of delayed gratification, Burke describes aesthetic pleasure among members of the more "advanced" cultures as something that can be "frequently interrupted by the faults which are discovered in the most finished compositions" (25). People who have developed a capacity for critical judgment are inclined to look for something better.

All this, arguably, would have been as familiar to eighteenth-century readers of Burke's *Philosophical Enquiry* as it is to most literary scholars today. My point in recalling the assumptions established by one of the acknowledged fathers of modern British aesthetics is to show how another group of writers appropriated those assumptions and made them work against themselves with an effectiveness, I believe, that modern literary history has yet to appreciate fully. In the hands of William Gilpin, the picturesque aesthetic incorporated both the primacy and the universality that Burke had given to sensation. But from among the capacious field of sensations established by Locke and adapted for aesthetic theory by Burke, Gilpin fixed on sight as the only sensation to be received from an object classified as picturesque. Objects were always more primary than their images for Gilpin, much as they were for Burke. Among all the objects capable of providing aesthetic pleasure, Gilpin argued that some objects lent themselves to the purely visual experience he called the picturesque. His three essays devoted to that topic sought to show that the source of aesthetic pleasure resided not in the qualities of such an object but in those of its image. Rather than working in opposition to judgment, moreover, such visual pleasure offered observers both "rational, and agreeable amusement" (46). Ideally, the pleasure that observers derived from their encounter with the picturesque would be enhanced by their critical apprehension of it.

With his claim to be adding one more kind of beauty to the existing catalogue, followed up by his insistence on the difference between an object and its image, Gilpin all but promised not to contest the territory mapped out by Edmund Burke's *Philosophical Enquiry*. Nor, then, could anyone suspect him of doing otherwise when he announced that his first of three essays on the picturesque would address the question, "*What is that quality in objects, which particularly marks them as picturesque?*" (4). To understand how thoroughly and by what means Gilpin's version of the picturesque transformed the traditional notion of beauty, we must first recall how hard Burke worked to distinguish aesthetic objects from those capable of arousing erotic yearnings:

> We shall have a strong desire for a woman of no remarkable beauty; whilst the greatest beauty in men, or in other animals, though it causes love, yet it incites nothing at all of desire. Which shews that beauty, and the passion caused by beauty, which I call love, is different from desire though desire may sometimes operate along with it. (Burke, 83)

According to Burke's visual aesthetics, the experience of beauty is ultimately far more dangerous to the sensibility of the perceiver than is the experience of the sublime, despite the sublime's dependence on objects capable of inspiring astonishment and horror. Although beauty arises from entirely different natural objects, the most vulgar response to beauty resembles what Burke regards as the highest form of aesthetic pleasure, insofar as the vulgar variety threatens to overturn the observer's rational command of the sensory universe. But because the sublime contains and aestheticizes what would otherwise prove horrifying, an encounter with the sublime allows the observer to enjoy the threat it momentarily poses to his rationality.[7] While the response to beauty is the less forceful of the two kinds of aesthetic pleasure and thus might seem the more likely to submit to rationality and self-control, beauty is, in Burke's estimation, the only form of aesthetic experience capable of eliciting erotic desire, which is the nemesis of rationality and self-control. In contrast with an aesthetic response, erotic attraction to an object of beauty blurs the distinction between art and life and therefore exerts a peculiar form of power over the observer. The mere act of seeing objects capable of eliciting such desire, according to Burke, "hurries us on to the possession of [those] objects" (83). Thus do objects capable of eliciting erotic desire put us at the mercy of the object world.

Gilpin, on the other hand, is completely promiscuous in identifying the objects capable of eliciting an aesthetic response. "We pursue
beauty in any shape," he declares, "admiring it in the grandest object,
and not rejecting it in the humblest" (46). Whatever value something
might possess in itself has nothing to do with its aesthetic value. The
aesthetic value of any object depends entirely on the quality of its
surface texture. In this respect, roughness is much to be preferred
over beauty's smoothness, and the rugged carthorse makes a better
subject for the sketching pencil than the glossy thoroughbred. "It is
the various surfaces of objects," Gilpin writes, "that give the painter
his choice of opportunities in massing, and graduating both his
lights, and shades . . . What the painter calls *richness* on a surface, is
only a variety of little parts; on which the light shining shews all its
small inequalities, and roughnesses" (20). Where an object's surface
has greatest variety, there we will find its visual information densest
and consequently yielding the most visual gratification. Thus to his
initial question, "What is that quality in objects, which marks them as
picturesque?" Gilpin replies by informing us that there is nothing in
the object; only the quality of its surface marks it as suitable material
for art. Having done away with distinctions that inhere in things
themselves, Gilpin then proceeds to blur the distinction between
aesthetic pleasure and that most vulgar of pleasures that Burke links
with eroticism. Gilpin identifies the desire for novel visual experiences as the "foundation" for both refined and vulgar pleasure (48).[8]
On this foundation, he builds a theory of cultural consumption that
mimics, mingles with, and finally uses a common form of visual pleasure to undermine Burke's claim for art's aloofness.

Where Burke had fastidiously separated the erotic from the aesthetic, Gilpin describes the experience of picturesque beauty as one
that elicits an aggressively sensual response. He is especially effective
in challenging the distinction between high and vulgar responses to
natural beauty when he compares the traveler's search for picturesque beauty with the pleasures of the hunt: "Every distant horizon
promises something new; and with this pleasing expectation we follow nature through all her walks. We pursue her from hill to dale;

and hunt after those various beauties with which she every where abounds" (48). Lest we miss the point of the feminine pronoun and heavy-handed references to ancient arts of venerie, Gilpin proclaims, "the pleasures of the chace are universal. A hare started before dogs is enough to set a whole country in an uproar. The plough, and the spade are deserted. Care is left behind; and every human faculty is dilated with joy" (48). Gilpin has a reason for reducing aesthetic pleasure to the level of the very kind of sensuality that Burke had set in opposition to it: Gilpin's point in thus making picturesque beauty universally available is to set seeing apart from every other form of sensuality. He begins by asking whether hunters really have more fun than gentlemen observers:

> shall we suppose it a greater pleasure to the sportsman to pursue a trivial animal, than it is to the man of taste to pursue the beauties of nature? to follow her through all her recesses? to obtain a sudden glance, as she flits past him in some airy shape? to trace her through the mazes of the cover? to wind after her along the vale? (48)

Yes, the picturesque aesthetic allows the man of taste to enjoy himself as much as the plebeian sportsman, and that is precisely the problem. We are "most delighted," Gilpin concedes, "when some grand scene, tho perhaps of incorrect composition, rising before the eye, strikes us beyond the power of thought" (49). "In this pause of intellect, an enthusiastic sensation of pleasure overspreads [the soul and] . . . we rather *feel*, than *survey*" the scene (50). In Gilpin's estimation, to see in this way, is not to see at all. Seeing involves partitioning, taking inventory, itemizing—in this way, taking visual and intellectual possession of what one sees.[9]

Gilpin finally takes what can only be considered a deliberate swipe at Burke, when he argues that we conduct a loftier relationship with the external world when we are less overwhelmed with emotion and therefore more likely to "allow the eye to criticize [the scene] at leisure" (50). At the heart of the picturesque aesthetic resides the insidious question of whether art is really separate from life, once we respond to both art and life as visual surfaces capable of yielding a curious blend of pleasure and judgment that is ultimately neither one. On what other basis than this radical hypothesis does Gilpin proceed to pronounce it more advantageous to examine nature piece by piece than to grasp it in one all-encompassing embrace?[10] This rejection of the Burkean opposition between critical judgment and aesthetic pleasure does more than link the two modes of understanding. Believing that aesthetic pleasure is actually increased when brought under rational control, Gilpin devises a method for transforming the tourist who responds with enthusiasm to a lovely scene into an observer who can reproduce the scene by recalling, not how he felt, but *how he saw it*. For the problem posed by his common garden variety of Romantic enthusiasm, Gilpin provides two antidotes.

One consists of record-taking procedures designed to reduce objects to the most rudimentary visual information. In Gilpin's words, "A few scratches, like a short-hand scrawl of our own, legible at least to ourselves, will serve to raise in our minds the remembrance of the beauties they humbly represent" (51). There may well be "more pleasure from recollecting, from a few transient lines, the scene we have admired," he insists, than in our first, unmediated encounter with those scenes. In order to experience what he calls "this secondary pleasure," Gilpin's tourist has to ignore "those enthusiastic feelings, which accompanied the real exhibition" and look at nature in a "calmer," "more uniform," and "uninterrupted" manner (51). Such composure is not difficult to achieve. By sketching the scenes that he finds especially pleasing to the eye, the tourist produces a kind of map enabling him to recall and share his experiences with friends and family: "After we have amused *ourselves* with our sketches, if we can, in any degree, contribute to the amusement of others also, the pleasure is surely so much enhanced" (52).

The scene thus rendered as an image offers such clear advantages over actually "traversing the wild, and savage parts of nature" that Gilpin feels entirely justified in displacing the original (51). Besides, the sketch provides another, more subtle way of converting the excesses of the tourist's enthusiasm for the original into what can only be called a productive form of pleasure. In order to produce a sketch that reproduces the visual pleasure of visiting the spot, the traveler needs little in the way of artistic training and talent. He must simply follow a set of procedures that trains him to look at other scenes in terms of their visual composition.[11] A picturesque scene could be adequately represented by such crude rules of visual composition because the beauty of that scene was wholly in its image. That image does not aim at recapturing the fresh smell of country air, the sound of birds, or the feel of grass underfoot, much less what associations these sensations might trigger in an individual perceiver. Rather than attempt to put an audience in touch with either nature or his own response thereto, the author or artist of the picturesque gives us a copy in the form of a general picture of an interesting view.[12]

Nothing better illustrates the specificity of the picturesque in this respect than a comparison of Gilpin's 1782 description of a tour of the countryside surrounding Tintern Abbey with Wordsworth's revision of this description in "Lines: Composed a Few Miles above Tintern Abbey, on Revisiting the Banks of the Wye during a Tour, July 13, 1798." In these well-known lines, Wordsworth pays tribute to the salutary influence of the setting that attracted the picturesque traveler of a generation before:

> . . . for she [nature] can so inform
> The mind that is within us, so impress
> With quietness and beauty, and so feed
> With lofty thoughts, that neither evil tongues,
> Rash judgments, nor the sneers of selfish men,
> Nor greetings where no kindness is, nor all
> The dreary intercourse of daily life,
> Shall e'er prevail against us . . .

With these lines Wordsworth is waging an argument with his more popular contemporary. Gilpin had described the place as one where "every thing around breathes an air so calm, and tranquil; so sequestered from the commerce of life, that it is easy to conceive how a man of warm imagination, in monkish times, might have been allured by such a scene to become an inhabitant of it."[13] That it takes a scholar specializing in late eighteenth-century British literature to hear this echo testifies to Wordsworth's stunning success in displacing the picturesque observer.[14]

In his preface to the poem, Wordsworth claims he wrote his lines "upon leaving Tintern, after crossing the Wye, and concluded [the poem] just as I was entering Bristol in the evening." The scene that matters most to him is therefore neither the one he sees while there, nor that which disappears behind him on departure, as does "a landscape to a blind man's eye." He makes it absolutely clear that he values precisely what is no longer visible. By way of contrast, Gilpin came down the river from Monmouth toward "the noble ruin of Tintern-abbey" bursting with anticipation at the thought of seeing what was even then, as he puts it, "esteemed, with its appendages, the most beautiful and picturesque view on the river" (*Observations,* 31). But the scene that greeted him fell significantly short of his visual standard:

> Though the parts are beautiful, the whole is ill-shaped. No ruins of the tower are left, which might give form, and contrast to the walls, and buttresses, and other inferior parts. Instead of this, a number of gabel-ends hurt the eye with their regularity; and disgust it by the vulgarity of their shape. (*Observations,* 33)

Given the abbey's lack of picturesqueness, the modern reader brought up on Wordsworth might well expect Gilpin to swerve from that unshapely architecture and ponder the surrounding landscape instead. That expectation would be disappointed.

The picturesque observer is curiously drawn to those things that spoil the view; he tends to dwell on the shortcomings and excesses of a scene which would then prompt him to imagine how the visual composition could be improved. Thus its deficiencies inspire what is perhaps the single most remarkable statement Gilpin makes about the abbey: "A mallet judiciously used . . . might be of service in fracturing some of [the gable-ends]; particularly those of the cross isles, which are not only disagreeable in themselves, but confound the perspective" (*Observations,* 33). What Gilpin found lacking in terms of picturesque beauty, Wordsworth's Romanticism supplied in terms of a compensatory personal experience that saw in the scenery traces of the sister who was no longer there. In this respect, paradoxically, Wordsworth comes to resemble "the man of warm imagination," that is to say, the man ill-at-ease with modernity whom Gilpin imagined beating a monkish retreat from "the commerce of [daily] life" (*Observations,* 32). Though written sixteen years before Wordsworth inscribed the landscape with familial memories, Gilpin's view, I am suggesting, is clearly the more modern of the two in that it looks ahead to a thoroughly commodified landscape.

In adding "one species more" to Burke's catalogue of beautiful things, Gilpin's theory of the picturesque identifies a source of pleasure that other eighteenth-century authors, intellectuals, and tastemongers had neglected.[15] Moreover, the observer responding to beauty in the picturesque sense of the term did not have to guard against responding in a way that might turn erotic and make him want to possess the things in view. The pleasure to be garnered from the picturesque is to be found neither in objects, according to Gilpin, nor in the fantastic images that artists produce by imitating and combining them. Objects matter only insofar as they provide certain kinds of visual information, and the artist's taste and imagination matter almost not at all. Indeed, he claims, "the more refined our taste grows from the *study of nature,* the more insipid are the *works of art*" (57). The less art enters into reproduction, then, the better—and more gratifying—will be the work of picturesque representation. "The copy," Gilpin argued, consequently "must be pure, if it do not disgust" (57). How to make the copy as untainted as possible by the artist's hand was not a question that concerned the mainstream of late eighteenth-century thought. According to the picturesque aesthetic, however, the mere fact that an object could be reproduced as an image—that it manifested reproducibility—was what gave it value. If objects were only as valuable as the quality of visual information they yielded, then the second guarantee of picturesqueness was the reproducibility inherent in that information rather than the sensitivity and talent of the individual who observed and copied it.

In formulating these two incorrigibly unromantic conditions for good art, Gilpin was proposing a kind of taste designed to transform the consumer into a producer of art. To share his experiences with others, it was not only necessary for Gilpin's observer to reproduce the object much as he saw it; he also had to see that object much as other people would. To standardize the act of seeing in this way, Gilpin's third essay on the picturesque developed a set of instructions that would lend a sketch or drawing an element of reproducibility. This method, which might be described as an early version of the paint-by-numbers method, was meant to be "attainable by a man of business" (90). Of course, his readers would have gathered well before this point that all three essays were directed toward a class of townspeople whose money came from business and trade, people with leisure time on their hands but without customary ways of occupying themselves. What Gilpin delivered was an aesthetic tailored specifically for such people, their lives, their incomes, their sexual practices, and their education.[16] Given that Burke as well as the Romantics formulated their theories at least in part to counter what they saw as the aggressive utilitarianism of an emergent middle class, we should not be shocked to find that Gilpin, in speaking precisely to these class interests, wrote in opposition to the logic of representation formulated by Burke and adapted for Romanticism. Once we grant that Gilpin's version of the picturesque did indeed revise traditional aesthetic theory to fit hand-in-glove with the economic practices of modern townspeople, however, we must confront the possibility that the reverse may be true as well: that the picturesque aesthetic aestheticized the lives of this class of people and, in so doing, made their taste into a national and international standard.

The Picturesque Imperative

Before it could produce this happy tautology whereby art appeared to reflect life and vice versa, the definition, purpose, and audience for the picturesque were hotly contested and its logic was adapted for a Victorian readership. During the first two decades of the nineteenth century, British intellectuals not only made these changes in what was fast becoming the first genuinely middlebrow aesthetic, but argued for parallel transformations in the English monetary system as well. It is fair to say that these debates within aesthetic and economic discourse, respectively, arose in response to the same question, how to evaluate representation once it has been detached from the objects in which value had traditionally been presumed to dwell. One's position in both debates ultimately depended on the ontological status one assigned the image: Was it merely being a copy of the original that gave an image value, or did the image acquire value in capturing accurately the essential features of the original? As it continued into the nineteenth century, the debate shifted away from this question of whether value resided in the object or in the image and took up an entirely different issue. A second generation of spokesmen for the picturesque was preoccupied with the question of how to distinguish between good and bad images: Was the image supposed to gain its authority from the object with as little mediation as possible, or was it supposed to beautify that object, thereby suggesting ways in which the original might be genuinely improved?

The fact that Parliament shifted from a gold to a paper standard during the same period when the picturesque challenged the secondary status of the image in relation to the object offers more than a suggestive parallel. The policies that brought about a standard paper currency in England dramatize the material effects of a system that allows certain copies to stand in for the original. I maintain, however, that no economic logic can explain why the shift from gold to paper failed to disrupt the economy and disturb the social order to the degree that Parliament had feared and bank directors had predicted.

The Prehistory of Realism

45

Value indeed proved to reside in representation. To understand why the English people were suddenly willing to put their trust in paper, after so many years and so much intelligent opinion to the contrary, we must turn to aesthetic theory. The shift in emphasis to the question of whether picturesque beauty resided in the good image or the bad indicated that English people had grown accustomed to the idea that certain copies could provide adequate semiotic substitutes for the original. With this change, one might say, realism was born.

We have already seen how Wordsworthian Romanticism refused to follow the semiotic pathway cut by Gilpin, preferring Burke's more traditional argument that locates the source of an aesthetic response in the nature of the object represented. Never mind that Burke and Wordsworth held two rather different notions of what the nature of an object might be; both still insisted energetically that art draws value from a source outside itself and must maintain its tie to that origin. The picturesque aesthetic, on the other hand, was openly unconcerned with origins (*Three Essays,* 47). Indeed, one might even say that the image gave value to an object within the logic of the picturesque aesthetic, insofar as that image measured up to a standardized image of that thing. Was it one of the unacknowledged coincidences of history that a similar rupture between sign and substance troubled the national economy from 1782 until the 1830s, the period during which England groped its way toward a modern monetary system? At the risk of oversimplifying what was actually an extremely complex process, I would like to identify two principles that surfaced in the monetary debates and the aesthetic discussions of the period, whenever the question of value arose.[17] The terminology may come from the monetary debates, but the same principles were at work in aesthetic arguments as well.

The first was the principle of restriction. Burke's aesthetic theory proceeds on the assumption that copies can proliferate without any loss of value, so long as the original objects retained their value and the sensations we receive from them were measured according to a fixed standard of taste.[18] In this respect, we can call his thinking restrictive. Presumably, such a standard was not entirely fixed during the 1750s, or he would not have taken such pains to distinguish common from refined taste. Some years later, when Gilpin turned to writing essays on the picturesque beauty to be seen in England's countryside, he too argued for a way of regulating taste. Rather than restrict the sources of aesthetic value, however, Gilpin could be said to have followed a second and presumably contrary principle often cited in the monetary debates. His theory of the picturesque proceeded on the assumption that one copy could be converted into another—that, indeed, the value of any such copy came from its convertibility. It was the principle of convertibility that he observed in determining that an image's capacity to please did not depend on the capacity of its subject matter to please, but rather on certain qualities of its reproduction. This same principle led him to conclude that a recognizable "composition" of visual information would come to serve as the standard any sketch or drawing had to meet if it were going to become a source of pleasure. Indeed, even when an object fell short of the picturesque standard, one could still take pleasure in those deficiencies and determine—as Gilpin did in describing Tintern Abbey—precisely where a scene would have to be improved to fulfill the visual standard. By adding one species of beauty more to Burke's catalogue, moreover, Gilpin expanded the provenance of the critical faculty, the agent of aesthetic taste, to include almost anyone with leisure time and the money to acquire polite forms of amusement.

This problem within the sign itself not only shaped aesthetic arguments during the last decade of the eighteenth century but also generated a set of positions on the variability of the gold supply and how to regulate it. Those who endorsed restriction initially prevailed, and the Restriction Bill of 1797 kept the Bank of England from giving out cash, even at the request of the government. The many small banks in rural areas dealing strictly in savings and loans were permitted to issue notes that could be converted only into Bank of England notes. For the first time, Bank of England notes began to circulate alongside various country bank notes instead of metal. As a result, the Bank of England note—and not its worth in gold—

became the measure of value. Accordingly, the monetary debate shifted its focus from the advantages and problems of restriction to the advantages and problems attending convertibility, the second principle at play in determining aesthetic value during this same period.[19]

Successive swings between inflation and depreciation apparently taught Parliament that the value of the English pound could not be controlled by restricting the flow of gold—not when there was too much paper in circulation. To sum up educated opinion on the matter in 1801, William Boyd employed a rhetoric that uncannily anticipates the opening lines of *Pride and Prejudice:* "That the augmentation of the quantity of money or paper performing the functions of money in a country has a tendency to depreciate that money or paper is a principle universally recognized."[20] To close the gap between sign and substance, in 1816 Parliament lifted the restriction on converting notes into metal. This method of ensuring convertibility replaced restriction of the legal tender of Bank of England notes as the preferred method for preserving their value. But because those who engineered the resumption of cash payments for notes regarded convertibility as an antidote to the policy of restriction, England found itself squarely back in the situation that had prompted the Restriction Bill. With the proliferation of paper money, the gap between the pound note and its value in gold had widened, causing a further drain of the English gold supply. The double bind created by the laws of restriction and convertibility reasserted itself, in other words, not only during the twenty-year period when England was off the gold standard, but also in the decades after 1816, when that standard was reinstated. Gold poured into England in the years following the French Revolution. With the renewal of public faith in the government of France, however, that gold was taken out of the Bank of England and returned to France. Despite the fact the flow of gold reversed itself, moving first in and then out of England, the gap between metal and paper remained a constant threat to the value of paper and vice versa, so long as there was such a flow to trigger either a further run on gold, in the first instance, or a surplus of paper, in the second.[21]

In this oscillation between a currency that stands in for gold and one whose value depends on what one gets for it in exchange, we can observe a more general change in the logic of representation.[22] I want to explore briefly the results of the monetary convertibility set in motion by the Restriction Bill of 1797, since those results worked not only in parallel but also in tandem with similar events in the domain of aesthetics. After 1797, the various tokens, bills of exchange, and local notes drawn by corn-dealers, cattle-drovers, brewers, or shopkeepers to provide currency for farmers and tradesmen could no longer be cashed in for coins, much less for gold. Metal was successfully restricted. These alternative currencies could, however, be exchanged for Bank of England notes and were all the more likely to be so converted in times of crisis. Thus, after 1821, T. S. Ashton observes, the ratio of English bank notes to bills of trade and other economic tokens steadily increased.[23] Cash in the form of metal coins and Bank of England notes soon came to occupy the symbolic position that gold had once occupied, as the standard and means of maintaining exchange value. This process of standardization involved a number of important institutional changes—determining who could issue notes and set the rate of discount on credit, what ratio of gold to paper should be maintained, and how to adjust the currency to fluctuations in the price of goods relative to the price of gold. Before England went off the gold standard, only people of property could draw notes of credit; the majority of the population operated within local currency systems, using strictly local coins, small notes, and tokens that could be redeemed by local vendors. Once England went off the gold standard, however, these currencies began to include English Bank notes, whose value depended on the principle of convertibility.

The increased accessibility of these notes seems to have had a twofold impact. The Bank of England note circulated within and between local economies, gradually breaking down the distinctions between city and country currencies. Eradication of these particular distinctions can be described as a centripetal process that reoriented all economic exchange in relation to an urban center that held the nation's supply of gold and issued bank notes according to a policy considered good for the nation as a whole. In this sense, the "nation" had never been imagined more materialistically. At the same time, standardization also exerted a centrifugal pull, drawing exponentially more individuals into a single currency system. Working together, the principles of restriction and convertibility helped to propel England toward a modern monetary system.[24]

Around the time of the Restriction Bill, we can observe the beginnings of a similar transformation of the semiotics of landscape in a second generation of authors writing on the picturesque. These authors took up the category and attempted to limit those who could recognize beauty and reproduce it for others. Among these men of letters, two stand out from the rest chiefly because of their quarrel with each other. Richard Payne Knight challenged Uvedale Price's belief that the pleasure of the picturesque derived from qualities inherent in the objects seen and the sensations they elicit from us.[25] Seeing could not be a natural process, in Knight's estimation, if what we see depends entirely upon the cultural equipment an individual brings to the act of seeing. Thus their debate initially pitted the cultural quality of perception against the nature of the object perceived as to which was the best way to restrict aesthetic value. Scholars of this period have established the grounds on which Knight challenged Burke in order to argue with his contemporary and rival, Price.[26] Much more interesting for my purposes, however, is the reason why and the strategy by which Knight's argument tried to pull the picturesque back within the very category of "beauty" that Burke had delineated. That the success of his endeavor depended on overthrowing the priority Gilpin had given to a highly textured surface is implicit in Knight's claim that "the beauty, spirit, and effect of landscape, real or imitated, depend upon a due mixture of rough and smooth."[27] That his *Analytical Inquiry into the Principles of Taste* begins and ends with attempts to reconcile what Gilpin had put asunder by preferring the cart-horse to the sleek Arabian, the Friezland hen to birds with an aesthetic lineage, or rugged wastelands to the well-groomed park and glassy lake, reveals the political edge of his argument. By arguing that it takes a noble object to make a beautiful representation, Knight was obviously attempting to restrict aesthetic subject matter to the traditional country houses and grounds that provided the ruling iconography of an agrarian England.[28]

The historical circumstances prompting this conservative position surfaced in Part II of *An Analytical Inquiry*, as Knight expressed aggravation at another well-known contemporary, the British landscaper Nathaniel Kent, a man we might expect Knight to have revered for his skill in painting. Instead, he charged Kent with encouraging a dangerous tendency among certain "improvers" to change indiscriminately the appearance of the English countryside. Thus, by the beginning of the nineteenth century, the question of whether and to what extent an aesthetic standard should be brought to bear on the object represented had become *the* issue that set the two definitions of picturesque beauty against each other. "Kent, it is true, was by profession a painter, as well as an improver," Knight explains, "but we may learn from his example, how little a certain degree of mechanical practice will qualify its possessor to direct the taste of a nation, in either of those arts" (255).[29] Kent, however, was not only as susceptible to popular whim as Gilpin, but he also conspired with people of money and little taste to remodel the countryside, first according to one fashion, then according to another. Thus, complains Knight, "he and his followers demolished, without distinction, the costly and magnificent decorations of past times, and all that had long been held in veneration" (249).

If the theory of the picturesque advanced by Gilpin prompted a whole range of people to place value in copies of the English countryside, and given that some of those people had enough money to carry out that aesthetic principle by landscaping country homes with the help of Kent and "his followers," then what could Knight do to prevent the desecration of traditional English beauty? Where Price sought to relocate value in the original, thus reestablishing the traditional mimetic priority of object over image, Knight sought to subordinate popular landscape designs to a pictorial standard. Knight's desire to stabilize the appearance of the English countryside in this way was no less intense than the desire of monetary experts to stabilize the English monetary system. He could not hope to solve the problem by limiting aesthetic sensibility to the landowning class, not in an age when nature was rapidly undergoing commodification. Thus he sought to make certain visual representations count more than others, when he claimed that "pictures" could solve the problem created when the location of value shifted from the object to its representation: "with respect to the art of improving, we may look upon pictures as a set of experiments of the different ways in which trees, buildings, water, &c. may be disposed, grouped, and accompanied in the most beautiful and striking manner" (6).[30] His solution proceeds by much the same logic pursued by those who established the English Bank note, in place of gold, as the means of stabilizing the value of English money. Changes in the landscape should be governed "by the general and unchanging principle, to which the effects of all visible objects are to be referred, but which are very commonly called the principles of painting" (250). The tradition of landscape painting should serve as the standard for distinguishing good pictures from bad.

It is in the light of this strategy for restricting the convertibility of land into landscape design that one can make sense of the "Appendix" to Knight's *Analytical Inquiry*, where he attempts to reverse Gilpin's claim that "the more we study nature, the more insipid are works of art" (*Three Essays*, 57). To counter what he considered an increasingly common tendency to naturalize aesthetic perception, Knight argued that apprehending picturesque beauty required an observer to do more than simply see; a person had to study art before he or she could appreciate nature. The advantage of becoming familiar with great works of art was "not merely to make us acquainted with the combinations and effects that are contained within them." On the contrary, a familiarity with artistic composition would guide our "search of the numberless and untouched varieties and beauties of nature" (4). While conceding Gilpin's point that "he who studies art only will have a confined taste," Knight maintained the contrary was also true, that "he who looks at nature only, will have a vague and unsettled one" (4). By the first decade of the nineteenth century, then, the burning question was no longer whether or not the picturesque should be appended to the category of "beauty," but rather which definition of beauty ought to be considered truly "picturesque."

In thus turning the tables on Gilpin theoretically, Knight sought to restrict not only which styles of landscape could be brought to bear on the countryside around him, but also who was qualified to judge the beauty of those surroundings. If Knight had anything to say about it, nothing on the order of Gilpin's rudimentary instructions for sketching could prepare an observer to recognize an improvement on nature; no lead pencil would allow him to produce one. The value of a visual reproduction does not originate in the surface of the object that we see so much as in our ability to see and often to improve on nature, which comes from an education in the arts. If the ability to recognize beauty in the world outside the picture frame requires familiarity with the highest quality of painting, then reproducing beauty could also require an elite education. The sketchpad artist has no hope of producing an image of aesthetic value, Knight insists, if he does not begin with a worthy object, say, a thoroughbred rather than a cart-horse, and understand just how "the Dutch Masters" added "a greater flare of picturesqueness to these beautiful animals" (404). Whereas Price had taken up the Burkean position that value resided in the object represented, Knight countered that we never see those things just as they are, but only as our education teaches us to see them. In boldly marking this aesthetic difference from Price, however, Knight was actually extending the same ideology that Price had tried to implement, when he sought to relocate value in the nature of the object. "In the last analysis," Ann Bermingham suggests, "'the association of ideas' outlined in Knight's essay was no more than the imaginative appropriation of the countryside by a class already responsible for its territorial appropriation."[31]

Using the same logic of representation that unfolded in the monetary debates, Knight's and Price's respective revisions to the theory and practice of the picturesque can be classified as restrictionist. Like the 1797 Restriction Bill itself, the claim that an education in the arts and a house in the country are necessary preconditions for experiencing aesthetic pleasure is a way to reunite the sign of value with its substance. This aesthetic theory was supposed to consolidate taste, like England's wealth, in a traditional landowning class, albeit one whose boundaries were made permeable to some degree by education, on the one hand, and by capital, on the other. But contrary to his intentions, when Knight sought to restrict the pleasure of looking at the English countryside to those whose land it was, thereby closing the gap between substance and sign, he made its representation more important than the thing itself. As in the case of English monetary policy, aesthetic restrictionism (the attempt to reunite the traditional art of landscape with its elite subject matter) led inevitably to convertibility (the displacement of that landscape by a form of representation that would provide the standard of all landscaping). As with the Bank of England note, however, the signs of aristocratic taste began to serve so well in place of the fact of an elite education that these signs, that is to say, the appearance of the landscape, became a source of value in their own right.

We may observe the beginnings of just such a process not only in Knight's disdain for Kent and all indiscriminate improvers, but also in Jane Austen's contempt for those people from town who have learned to manipulate the signs of taste and discretion so as to imply an elite essence in which they felt lacking. Such heroines as Fanny Price, Elizabeth Bennet, and Catherine Moreland, on the other hand, prove themselves worthy of a well-born husband, as they acquire certain elements of his education and learn to reproduce his taste. During one well-known instructional moment, Henry Tilney delivers "a lecture on the picturesque" in response to which Catherine Moreland displays, albeit a bit too enthusiastically, the ability of an Austen heroine to reform her way of seeing on the spot. Indeed, she

> voluntarily rejected the whole city of Bath, as unworthy to
> make part of a landscape. Delighted with her progress, and

fearful of wearying her with too much wisdom at once, Henry suffered the subject to decline, and by an easy transition from a piece of rocky fragment and the withered oak which he had placed near its summit, to oaks in general, to forests, the inclosure of them, waste lands, crown lands and government, he shortly found himself at politics.[32]

In summarizing the politically divisive issues of land use that were simultaneously created and suppressed by the picturesque aesthetic, this one brief paragraph also tells us that the term "picturesque," though saturated with the ideological contradictions of the age, had become pretty common knowledge, fit for a young woman's education. Was it the conservatism of their definition of that term that proved so fatal to the very notion of gentility which the second generation of picturesque philosophers sought to preserve? If so, then we face a more perplexing question: how could such aesthetic conservatism lay the foundation for a commonplace so common that all novel readers might enjoy it?

In his effort to reconcile the picturesque with an utterly traditional notion of beauty, Knight evidently decided it was a bad idea to locate aesthetic value where it could be seen by the ordinary observer. He argued that not just anyone could see aesthetically, and he used the tasteless experiments with landscape to demonstrate the point. In overturning Gilpin's claim that to see nature was to enjoy a thing of beauty, however, Knight could not relocate aesthetic value in the kind of nature that celebrated an aristocratic England, any more than Ricardo and the bullionists could return the English monetary system to its former dependence on gold, once the Bank of England note had proved an adequate semiotic substitute. On the contrary, Knight located value in education, the visual representations he had seen, the way he had been taught to see them, and the quality of the visual standard he consequently observed. As a result, the image rather than the object remained the source of aesthetic value in Knight's revision of the picturesque aesthetic, even though the kind of image he proposed was available only to a propertied elite.[33] Much as they disagreed on the qualities specific to picturesque beauty, its proper subject matter, and the names of its true practitioners, Knight, Price, Horace Walpole, Ann Radcliffe, Austen, and everyone else who argued about the picturesque were arguing about the kind and quality of visual information. By doing so, they put Gilpin's argument with Burke and the Romantics in the past.[34]

This change in the poles of the debate over the picturesque marks a change in the status of the visual representation itself.[35] If the English Bank note's convertibility made it more than a mere certificate for value in gold, then a sketch or painting of the tastefully positioned and appointed country house became something more than a representation of a piece of rural property. That image had been instrumentalized. Rather than simply reproducing the visible surface of a particularly well-textured landscape as Gilpin had proposed, this image began to behave like a plan or model, capable of bringing the landscape in line with a visual standard—whether the tasteful composition defined by painting for which Knight had argued, or the spatial design that stressed the connections between landlord, tenant, and laborer that Kent and Price endorsed. At the point when the model precedes its material realization, it is fair to say that the copy has replaced the original. Thus the English landscape began to copy art almost a century before Oscar Wilde called attention to the fact. But the question of how the country house became a standard capable of absorbing local symbolic economies—in the manner of the Bank of England note—requires a discussion of its own.

Picturesqueness in the Age of Realism

To pursue the picturesque into the Victorian period is to watch it lose coherence as a theory, manifest itself in ways that seemed entirely unrelated, and finally saturate every domain of cultural production. The reasons for the disintegration of what was the most politically charged aesthetic argument waged during the late eighteenth and early nineteenth century have everything to do with its success. Indeed, the widespread acceptance of the picturesque in one form or another is directly related to the cultural consolidation and economic entrenchment of the very people for whom the theory of the picturesque was first intended. By pointing out certain parallels between events occurring in the domains of money and aesthetics, respectively, I have tried to demonstrate how, during the early nineteenth century, English culture underwent a shift from gold and land to capital and cultural capital. Only such a transformation at the level of representation could have produced the topographical changes that ensued. It took more than a new system of currency and the commodification of land to make the cultural geography of England into one that served the banking and commercial centers, and thus the class of people who prospered from their growth. Such a change also required a standard of taste capable of refiguring the English countryside as a space at once therapeutic and aesthetic.

I have been using the word "landscape" as if it were a self-explanatory term for the arrangement of the natural surroundings for a building of some significance, but this specific meaning was produced during the early years of Victoria's reign by the intersection of several cultural and economic events. Presiding over these events was John Loudon, who during the 1830s and 1840s edited two extremely popular pamphlets on gardening and launched a series of cheap editions that he hoped would include "all the best work on Landscape Gardening which have hitherto appeared."[36] Until the first decade of the nineteenth century, according to Loudon, "landscaping" was used as a term for "the art of laying out the grounds which immediately surround a country residence" (v). Thanks to such proponents of the picturesque aesthetic as Knight and Price and such landscapers as Nathaniel Kent, who laid out the grounds for the owners of large country estates, "landscape" began to acquire its distinctively modern meaning, a process which Loudon outlines in the introduction to the first book in his series of reprints of earlier works on landscape gardening.

According to Loudon, cultivated and refined countries prefer "The Modern, English, Irregular, Natural, or Landscape Style," pre-

The Prehistory of Realism

57

cisely because more advanced nations practice modern agricultural methods which tend to mark the countryside with regular lines and disrupt its natural contours with enclosures (v). Such nations also tend to develop landscaping practices that conceal these signs of labor and perpetuate the natural beauty of an earlier historical period. In an advanced nation, then, plowed fields and a copious harvest table could not serve as signs of wealth and well-being; wastelands were more prestigious. As Loudon explains, "Where society is in a higher state of cultivation, the natural, or irregular style, from its rarity in such a country, and from the sacrifice of profitable lands requisite to make room for it, becomes equally a sign of wealth and taste" (vi). As England entered the nineteenth century, two styles of landscape emerged to do the work of suppressing the signs of agricultural production. The School of Nathaniel Kent cleared away all foliage and architectural appendages so that the English house "rose directly from the grounds" (vii). As Loudon tells it, "the smooth, bare, and almost bald appearance, which characterized Kent's School, soon gave rise to one distinguished by roughness and intricacy, which may be called the Picturesque" (vii). But Loudon's story does not end with the rise of the picturesque. Fortunate though the picturesque turn may have been, in his estimation there was another and still more important aesthetic development in store for Victorian homeowners.

The modern style of landscape might well have begun with Gilpin's Essays, which, Loudon tells us, "may, very properly, form another volume of the series" (vi), but it is the work of Humphry Repton, a contemporary of Knight and Price, that combines "all that was excellent in the former schools." In this respect, Repton was the father of what Loudon calls "the Gardenesque," the style of landscaping that superseded the indiscriminate mixtures and crowded vegetation characteristic of all those, including even Repton, who observed the picturesque aesthetic. The gardenesque places the emphasis on individual plants—often imported, always improved by botanical knowledge—in careful juxtaposition with local species. Repton anticipated the gardenesque when, for instance, he tackled the problem of "the browsing line," created when cattle were allowed to chew off the branches of various trees at the same level. Only the removal of the cattle would allow trees to achieve the shape appropriate for their "different ages, characters, and heights."[37] Having argued for human intervention in this respect, Repton further anticipates the gardenesque school when he outlaws such intervention in the form of stylish pruning: "I am sorry to have observed, that when trees have long been used to this unsightly [i.e., unnatural] mode of pruning, it is difficult, or indeed impossible, to restore their natural shapes" (*Observations on the Theory and Practice*, 177). Whatever disfigures the natural shape of the plant, as agricultural production invariably does, is bad landscaping. Its tendency to deal in these smaller units and arrange them according to a natural standard explains why, in Loudon's words, "the Gardenesque School of Landscape has [not only] been more or less adopted in various country residences, from the anxious wish of gardeners and botanical amateurs to display their trees and plants to greatest advantage," it is also "particularly adapted for laying the grounds of small villas" (ix). As incorporated in the gardenesque school, the picturesque aesthetic becomes a method uniquely capable of rendering the traditional country estate in miniature, and aesthetic reproduction replaces agricultural production.

To appreciate fully the historical consequences of the picturesque, then, we must consider how that theory lived on in those qualities of Repton's theory of landscaping and provided a basis for the gardenesque aesthetic. His extensive writing on the topic transformed a theory instructing travelers how to derive pleasure from looking at the English countryside into something more on the order of a "how-to" book for gardeners. Already blended with features of the Kent School which aimed at displaying the owner's residence, the picturesque aesthetic underwent further dilution and dispersal as Loudon assembled Repton's work in a single volume, complete with a "copious alphabetical index." This volume was in turn scheduled to become but one of five in "as complete an Encyclopaedia of Landscape Gardening as the present state of our knowledge, in that art, will admit" (xi). What attracted Loudon to Repton in the first

The Prehistory of Realism

place was his systematic revision of the traditionalism of the improvers. Loudon finds much to admire in the writings of William Gilpin and Uvedale Price, only to deem the theories of Repton's contemporaries lacking on the same grounds Repton himself does. "The fatal rock on which all professed improvers are likely to split, is," in Repton's view, "system: they become mannerists, both from getting fond of what they have done before, and from the ease of repeating what they have so often practised."[38] He reduced the traditional method of landscape design that Knight had sought to perpetuate to a style, or mannerism. This argument on behalf of a picturesque plan that appears to be no plan at all, but rather the natural arrangement of objects, is clearly one reason why Loudon chose to disseminate Repton's advice to a middle-class readership.

In addition to this characteristic of his method, however, we must hold a second factor responsible for setting Repton apart from other improvers and giving him particular appeal for people who were building homes on the outskirts of England's commercial centers during the period when Loudon's pamphlets and cheap editions were in high demand. In rewriting the picturesque aesthetic, Repton replaced the term "improvement" with "appropriation." In a list appended to his 1795 *Sketches and Hints on Landscape Gardening,* he included the term and defined it as

a word ridiculed by Mr. Price as lately coined by me, to describe extent of property; yet the appearance and display of such extent is a source of pleasure not to be disregarded; since every individual who possesses anything, whether it be mental endowments, or power, or property, obtains respect in proportion as his possessions are known, provided he does not too vainly boast of them . . . The pleasure of appropriation is gratified in viewing a landscape which cannot be injured by the malice or bad taste of a neighbouring intruder; thus an ugly barn, a ploughed field, or any obtrusive object which disgraces the scenery of a park, looks as if its pleasure derived from appropriation, or the unity and continuity of unmixed property.[39]

Although we find "Picturesque Effect" near the top of his list of desirable features, his inclusion of "Appropriation" demonstrates the difference between Repton's readership and those who, like Gilpin, took optical pleasure in the English countryside just as it was—even if that pleasure involved taking a mallet to an abbey here or there. In seeking the pleasure of the picturesque, Gilpin's traveler took for granted the absolute difference between the pleasure of looking and the kind of gratification that came with possessing what one saw. For Repton's wealthy rural clientele, however, the two forms of pleasure easily collapsed into one, aptly named the pleasure of appropriation.

Throughout his work, Repton straddled this contradiction with perfect ease, arguing on the one hand, that the signs of enclosure should be suppressed, and on the other, that the visual field resulting should be privatized.[40] Indeed, given his inclination toward a future whose contours were shaped by this paradox, it does not take a great stretch of imagination to understand why Loudon would consider this particular man ahead of his time. Repton's view of the English countryside was in certain ways more suburban than rural, because he saw the countryside as a limited commodity. It offered a sanctuary from the public view to those with the resources to buy one: "A view into a square, or into parks, may be cheerful and beautiful, but it wants appropriation; it wants that charm which only belongs to ownership, the exclusive right of enjoyment, with the power of refusing that others shall share our pleasure" (*Fragments*, 601–602).[41] In the sections of his *Fragments on the Theory and Practice of Landscape Gardening* written just prior to his death in 1818, Repton reflects back on the term "appropriation," which he had used over twenty years earlier "to describe that sort of command over the landscape, visible from a window, which denotes it to be private property belonging to the place" (*Fragments*, 601). The tendency toward appropriation had apparently become so pronounced, the methods of achieving that pleasure so successful, that Repton modified his earlier position in terms that bear quoting at some length:

> It was, formerly, one of the pleasures of life to make tours of picturesque inquiry; and to visit the improvements in different parts of the kingdom: this is now changed to the residence at a watering-place, where the dissipation of a town life is cultivated in a continual round of idle, heartless society; without that home which formerly endeared the life of a family in the country. (*Fragments*, 602)

Repton now blames "appropriation" for depriving townspeople of the pleasure of traveling the English countryside in the manner that Gilpin had once recommended: "For the honour of the country, let the parks and pleasure-grounds of England be ever open, to cheer the hearts, and delight the eyes, of all who have taste to enjoy the beauties of nature" (*Fragments*, 602).

At the same time, he recommends further "appropriation" as the solution to the problem created when the town infiltrated the country and carries out this method in designing the landscape surrounding his home: "And, after all, the most romantic spot, the most picturesque situations, and the most delightful assemblage of nature's choice materials, will not long engage our interest, without some appropriation; something we can call our own; and if not our own property, at least, it may be endeared to us by calling it *our own home*" (*Fragments*, 602–603). In creating such a picturesque assemblage of nature's choice materials before his home in Harrestreet, Repton apparently had to close off common lands and reroute a street to suppress the signs proclaiming other people's use of the land (see Figures 1.1, 1.2). Privatization of the visual field had become, by this time, a class-specific phenomenon which betrayed a fundamental shift in the position from which the countryside was visualized. In this later "fragment" Repton regards the country house from outside that house, as a space where privatization obstructs the view. But when it comes to the grounds surrounding the villa, home, or "humble cottage," he views the natural surroundings, contrastingly, from the inside out, expanding the prospect of the homeowner and inflating his sense of proprietorship. Thus the traditional agrarian countryside that belongs to all of England coincides in Repton's theory of landscape with a bourgeois pastoralism that dreams of converting features of the unbounded countryside into private sanctuaries.[42] As if linking his own passing to that of the aristocratic landscape he helped to transform, he confesses, "I have lived to reach that period when the improvement of houses and gardens is more delightful to me than that of parks and forests, landscapes or distant prospects" (*Fragments,* 605). Within a decade a readership was in place, eager to buy Loudon's encyclopedia of landscape gardening, and the natural features of the English countryside had clearly begun to authorize an entirely new group of people.[43]

More than forty years separated the publication of Repton's first works, which gave landscapers of large country estates advice on how to practice the picturesque, from the publication of his collected works in a cheap edition describing the methods that Loudon dubbed "the gardenesque." There is abundant historical evidence to suggest that this period saw the consolidation as a class and entrenchment of the very kind of city people for whom Gilpin wrote his essays on the picturesque.[44] It is clear that a way of seeing the countryside specific to this class preceded their possession of the means to transform it accordingly. I have already suggested in referring to Austen's *Northanger Abbey* that the picturesque helped to bond together the very groups among whom it made careful distinctions. One can also witness such consolidation in *The Mysteries of Udolpho,* where Radcliffe crafts a suitable husband for her genteel heroine by dispatching a country gentleman to the city for a tour of duty. Only when he has been sufficiently modernized by conducting business in the city can Emily St. Aubert's ancestral manor in the country provide a sanctuary for his body and redemption for his soul, though not his means of income. Although they steadfastly eschew men who work in business and trade, Austen's heroines preside over equally confusing ideological mixtures, were one to judge them against the class system established by industrial capitalism.

The Prehistory of Realism

By the 1830s, the very people who appeared at the limits of the
social world imagined by Radcliffe and Austen were not only in
charge but also using the difference between town and country to
separate work and politics from domestic activities. The homes of the
newly prosperous urban classes simultaneously copied the English
manor house and displaced it as the sign and instrument of economic hierarchy. The ornamental garden that had been part of the
eighteenth-century estate became the entire grounds for the miniature manor houses springing up in the suburbs around the Victorian cities. There was, of course, a crucial economic difference between copy and original. The kind of home in which Repton lived
out his days announced a prosperity that was not produced in the
surrounding fields and outbuildings but at a significant remove from
the family residence, a prosperity, moreover, directed inward toward
the immediate family members dwelling within the house, not outward to embrace those whose lives depended on working the land.
Manifest in the home, its landscaping and garden, and its appoint-
ments, capital was converted into cultural capital.[45] The Loudons

View from Mr. Repton's cottage, at Harrestreet, as improved by him (1816). Humphry Repton.

aided and abetted this process when, as editors, they issued the promise, "We shall prove in this work that a suburban residence, with a very small portion of land attached, will contain all that is essential for happiness."[46]

Schooled in the picturesque, Loudon's readership put into practice a form of improvement that was not restricted to those who owned large tracts of land but could be practiced by anyone with sufficient money and the inclination to convert it into this form of cultural capital. But while the improvers failed to limit the practice of the picturesque aesthetic to those with both educated taste and tracts of land, their modification of Gilpin's theory nevertheless helped to convert the picturesque aesthetic into a set of practices capable of appropriating the cultural geography of England for a class of people whose wealth had its source in the city. Indeed, it is fair to say that even Burke himself played a part in shifting the cultural scales in favor of those whom he criticized for destroying the beauty of the traditional landscape. Rather than whether or not to remake the traditional countryside of England, the debate was a question of how to do a good job rather than a bad one at remaking it. Thus the die was cast: the picturesque aesthetic would determine the procedures and standard according to which the English countryside would be transformed.

By the mid-nineteenth century, the picturesque had undergone a double permutation. With a little instruction, Gilpin had argued, all members of the literate classes could have access to a world removed from the concerns and privations of city life and find immediate gratification there. With the rise of these people to a position of authority, picturesqueness apparently acquired the capacity to be converted into cultural capital and lost its former power to offer the viewer an ideal world apart.[47] As it remodeled the English landscape, however, the picturesque also retained its logic as an aesthetics of the surface, lost the place it had acquired as "one species more" of beauty, and devolved into a spectrum of more or less pejorative meanings, ranging from the nostalgic (objects of beauty no longer with us), to the conventional (objects of beauty too often reproduced), to the deceptive (objects of beauty that misrepresent the ugly facts of social life).[48] Once it began to efface the distinction between image and object that Gilpin had so carefully maintained, something that was picturesque could not be construed as either real or ideal in nineteenth-century terms.

In his 1856 essay on the "Turnerian picturesque,"[49] John Ruskin cracks open the contradiction that Repton managed to straddle without too much rhetorical stress. Ruskin was perhaps the first to understand exactly how the interaction between the principles of restriction and convertibility had played itself out in art, where the restriction of taste to an educated and propertied elite simply established certain aspects—all of them superficial—of that way of life as a form of cultural capital, into which various forms of economic capital might be converted. I have already described some of the ways in which one form of domination, embodied in the large estates of an agrarian economy, was replaced by another cultural geography that supported and was supported by industrial capital. This change was accomplished at least in part by implementing the picturesque aesthetic. Doing so on a sufficiently wide scale changed not only the meaning and value of the English landscape, I have suggested, but also how it looked, who inhabited it, and how it was used.

Ruskin was among those intellectuals who felt committed to an art form that opposed both the restrictive character of a culture that had divided English society into the observers and those who were observed, and the convertibility that had, he felt, eliminated the traditional sources of aesthetic value to be found in the English countryside, even as it narrowed down the group of those who could consume its beauty.[50] His comparison of two paintings—one by Stanfield Clarkson, whom Ruskin anointed "the first master of the lower picturesque," and the other by the still-esteemed J. M. W. Turner—dramatizes the aesthetic logic dominating his age as well as the counter-logic by which he imagined art could break up the conspiracy between restrictionism and convertibility that he attributed to the picturesque (7). It is significant that what Gilpin had characterized as but "one species of beauty more" had, by the 1850s, become the master category. In Ruskin's analysis, it takes a new version of the picturesque to counter the "lower school of the superficial-picturesque."

Clarkson's painting depicts a mill that is old and worn. Its sails "are twisted into most effective wrecks, as beautiful as pine bridges over Alpine streams." Its walls are similarly appealing to the eye, "as beautiful as a chalk cliff, all worn into furrows by the rain, coated with mosses, and rooted to the ground by a heap of crumbled stone, embroidered with grass and creeping plants" (7). All this beauty would no doubt have met with Gilpin's approval, yet these very features of the painting are precisely what, according to Victorian aesthetic theory, devalues Clarkson's mill. Ruskin completely agrees with Gilpin that "the essence of picturesque character is not in the nature of the thing, but caused by something external to it" (2). He insists on the secondary importance of the object represented, however, in order to refute the most fundamental principle of the picturesque tradition, namely, that aesthetic value resides in the image, or the quality of surface that we see.

Ruskin uses Clarkson's depiction of the mill as an object lesson in what happens to the traditional relationship between English people and their land when the landscape is converted from real to cultural capital. This example of the lower picturesque acquires its picturesqueness—for example, tattered sails, crumbled stones, creeping vines—by picturing the mill as one that no longer works. Its primitive machinery is obsolete, allowing one to enjoy it purely as an object. By stripping his subject matter of any other value, moreover, Clarkson offers the observer an aesthetic object he can imagine possessing for himself. As Ruskin portrays him, such an observer

> evidently thinks it the most fortunate thing possible. The owner is ruined, doubtless, or dead; but his mill forms an admirable object of Brittany. So far from being grieved about it, we will make it our principal light; . . . we illume our whole picture with it, and exult over its every rent as a special treasure and possession. (8)

So pervasive is this "heartless" way of seeing, according to Ruskin (9), that Turner felt compelled to combat it. In order to produce an image that was noble as well as picturesque, he figured out a way to make his mill resist such appropriation.

Turner's mill, as Ruskin describes it, is "serviceable" (8). The painter of the "noble picturesque" articulates its parts, not as a differential system of visual information, or image pattern, but in a manner that requires the viewer to visualize the mill as an assemblage of working parts. What appears primitive and fragile about the mill, as Clarkson rendered it, testifies in Turner's painting to the harshness and insecurity experienced by those generations who labored at the mill. In his struggle to make the landscape conventions of his age display what Ruskin calls a "visible pensiveness," the image itself became an obstacle that Turner had to paint his way around: "because he could not get the windmill dissected, and show us the real heart and centre of the whole, behold, he has put a pair of old millstones, *lying outside,* at the bottom of it" (8). What distinguishes the "noble" from the "lower" picturesque are the same features of the image that make us conscious of what cannot be seen on the surface of Turner's mill. Much like the stony remnants of the sheepfold in Wordsworth's "Michael" or, to borrow Ruskin's own allusion, the stones of "a ruined abbey," Turner manages to infuse the image of a mill "with the pathos of character hidden beneath" (6). Indeed, like Wordsworth, Ruskin defines art as a form of representation in which something external that has its source in the poet's "sympathy" supplements the superficial image one ordinarily sees. "The dignity of the picturesque increases from lower to higher," he contends, "in exact proportion to the sympathy of the artist with his subject" (12). Like Wordsworth in another respect as well, Ruskin finds this supplement significantly lacking in that representation which fills "ordinary drawing-books and scrap-books, and employs, perhaps, the most popular living landscape painters of France, England, and Germany" (9).

To argue that both Wordsworth and Ruskin locate truth in an aesthetic domain beyond the image, however, is to imply a philosophical continuity between them that is ultimately misleading. That Ruskin portrays Turner as a hero for using the visible surface of the mill to reveal the invisible depths indeed betrays Ruskin's mistrust of picturesque representations of the natural world. By the same token, Turner's addition of two well-worn millstones in the foreground of his painting suggests he was after a form of truth concealed behind the visible surface of his subject matter. His dissatisfaction with the tradition of visual representation finds expression in a truth specific to the age of realism, precisely because it is ultimately a truth that can be visually represented. In Turner's painting it takes a specialist at seeing to select the details which will shatter the surface tension of conventional images, thereby forcing the world of objects to tell a human story—to perform, that is, what Ruskin describes as "the unconscious confession of the fact of distress and decay" (6). Thus in Turner's version of a crumbling mill, we find something of the ugliness Gilpin once saw in Tintern Abbey, instead of the beauty

Wordsworth abstracted from the natural mementos of his relationship with Dorothy.

To oppose the popular, or surface-picturesque, the great Victorian landscape painter equated a specific brand of ugliness with the kind of social meaning from which Gilpin's traveler sought and found an antidote in images. Where the roof on Clarkson's mill is "nearly as interesting," according to Ruskin, "as a piece of the stony peak of a mountain, with a châlet built on its side; . . . exquisitely varied in its curve and swell, Turner's roof, on the contrary, is a plain ugly gable,—a wind mill roof, and nothing more" (7). In comparing the two mills, Ruskin demonstrates that Clarkson simply got his details wrong. During the age of realism, the difference between high art and low was not the difference between art that aspires to beauty beyond the surface, as Wordsworth thought it should, and art that settles for a pleasing surface. The difference between high art and low, according to Ruskin, is the difference between two renderings of the visible surface—a difference, that is, between two versions of the picturesque.

Realism, I am suggesting, was more dependent on images than Romanticism and yet was equally contemptuous of representation that stressed the superficial appearance of the object world. If the image-based theory of the picturesque struck the Romantic poet as an unimaginatively materialist view of nature, then the same suppositions seemed heartlessly idealist to Victorian intellectuals. Truth was there for the new ruling class to see, but bad images allowed them to ignore it. To represent the truth residing on the visible surface of the world, novelists as well as painters had to counter bad images with good ones. Sir Arthur Conan Doyle's detective stories provide a revealing paradigm for this substitution. Consider a passage from "The Disappearance of Lady Frances Carfax," where Holmes recounts how he nearly permitted the standard image of a coffin to obscure the peculiar differences of the coffin intended for this missing lady, thereby sending truth, along with that lady, to an early grave. "Such slips of the eye," as he explains to Watson, "are common to all mortals, and the greatest is he who can recognize and repair them. To this modified credit I may, perhaps, make some claim. My night was haunted by the thought that somewhere a clue, a strange sentence, a curious observation, had come under my notice and had been too easily dismissed. Then, suddenly, in the gray of the morning, the words came back to haunt me. It was the remark of the undertaker's wife, as reported by Philip Green. She had said, 'It should be there before now. It took longer, being out of the ordinary.' It was the coffin of which she spoke. It had been out of the ordinary . . . But why? Why? Then in an instant I remembered the deep sides and the little wasted figure at the bottom. Why so large a coffin for so small a body? To leave room for another body. Both would be buried under one certificate."[51]

In "seeing" that he had allowed the standard image of an object to obscure the details that lent this object its sinister particularity, Holmes has assumed the position of the author of a work of realism. Already predisposed to discard the conventional images that make the world deceptively familiar, the detective is receptive to the verbal information provided by an undertaker's wife sensitive to the variations in this one commodity. This in turn allows him to seize on just those details required to read the truth and tell the story inscribed on the surface of the object world.

This same talent for selecting the telling detail explains how Dickens can both be called the master caricaturist and assigned a prominent place among the authors of English realism. The famous definition of a horse provided by a tormented schoolboy in *Hard Times* equates a superfluity of "facts" with a lack of specificity that renders a description useless: "Quadruped. Gramnivorous. Forty teeth, namely twenty-four grinders, four eye teeth, and twelve incisive. Sheds coat in the spring; in marshy countries, sheds hoofs, too. Hoofs hard, but requiring to be shod with iron. Age known by marks in mouth."[52] Having demonstrated that such an abstraction offers no coherent description of the animal in question and thus no definition at all, Dickens shifts the topic of the classroom examination from actual horses to their representation: "That's a horse. Now let me ask you, girls and boys, Would you paper a room with representations of horses?" (10). When the answer turns out to be an emphatic "no," Dickens has made his point. The man is a philistine. Rather than even temporarily allow this aesthetic to win the day, Dickens forces the school inspector to step forward and demonstrate that those who use general descriptions are also likely to confuse those images with the objects they represent: "'I'll explain to you then,' after another and a dismal pause, 'why you wouldn't paper a room with representations of horses. Do you ever see horses walking up and down the sides of rooms in reality—in fact? Do you?'" (10). Having demonstrated what is wrong with standardized images— whether sentimental or purely utilitarian—Dickens offers as an antidote his own description of those who reproduce such images. Successfully completing the required definition of a horse, the tormented schoolboy blinks at his interrogator "with both eyes at once, and so catching the light upon the quivering ends of lashes that they looked like the antennae of busy insects, put his knuckles to his freckled forehead, and sat down again" (10). In the service of good images, Dickens reduces all purveyors of bad images to similarly memorable clusters of visual details.

It is tempting to consider the photograph as the perfect realization of the picturesque tradition and the aesthetic practices it spawned. In keeping with that tradition, the photograph overvalued the surface in a way that fed and fueled the desire to see, even as it blurred the distinction between the producers and consumers of such images in much the same way that Gilpin's theory did. When considered within the problematic I have been describing, however, a problematic generated by and in reaction to the picturesque, the photographic image must be seen as a counter to the picturesque, an attempt to get in touch with the very people, things, and settings the picturesque displaced.

In his account of how he came to discover the English calotype process in 1839, we can see William Henry Fox Talbot take up such a position—at once dependent on and hostile to the picturesque—as he recalls his frustration with the popular sketching device known as the camera obscura. The instrument so "baffles the skill and patience of the amateur to trace all the minute details visible on the paper," he complained, that "my faithless pencil only left traces on the paper melancholy to behold."[53] Simultaneously driven by the picturesque imperative to capture a scene or object in all its particularity and frustrated by his inability as an artist to do so, he found himself at a cultural-logical juncture where it only made sense to eliminate the middle-man, allowing nature to imprint its image directly on a piece of paper. If what Repton created by turning the picturesque into a method of appropriating the English landscape can be called a form of mediation—mediation uniquely capable of displacing what it rep-resented, as no form of mediation before it was able to do—then what Talbot sought to eliminate from the picture by creating his calotype process must be called mediation as well. *The Pencil of Nature,* the title of this first album of calotype prints, captures the logic by which Talbot sought to counter the effects produced by one form of mediation—which he calls "faithless"—with a new image that is com-pletely faithful to its object.

In a well-known article appearing in *The Quarterly Review* (1857), Lady Elizabeth Eastlake takes on the question of "how far photogra-phy is really a picturesque agent." She seems to regard photography as less than the faithful mediator that Talbot intended. It not only falls short of the details required for an aesthetic experience, creat-ing "a general emptiness of the scene," but also offers a surplus of "the most elaborate detail, and of every size not excepting life it-self."[54] On these grounds, Lady Eastlake removes photography from the domain of art in order to enshrine it in the domain of fact, as a historically "new form of communication between man and man—neither letter, message, nor pictures." Photography, she contends, "is made for the present age, in which the desire for art resides in a small minority, but the craving, or rather need, for cheap, prompt, and

The Prehistory of Realism

73

correct facts resides in the public at large. Photography is the purveyor of such knowledge to the world. She is the sworn witness of everything presented to her view."[55]

It is true that Dickens attacked the tyranny of facts over the nineteenth-century classroom and would hardly subscribe to the kind of realism Lady Eastlake ascribed to photography. We should keep in mind, however, that whenever he lashed out at facts, he invariably did so on grounds that they were not realistic enough, and he endorsed imagination, because it allowed one "to see the texture of daily life" that was otherwise occluded by utilitarian abstractions. Indeed, we might read the images that accompany the curiously attenuated ending of *Hard Times*—"Did Louisa see these things? Such things were to be."—as a sequence of photographs for which those readers of imagination will have to supply the referents.

CHAPTER TWO

The World as Image

SO LONG AS VISUAL REPRESENTATIONS POINTED TO THINGS IN much the same way that verbal representations did, the relationship between representation and world represented was relatively unproblematic. In looking at a picture, the observer was looking at an object as it was seen by another observer, albeit someone with special access to the subject matter and ability to represent it. According to Jonathan Crary, this traditional mimetic relationship between copy and original remained a rather stable one until 1839, when Henry Fox Talbot and Louis Daguerre developed the methods that would supplant the tracings made with the assistance of a camera obscura as the most exact way of reproducing what the eye could see. The camera obscura existed in analogy with the human eye. The underlying assumption was that the image traveled directly from an object in the world to a screen at the back of a darkened room, where the artist sketched it on a blank piece of paper, in the first instance, and the rational faculty re-inverted and classified the image, in the second instance. Thus, one might say, the camera obscura constituted an ideal "eye" that simultaneously subordinated the ordering faculty of the individual mind to the natural order of the world and the hand-sketched copy of the object to the original. When Talbot imagined the light entering the darkened box of that device and inscribing itself directly and durably on photosensitive paper, he unwittingly destroyed the very analogy that led to his invention. The calotype process, as he envisioned it, replaced the human eye and hand with a chemical process set off by light.

Crary calls attention to the difference between "visibility," a theory and practice of representation modeled on the natural process of seeing, and what he calls "visuality," a theory and practice of imaging that visualized what could not have been seen without the help of certain technological advances, at least not by so many people and from the same perspective. He uses the difference between visibility and visuality to describe a general and pervasive transformation of seeing that occurred at some point in the mid-nineteenth century:

> During the seventeenth and eighteenth centuries th[e] relationship [between eye and optical apparatus] had been essentially metaphoric: the eye and the camera obscura or the eye and the telescope or microscope were allied by a conceptual similarity, in which the authority of an ideal eye remained unchallenged. Beginning in the nineteenth century, the relationship between eye and optical apparatus becomes one of metonymy: both are now contiguous instruments on the same plane of operation, with varying capabilities and features. The limits and deficiencies of one will be complemented by the capacities of the other and vice versa.[1]

It is true that viewers were already accustomed to looking at people and things in the ways photography represented them. It is also true that photographic technology increased exponentially the separation of the senses that privileged seeing. In these respects, photography was only reproducing a well-established relationship between seeing an image and knowing an object. Throughout the nineteenth century, however, optical science and aesthetics came to think of the eye as increasingly embedded in a highly individuated physical body subject to mood swings, flagging attentiveness, hallucinations, and a variety of outside pressures;[2] it was no longer anything like the sensory receptor that simply saw whatever was out there to be seen. In comparison with the eye, the modern optical apparatus seemed relatively neutral and impervious to such influences, as only a machine could be. What is more, the modern camera substituted an image for the object represented, as if to say that an observer could learn more and better from the former than from the latter. That image visualized persons, places, and things inaccessible to the ordinary observer, thus expanding the observer's visual universe. At the same time, that image determined *how* one saw things, since it reproduced not only the image of some person, place, or thing, but also a way of seeing subject matter of various kinds.

Alongside developments in the theory of optics that individuated human vision, improvements in photographic technology expanded the range of people and things whose images could be mechanically reproduced, made these images cheap and available, and thus established certain ways of seeing as the standard.[3] Before very few decades had passed in this new relation between eye and camera, most literate individuals saw most of the world as photographic images, or so the evidence will suggest, and on the basis of that information they knew the world and understood their place within it.[4] The English calotype process created a negative capable of generating a number of prints, and these copies themselves replicated the same kinds of images with which the Victorian readership had become familiar through lithography, fiction, treatises on the physical and moral condition of the poor, and accounts of colonial exploration.[5] It was perhaps because photography was anything but original and made no claim to creativity of any kind that it so quickly acquired the authority to represent what was real; it could take whatever had already been seen in even the most artificial and stereotyped way and provide those people, places, things, scenes, and events with material grounding and particularity. It could do to the sordid, the exotic, and the private pockets of nineteenth-century life what the eye could do to the most accessible of public spectacles.

Even though the new images drew on a well-established pictorial

The World as Image

tradition and for the most part portrayed familiar subject matter in predictable ways, photography did not leave the world as it found it. Simply by substantiating certain ways of seeing the world, photographic images changed the world that members of the literate classes saw, a world that included themselves as observers. After the advent of the photograph, the accuracy of any image, whether sketch, painting, or photograph, would be determined by way of an implicit comparison with an unmediated image—or photograph—of that object. An image's quality was measured against other images, not by its resemblance to those people and things it claimed to represent. Witness the fact that within a mere ten years or so after the invention of photography and well before it had usurped lithography's authority to say what something looked like, a number of prominent Englishmen—the Prince Consort among them—were caught up in a lively debate concerning whether and on what grounds photography could be considered art rather than merely documentation.

Early on in the debate, one British magazine had these disparaging words to say of the camera: "We altogether doubt that any contrivance of the kind will produce a portrait half so good, natural, or expressive, as a decent artist might produce with a burnt stick."[6] In explaining the untapped potential of the new medium, however, an essay published less than a decade later, in 1851, goes to the other extreme and recommends enthusiastically that artists should copy photography:

> But stay. On yonder bridge, listlessly leaning against the balustrade, two friends have met and are conversing. Ere they pass on, our instrument has secured the imprint of them—or all, and more than all, we have described . . . How long it would have engaged a practiced hand to achieve a similar exploit we know not; but we can aver that an artist of some experience was occupied fully during eight summer days in copying this photograph.

This author regards the painting based on actual objects as inferior to one copied from the photographic image: "In the latter you feel that there is no straining after effect—that nothing has been introduced in obedience to mere conventional rules—that nothing, however trivial, has been omitted nor neglected. It is impossible, however great our faith in the painter, that we can ever place similar reliance on his work."[7] Writing in 1859, still another commentator dismissed out of hand "the photographic pictures which swarm on every drawing-room table and in every portfolio." Voicing what was also common opinion, he rejected the photographic image on grounds of inaccuracy. It was no less, he felt, than "a ghastly misrepresentation of nature, little more true to the reality than was an automaton doll with an artificial voice exhibited a few years since in London." The way to correct this problem was for photography to copy art rather than attempt to rival it. As he explains, "perhaps the most valuable application of photography is one in which it has already been very successfully employed,—the reproduction, namely, of facsimile drawings after Raphael and the other great artists. . . . Here the photograph is an unrivaled, an unapproachable transcriber."[8]

The debate gathered new energy as a result of the International Exhibition of 1862. Having borrowed their categories from the Great Exhibition of 1851, Her Majesty's Commissioners reserved Section 4 for the "Fine Arts," which included all traditional artistic media. They created quite a row when they assigned Class No. 14, "Photographic Apparatus and Photography," to Section 2, the place in the exhibition reserved for "Machinery." Whereas the Commissioners considered photographic images a product "on par with the machinery of its manufacture," the British photographic community distinguished between the camera and the camera's image. Although the Commissioners refused to reclassify photography, they did agree to give it a separate space within Section 2. This placement apparently inspired British reviewers to "give high praise to the great variety of images produced by their compatriots, especially over their traditional rivals from France. By the time the exhibition closed its doors, over one million visitors had the opportunity to examine the photographs."[9] Although it achieved only the most temporary and provocative resolutions to the question of whether photographic images were art, this debate was quite successful in repositioning visual art of any kind in relation to the apparently unmediated image produced by photography.

What the production of photographic images did to painting, it did to visual representation more generally as well. Photography endowed the image with a capacity to reduce its subject matter to the visible traces of virtually any person, place, or thing, much as if an adjective were replacing a noun. Rather than the image of an object pure and simple, a photograph offers its viewer an image marking a specific position within a larger field of vision, a position the viewer could recognize instantly. In this respect, a photograph objectifies what is commonly known as "the gaze," which structures the field of vision so that we can make a match and acknowledge the identity of the object seen. At the same time, a photograph also offers its viewer an engaging surface across which the eye can travel, much as it would in encountering sensual variations in the object world. This way of engaging the field of vision is sometimes called "the glance."[10] Where the gaze presupposes a world whose visual order exists separate and apart from any individual apprehension of it, the glance implies an object world in which the eye can wander and be ordered by that world. In the first instance, then, vision behaves taxonomically to establish a fixed identity, while the second allows perception to encounter things according to individual predilections, revealing at once the individual's expressive range and the new possibilities for perception one may encounter in the world. At the level of common sense, these two quite different scopic activities seem to oppose each other. One cannot very well look beyond the surface of visual experience to the categories that organize it and also revel in the surface details that express the conditions of the moment and one personal habit of mind. That would be tantamount to ordering the world as a static field or world picture while, at the same time, discovering the options and limitations of that field as one moves through it.

But perhaps it is possible to look at a position on the map while enjoying the view from the road. History suggests the Victorians did. Though logically opposed, these scopic activities took up a conspicuously interdependent relationship with the advent of photography. In looking at the various shops, stores, homes, parks, and tenements surrounding them, Victorian observers were consuming what they saw along the way. We may presume, however, that those observers had already seen sufficiently similar people, places, and things in photographic reproduction to allow themselves to be captivated by anomalous occurrences and fascinating details within a familiar set of visual categories. It stands to reason that this normative viewpoint would have quickly lost its grip on the real had not that picture of the world been forced to account for a constant influx of new visual information. The idiosyncratic viewpoint would no doubt have generated in its turn unresolved anxiety, if observers did not have the assurance that everything could ultimately be contained, placed, and explained in a single picture. Photography conferred the new reality on objects of having been seen in a particular way. Thus the invention of photography not only placed the camera on the same terrain as the eye, as something that could see for itself, it also shifted the camera into a position of potential superiority, where it decided that objects would henceforth be seen in the ways in which photographs either had or would picture them.[11]

It is now a commonly accepted truth that various visual media and forms of visual display developed during the nineteenth century to aid and abet colonial domination. According to this view, photography was one among a number of such means by which Europe subordinated other cultures.[12] Pierre Bourdieu offers what I consider a better way of explaining the relationship between photography and cultural imperialism. Indeed, he complains that historical accounts generally posit more fundamental psychological and economic causes for the rise of "photographic practice, subject to social rules, invested with social functions, and therefore experienced as a 'need.'" He contends that, on the contrary, this need arises from "something that is actually its consequence, namely the psychological satisfaction that [such imaging itself] produces" in modern middle-class observers.[13] I find Timothy Mitchell's work particularly helpful in this regard, because he, like Bourdieu, rejects any simple cause-effect relationship between desire and visual representation, especially when it comes to understanding Western Europe's fascination with "the Orient." Mitchell explains how the exhibitions of Islamic culture staged during the nineteenth century in some of the major cities of Europe generated desire for more such exhibitions.[14] From poring over their travel accounts, he concludes that Egyptian visitors to late nineteenth-century Paris or Copenhagen often encountered some kind of exhibit containing certain pieces of their own culture—the false front of a mosque or perhaps a mock casbah—and such encounters inadvertently gave these North African travelers special insight into their European counterparts. As he explains, "The Europe one reads about in Arabic accounts was a place of spectacle and visual arrangement, of the organization of everything and everything organized to represent, to recall, like the exhibition, a larger meaning" (295).

To reassemble bits and pieces of Middle Eastern culture as an exhibition was to resituate those bits and pieces within the domain of realism. Despite the fact that they replicated the object represented and were even made of elements of the original, the scenes of Cairo on exhibition acquired the effect of the real chiefly because their meaning resided in a world prior to and outside the exhibition. Exhibitions doubled the visible world, offering a copy of a reality presumed to be somewhere else, where most Europeans could not see it. By appearing to put viewers directly in touch with its subject matter, the exhibition collapsed seeing into knowing. The visitor to the Cairo exhibit in Paris could see what he would see were he actually to go to Cairo. But the exhibition not only set the world on exhibition outside and apart from the viewer as a spatial field the viewer could survey, it also represented that world as though it actually existed primarily to be seen. Convinced of the fundamental difference between text and world, Europeans began to go looking for the world in other places and usually found it disappointing.[15] Observers came to expect what they encountered outside the domain of their visibility to look like the system of objects on display within the European metropolis, and the world invariably let them down. According to Mitchell's research, the sense of emptiness Nerval experienced on nearing the end of a visit to Cairo was more typical than not: "Just as well the six months I spent there is over; it is already nothing, I have seen so many places collapse behind my steps, like stage sets; what do I have left of them [but an] image as confused as that of a dream."[16] In place of the elation anticipated from confronting the thing itself, the Cairo that Nerval encountered in Africa offered the predictability of images he had already seen. The place was damned if it did conform to an exhibit, and it was damned if it did not.

When Egyptians observed one of the great European spectacles, they knew perfectly well that things, real or fabricated, were not the things themselves but components of an exhibition. Disappointment welled up in the gap between visuality and visibility; the original was likely to strike the European viewer as nothing but a debased version of the copy; and that viewer was likely to respond by yearning to see an original that exceeded the standard set by the copy. But, as Nerval realized to his great dismay, the new object of desire was destined to be a copy too, since the copy and not the original had set the visual standard for originality. One Egyptian remarked that "every year that passes, you see thousands of Europeans traveling all over the world, and everything they come across they make a picture of" (304). European tourists evidently began sketching scenes and eventually taking photographs, preferring, one might speculate, to harbor the illusion of the real promoted by the copy than to experience the letdown of encountering things that paled before their replications.

Neither the class of people who produced and consumed photographic images nor the spaces those people inhabited in Europe were immune to the effects of being visually objectified. The people who consumed photographs also produced significantly more images of themselves, their families, homes, shops, parks, and thoroughfares than they did of other peoples and their exotic habitats.[17]

In representing their own environment in certain ways, those who produced and consumed the spectacles of primitive and Oriental cultures also divided that environment into "us" and "them" on the basis of rather crude visual distinctions.[18] As they did so, these same people grew fascinated with life in the squalid neighborhoods, and they made those economically just below them want to occupy the well-ordered spaces of that city, possess the goods, and inhabit the bodies of men and women stationed luminously above them.[19] According to the theories most often used to think about urban life during the nineteenth century, this image-object, the subject of photography, would have to be classified as idealism pure and simple, were it not for the fact that social spaces developed to display things and people as they had or might be photographed. Though clearly belonging to the domain of mediation, representation, or discourse, the new means of making social and cultural distinctions cannot be so easily dismissed. Henri Lefebvre contends that social space is neither a thing among other things nor a product among other products, but instead "subsumes things produced and encompasses their interrelationships . . . and thus cannot be reduced to the rank of a simple object." While he refuses to locate social space on the materialist side of the ideal versus material divide, Lefebvre also insists "there is nothing imagined, unreal or 'ideal' about it."[20] Any group that claims to be real has to produce its own social space; otherwise that group is doomed to remain confined to the purely ideological or cultural domains, where its status inevitably dwindles to that of folklore.

In what is still one of the most important descriptions of the urbanization process, David Harvey relies on a similar model of modern culture to argue that in London the class struggle turned into a struggle for land. But this was not, as we might assume, a struggle that depended on who could possess the most land through either ownership or resistance. On the contrary, this struggle was waged and won by converting land into cultural space. Under these circumstances, one could possess land, only to discover it had been redefined as either too expensive to rent, on the one hand, or unfit to inhabit, on the other. Victory went to those who possessed the cultural means to divide the city into parcels of private property and so placed value on certain residential areas over others. Victory went, in Harvey's words, to the class who established "the authority of the spaces it could control over the spaces it could not."[21] The various genres of urban photography provide a record of the production of city space and the struggle that put certain kinds of space in charge of others, but this is certainly not all they do. Their utter pliability, the fact that the camera could only copy what was put before it and could only do so from a perspective that made sense to a photographer and his customers, is what allowed photography to emerge from the category of a curiosity or fad, to infiltrate virtually every aspect of modern life, and to establish the way in which that reality was most truly and accurately perceived.

The Order of Things Urban

It can be argued that what the European exhibitions did to Cairo, the camera could in theory do to anything—including the exhibition. Judging from the sheer redundancy of certain kinds of photographs, the camera was just as selective as the exhibition hall, and photographers did indeed seek out rather limited kinds of subject matter. These images also converged to form an entire world, much as objects did in the exhibition. In England, moreover, photographs constituted a small but significant and already contested part of the exhibition that inaugurated the age of exhibitions. His comments concerning the catalogue to the Great Exhibition of 1851 make it clear that Dickens agreed with Her Majesty's Commissioners that photographic images should be included in the exhibit devoted to "Machines" rather than among the "Fine Arts":

> The Commissioners caused to be prepared, for presentation at foreign courts, and to a few distinguished bodies, magnificent copies of the illustrated Catalogue and the Jury Reports, adorned with a large number of photographs relating

to exhibited articles; of these photographs there were as many of each taken as there were presentation copies of the whole work; and thus there was a duplication, or publication, equivalent to that whereby prints of the ordinary kind are diffused among the nations of the world. The great power of multiplication is one secret of the importance of the more recent photographic processes.[22]

Precisely because he thought of photographs as products rather than as reproductions of the world, Dickens could appreciate the photograph's power to substitute an image for an object. He correctly foresaw how the reproducibility of those images would increase the power of the exhibition proper as they made it both cheap and portable. Photographs were not only a part of the exhibition, in other words, they were also a less conspicuous and yet more powerful form of exhibition in their own right.

In the rest of this chapter I will try to provide a sense of how these images piled up around certain sites and converged to incorporate all the ideological contradictions of the moment as hostile states of being that nevertheless formed an internally coherent entity, or world. Fundamental to photography's success in this endeavor was the fact that photographs were not original and never tried to be. These images sought out and laminated themselves to certain elements of other media and genres—the painted portrait, the line-drawn or lithographed specimen, the gnarled objects favored by the picturesque tradition—and transformed these materials into a vast new visual order with the city at its center. This process of appropriation, repetition, and synthesis did not happen in an orderly sequence, and it would be erroneous to understand it as such. Instead, I will identify what I take to be the most basic and enduring components of a visual paradigm, explaining how they might have developed in collaboration with other forms of verbal and visual representation to reconstitute the world as image.

If photography arose and thrived in response to a desire to put the world itself on exhibition (Figure 2.1), then photographers took their most obvious shot at fulfilling that desire in making panoramic photographs. This kind of image emerged as a novelty in a market for topographical images that flourished during the mid-1860s, when a number of large commercial firms in England, France, and Italy were producing and publishing such photographs for purposes of tourism. At first, photographs of the urban landscape stuck close to the guidelines for drafting city streets and important buildings. But since these images were produced chiefly as a means of persuading tourists to come and see the city for themselves, photographers soon developed their own strategies of enticement. Street views were characteristically shot from a second-story window or some other elevated vantage point, the better to capture the spatial character of the modern thoroughfare. During the 1860s, a shorter exposure time and the perfection of combination printing allowed photographers to maximize this effect in panoramas that could compress and encompass a substantial piece of the city into one horizontally extended view. M. Christine Boyer compares the resulting cityscape to "pictures that hung in art galleries, a series of encircling spaces that contained their spectators, regulated their pleasures, and focused their gaze." The point of her comparison is to emphasize the aesthetic displacement involved in technically increasing the size of what one could see: "The real city, never actually displayed, gradually disappears from view: its chaos, its class distinctions, its snares and vices, all of these lay outside the circular frame beyond the horizon that dominated the spectator's gaze."[23] It is true that the panorama produced a purely artificial picture of the world by providing observers with a viewpoint which they could not achieve unaided by photographic technology. On the other hand, these images, in collaboration with the great exhibitions, soon began to determine what the urban middle classes thought a city was, how they lived, where they went, and what they saw when they were there. In this sense we would have to identify the city on display as indeed the real one. There is every reason to think that as photography took its shape from the modern city and the genres that were rising to the occasion of representing it, photography also gave shape to that city.

FIGURE 2.1   East Hill, Colchester (c. 1860).

"The emphasis on the notable and the new," writes Eve Blau, "resulted in representations of cities that not only were incomplete and partial collections of major monuments, public buildings, and grand new boulevards—but that also made every city look alike."[24] While this was true of modern cities in general, the creation of a visual standard for "the city" also endowed certain cities with a distinctive national and even individual appearance. Malcolm Andrews notes, for example, how "aggressive individualism, backed by private wealth, was giving a distinctive character to the redevelopment of nineteenth-century London. The city was celebrated for an idiosyncratic splendour wholly unlike contemporary Paris under Napoleon III's great rebuilding programme." The result was an architectural rebellion against what Victorians regarded as "the drab uniformity and constraints of the previous age," which was expressed, Andrews tells us, "in a bizarre range of pre-Georgian architectural styles. The new age had no architectural language of its own, except this revivalist eclecticism."[25] Noting that both the panorama and the city design were anything but picturesque, we might assume that by condemning dilapidated buildings the urban renewal process erased the signs of picturesqueness from the city. Having done so, however, this effort at modernization smuggled the picturesque aesthetic back into the picture as a style of renovation that was distinctively English. In 1900, Sir George Lawrence Gomme could recommend with utter confidence that "[a] ride on the top of an omnibus through any of the great routes . . . reveals, to those who have the feeling for the picturesque, beauties in London streets which are wholly local in character."[26]

The result was to transform the city from a visible space that surrounded the observer into a space he could step back from and view in much the same way he would an exhibition. In the panoramic photograph as in a picturesque landscape, details became important not in and of themselves but in aggregate, because there were simply too many for any one feature to count. In excess, such details constituted an abstraction for the volume of things that were transported rapidly through a relatively wide thoroughfare that either spanned the image or cut through it along an imaginary line from front to back. What we see in these images, then, is what might be called the flow of the modern city. Conceptualizing the city much as Charles Babbage, whom we credit for discovering grease, had imagined a factory through which materials were conveyed by a lubricated belt from work station to work station, the panoramic photographer visualized the city as a space in which an enormous variety of things were being distributed from suppliers to shops to consumers. This kind of motion was seen as the vitality of commercial blood coursing through the nation's veins.[27] The result, as in Babbage's factory, was a unitary space capable of both moving and immobilizing the objects and people stationed within it. Needless to say, these spatial images referred to something that was not really there to be seen until the panoramic shot allowed the middle classes of Europe to think of their major urban centers as the giant social, economic, and cultural hearts of the country through which all its people, goods, and information flowed. Because a space so organized was both *a* city in which they happened to be located and *the* city in terms of which they understood their relation to the real, Europeans began looking for similarly organized nodal points both elsewhere in Europe and throughout the Middle East. Their diaries reveal that Europeans visiting Cairo immediately sought a position from which to view the city panoramically, as if they could not really see it from traveling through its winding streets and bazaars.[28] In doing so, they were also differentiating a much older city structure from the one they associated with Europe, commercial vitality, and modernity. As Tom Gunning explains, "Any number of the *topoi* of modernity that cluster around the second half of the nineteenth century can be approached as instances of circulation: the boulevard system in the Haussmanization of Paris, which allowed a previously unimaginable expansion of traffic; the new modes of production of goods in the work process of the 'new factory system,' which demanded that individual workers perform simple and repetitive tasks as material passed before them; or innovations in systems of rapid transportation."[29] All the distinguishing features of the modern city are forms of circulation that transform one thing into another: bodies into work, work into goods, goods into money, money into goods, and so forth. Like everything else that took part in this process, photography was at once a cause and an effect, a means and an object of circulation.

By turning from the panorama to a very different kind of photograph, we can begin to understand what this reconception of the city as a panoramic photograph did to the people and things who were turned into images and put in circulation as such. Recalling that the population of Paris doubled and that of London tripled during the nineteenth century, we can certainly understand why the old city centers might have required renovation. Not so evident is why photographers were routinely commissioned to make a historical record of each plot of land, alleyway, and tenement slated for demolition.

The thirty-one photographs of old Glasgow taken by Thomas Annan between 1868 and 1874 record the first major redevelopment scheme in Great Britain and provide an exceptionally eloquent example of what was in fact a massive enterprise of converting the historic city into a visual record of the past. Empowered to acquire property, pull down buildings, and realign streets, the Glasgow city government put in thirty-nine new streets, widened a dozen more, and cleared a substantial amount of land for sale or lease to private owners. As first arranged in an album, Annan's images provided a record of those parts of the city that had not yet been touched by modernization. To offer such a record, he began with a shot of a main thoroughfare that panoramic photography would have displayed for purposes of attracting tourists. From there, however, his camera veered sharply onto numerous narrow, dark, and crooked passageways which seem to lead the eye into another city (Figure 2.2). Whereas panoramas displayed the new city bursting with people and things, all coursing toward some destination, this kind of photograph represented the old city centers evacuated of people and the objects on which they depended for a livelihood. It could be argued that the lack of human life in Annan's photographs was a function of slow exposure time rather than a matter of his aesthetic choice. By comparing these images of abandoned alleyways with panoramic depictions of the blur of commercial traffic on modern thoroughfares, however, one comes to understand the difference between them not only as a difference between photographic genres but also as a difference these genres helped to reproduce as the diverse contexts in relation to which each could be seen as an accurate reflection.

Since these images were supposed to be historical records pure and simple, we might expect them to adhere most closely to the doctrine of realism. No doubt men such as Annan tried. But the fact that he was recording a place and a whole way of life marked for obsolescence seems to endow these images with a fantastic quality that puts them at the opposite pole from realism. Eve Blau reminds us of the convention-setting power of Annan's work: his images, stark in comparison to the more nostalgic photographs of this kind, were

FIGURE 2.2   *Close No. 193, High Street* (1868).
Thomas Annan.

bound in a volume compiled in support of the redevelopment project.[30] Soon after they were taken, this photographic record was apparently all that remained of the wyndes and vennels of medieval Glasgow and the stone tenements that had been home to wealthy
merchants up through the eighteenth century. What Annan considered a purely documentary project joined a well-established category
of writing and illustration that had already made the most abject
pockets of urban decay seem fascinating to the middle-class observer.[31] In photographing the slums and tenements of the modern

FIGURE 2.3   *Bluegate Fields* (1872), Gustave Doré.

city, photographers reworked conventions established when Friedrich Engels and James Kay Shuttleworth described the condition of
the working classes and Dickens, Elizabeth Gaskell, and Benjamin
Disraeli, along with the popular engraver Gustave Doré (Figure 2.3),
turned these scenes of misery into popular entertainment. These
and many other artists and intellectuals had produced what might be
called the urban gothic, a genre to which photography came late but
nevertheless made a unique contribution. While Engels, Dickens,
and Doré all dealt in excess and endowed the most depressing sec-

The World as Image

tions of the city with preternatural life, Annan evacuated all signs of life so as to present his viewer with something more in keeping with the traditions of the haunted house or the deserted village.[32] Though commissioned to record those sections of the city that were about to be demolished, Annan's images not only lent material substance to the descriptions of Dickens and Doré, his photographic record also represented human misery, filth, and disease in highly idealized terms. However unconsciously, he exploited the difference between the vibrant fullness of the commercial city and the inert fragility of the quarters housing the poor to define the difference between past and present.[33] In doing so, it could be argued, photography such as Annan's helped to overcome the friction that kept people and goods from circulating freely throughout the city. If things in motion sometimes appear as streaks of opacity in panoramic shots, where the flow of traffic appears as just that, a flow, then an object's movement in the gothic image renders that object translucent so that one could see right through it to an open space beyond and imagine city space with that object gone.[34]

It is worth noting how, in using the image to assign a space to its subject matter, the camera automatically gendered that subject matter. Photographically speaking, gender might well depend on the degree of opacity an object acquired or failed to acquire in becoming an image. In linking nineteenth-century photography to the culture's fascination with spiritualism, Gunning has called attention to the fact that communion with the dead implicitly feminized the medium: "The medium was passive, but passive in a particularly dynamic way. She was receptive, sensitive, a vehicle, a medium by which manifestation spread. All mediums, men or women, had to be, in Spiritualist parlance, feminine, or negative (borrowing again from electricity and magnetism a technical term which also has implications for photography) in order to let the spirit world manifest itself."[35] Gunning's remarks cast an interesting light on the nineteenth-century view of the "medium" of photography itself, which can certainly be considered "passive in a particularly dynamic way." He also offers a suggestive analogy by which we might understand what photography accomplishes in semiotic terms when it selects certain objects for the kind of transparency that indicates there is nothing of substance behind the image. Whether male or female, rich or poor, people are rendered feminine in opposition to figures that other images endow with the opacity of material things.

The spatial divide between the commercial vitality associated with England's future prosperity and the poor who were simultaneously increasing in number and losing materiality within the new visual order was far from a simple one. Complicating the situation was the picturesque aesthetic. We have already followed that tradition through Humphry Repton into John and Jane Loudon's popular gardening books, where it appropriated certain features of aristocratic iconography and made them available for suburban display. Later in this chapter, I will explain what happened to that version of the picturesque as it infused the new art of photography and was brought inside the urban home. For the moment, however, I want to examine briefly what the picturesque tradition did to the urban poor. From its inception, the picturesque aesthetic had been uniquely geared to the task of turning poverty into art. I have argued that William Gilpin might be credited with founding the first middlebrow theory of art, when he explained that to see something as picturesque, all the observer had to do was to select a view featuring irregular shapes and highly textured surfaces. Equally important is his suggestion that things which were rugged, rustic, worn, and old tended to yield such a surface. This subject matter makes it possible to reduce what we see to "a variety of little parts; on which the light shining shews all its small inequalities, and roughness."[36]

The camera brought the principles of the picturesque into the city streets and broke down the complex and fluid social life transacted there into purely visual components. A photograph immortalizing the no doubt pungent mortality of a butcher shop demonstrates what happens to the relationship between people and things as the photograph disperses the gaze across an almost entropically detailed surface (Figure 2.4). The reduction of everything within the frame to such information creates a strange equivalence between those rather meaty butchers and the slabs of meat they seem so eager to display. But savoring this "richness of surface" detail is only half of the picturesque experience. To complete the aesthetic process, according to Gilpin, one must recombine those parts into a highly abstract visual object. Those who want to grasp the picturesque element of any scene should also look for general shapes, dresses, groups, and occupations, for these constitute "the idea of *simplicity;* from which," he says, "results the picturesque."[37] To make poverty interesting to look at, these same techniques set the poor apart from prosperous people in terms of a historical perspective (in that the poor were more primitive than modern) and a spatial one (in that their homes were not private enclosures, but a space that could be penetrated by the tourist and the sociologist, as well as the photographer).

Onto the urban poor were projected many of the same qualities that English tourists found so fascinating both in exotic cultures overseas and in the rural folk communities of Great Britain, qualities the middle classes imagined they themselves had overcome. So says an anonymous reviewer of *Hard Times* in praise of Dickens's representation of the working classes:

> In humble life, different occupations, different localities, produce marked and distinct hues of character: these differences are made more apparent by the absence of those equalizing influences which a long-continued and uniform education, and social intercourse subject to invariable rules of etiquette, produce upon the cultivated classes. Original and picturesque characters are therefore much more common among the poorer orders; their actions are simpler, proceeding from simpler motives, and they are principally to be studied from without.[38]

By the time *Hard Times* was published, however, middle-class enthusiasm for slumming had been dampened by the links established between the spectacle of crumbling buildings and the cholera epidemics of the 1840s as well as between the distorted and ragged bodies of the poor and the Chartist uprisings of that decade. Such factors

FIGURE 2.4   A butcher's shop (c. 1900).

forced spectators to imagine the peril that lay beyond the fascinating surface of the slums.

The same combination of historical factors paradoxically gave rise to the tradition of illustration that Malcolm Andrews has aptly named "the metropolitan picturesque."[39] Exploiting the picturesque appeal of urban poverty, any number of photographers made slum life safe for middle-class observers. Here was the same aesthetics of the surface applied to those sectors of the city too dangerous to inhabit and to the people who inhabited them. These people are available to the public view, and the camera could easily resituate them in much the same kind of space occupied by objects from Cairo at the Paris exhibition. Of the many photographers who worked in this genre, John Thomson and Paul Martin are among the best known and can serve to demonstrate how the principles of the picturesque aesthetic informed this particular genre of photography. True to tradition, Thomson and Martin display the elements of street life not as an aggregate, or flow, but as single figures frozen in isolation in a public place. These figures do not ask to be photographed; they are caught in the act of living their lives and seem unable to resist being turned into images.

In the photograph of a chimney sweep, who appears to have been on his way to work when his sooty exterior, oddly-shaped pack of tools, and impish apprentice caught Thomson's eye (Figure 2.5), all the features that make the photograph interesting to view, including the sweep's mildly startled expression, are directly related to his work—his grime, his tools, his assistant—and yet the photograph strips them of all use value. All signs of their capacity to labor, the public service performed by these particular people, have become visual curiosities in keeping with the spirit of the picturesque tradition. The same can be said of Thomson's memorable portrait of a working-class woman listlessly cradling a child in her lap (*The Crawlers,* Figure 2.6).[40] Scholars place Martin's photographs of London street life alongside Thomson's in the tradition of documentary photography and read them as records of how the working classes actually lived. Moreover, both photographers are generally considered reformers for having exposed middle-class viewers to the harshness of the life to which they had condemned so many people.[41] Rather than revealing some basis for sympathy between one class and another, however, Martin's method of representing labor demonstrates why the picturesque tradition has rarely been known to inspire reform, even when reform is the professed motive for taking such a photograph. Imitating the treatment that he had seen given to

FIGURE 2.5   *The Temperance Sweep* (c. 1876–1877).
John Thomson.

FIGURE 2.6   *The Crawlers* (1876). John Thomson.

FIGURE 2.7   *Loading up at Billingsgate Market, Cutout Figure*
(c. 1894). Paul Martin.

photographs of statuary, the story goes, Martin decided to set the
working man apart from the welter of visual information with which
the laboring body tended to merge (Figure 2.7). In so resisting the
tendency of the picturesque to reduce people to the status of objects,
however, he extracted labor, in the figure of the worker himself, from
the situation in which that labor had been performed. Indeed, looking at their images removed from the visual space that presumably

The World as Image

defined them, it is difficult to tell what such people were doing when Martin happened upon them with his camera. This effort to monumentalize them paradoxically did to working people exactly what the picturesque did to the windmill in Clarkson's painting: it detached Thomson's subjects from the symbolic economy in which they once had human purpose and labor value.

That photographs of London street life did not present a pretty picture was a large part of the fascination they held for the Victorian readership.[42] In contrast with portraits of the respectable classes, photography pictured urban types with irregular physiognomies—especially facial features—that produced the same sense of colorful heterogeneity that Dickens's reviewer associated with working-class culture. As Andrews points out, "natural Picturesque variety and individuality in the social . . . context was thought to have survived only outside the culturally dominant middle classes, and particularly amongst the poorer classes."[43] The individuals who appeared within such a framework were not representatives of the modern working class, paradoxically, but the very people—artisans, independent laborers, and petty tradesmen—who were often the casualties of modernization. Given the fact that the visible signs of such individuality were no less fleeting than the demand for the work these people performed, and thus likely to vanish with the next migration of the affluent population to the other side of town, it is particularly ironic that this genre of photography should make the bodies of these particular people appear more durable than those of the fashionable and well-to-do. It was almost as if the closer to matter an individual body appeared to be, the less it actually mattered.

Before considering where photography locates the observing subject within this differential system of images, let me emphasize how various, how contradictory, and yet how seamless was the world of objects captured and solidified in countless photographs. We should remember that photography performed this magic at the very moment when other forces of modernization were infusing the observer's world with an amazing array of new objects, breaking up land into parcels for lease or sale, forcing city people to migrate from one section of the city to another, and altering their sense of group identity as they did so. The more completely the visible facts worked in the service of a photograph's public meaning, the more subtle and yet potent was the photographic effect. By comparing the image of the butcher's stall first with Thomson's portrait of the chimney sweep and then with Martin's photographic statuette (see Figures 2.4, 2.5, 2.7), we can observe the progressive disappearance of the context for the human figure.[44] Scholars tend to respond to this decontextualization by putting Martin's figures back into the larger photograph from which he excerpted them (Figure 2.8). To replace the figure of a worker in the photographic context from which it was taken is to place it within the same system of images that Victorian photographers and their customers did, which does nothing to locate the working classes within the symbolic economies from which they were taken when first selected for photographic subject matter. As it made the poor visible, Victorian photography also rendered invisible the local cultures in which most of the population actually worked and made sense of material things. Another of Thomson's photographic projects should suggest another reason why the appropriation of local cultures by the new visual order was so effective.

Thomson is as well known for his ethnographic descriptions and photographs of China as he is for *Street Life in London* (1877). The popularity of his work suggests that despite the many interesting details by which he differentiated East from West, even those English men and women who visited China saw the Asian landscape and people much as Thomson had portrayed them. Dickens surely spoke for many when he equated the experience of seeing a photograph of some foreign scene with having actually been there. Told of the photographs of a suspension bridge being constructed by an English engineer over the Dnieper, for example, he marveled that "two thousand miles of distance were thus practically annihilated; the Czar could know all that was going on, without stirring from his palace at St Petersburg, by comparing the photographs successively forwarded to him."[45] Upon returning from his ten-year stint in East Asia, Thomson turned for his subject matter to the working-class people of Lon-

FIGURE 2.8   *Loading up at Billingsgate Market* (c. 1894). Paul Martin.

don's East End. In doing so, we might imagine, he brought the same kinds of shots to bear on the culture of poverty within the modern city. The techniques by which he sought to familiarize readers with the social distinctions among the people of China served to estrange respectable observers from local English street types. By comparing his collections of English and East Asian types, one finds that he has captured his chimney sweeps and crawlers in much the same pose and in a similar setting as those he chose for portraying this Chinese holyman (Figure 2.9). Thomson sets both apart from the members of a respectable family. That he himself saw two such different cultural categories of individual in much the same terms is evident in

FIGURE 2.9   *A Mendicant Priest* (1873–1874). John Thomson.

the ethnographic commentary he wrote to accompany this image of "A Mendicant Priest":

> This priest is attached to the Kuan-yin Temple; his duty is to beg for the benefit of the establishment, and to perform unimportant offices for the visitors to the shrine, light incense-sticks, and teaching short forms of prayer. I paid him half-a-dollar to stand for his portrait. He was very wroth,

declaring the sum quite inadequate, as the picture had bereft him of a portion of his good luck, which he would require to work up again with offerings. He further informed me that a good run of praying visitors would have paid him much better for his time. He was undoubtedly of an avaricious disposition, and well up in his profession of begging. I would judge, however, from his starved miserable appearance that he was a faithful disciple of Buddha, and that a very small portion of his gains was devoted to his dress or sustenance. He is a type of thousands of the miserable, half-starved hangers-on of monastic establishments in China. Equally indispensable are tribes of loathsome beggars infesting the gates of the temples, and herds of hungry, howling dogs, that live, or die rather, on temple garbage and beggar's refuse.[46]

This passage systematically translates the spiritual practices of the Chinese mendicant—his "unimportant offices," his resistance to the photographer, his dissatisfaction with the photographer's sum—into modern economic terms and, from those terms, derives an explanation (superstitiousness, laziness, and "avariciousness") for the signs of poverty which the man may in fact have displayed with pride.

The point was to divide this Chinese subject matter into two mutually exclusive kinds of people: respectable and poor. When a figure happened to be both respectable and poor, as in the case of the mendicant priest, the urban picturesque invariably placed that individual among those lacking respectability, should he or she happen not to be white.[47] The result was not only to attach a class to racial difference, but also to affix a racial marking to class difference. In picturing the world, photography consequently fractured and dispersed existing people and groups of people among ontologically incompatible spaces. At the same time, as these images piled up around certain sites of visibility, they converged with one another to make a world that could in theory be visualized in its entirety. Oscar Rejlander was among those who attempted this feat with a single image when he used a method of printing that combined pieces

FIGURE 2.10   *The Two Ways of Life* (1857). Oscar Gustave Rejlander.

carefully cut from different photographs to produce the seamless collage that Prince Albert commissioned for the Royal collection (Figure 2.10).

The Abode of the Observer

Despite the fact that the respectable classes compulsively photographed themselves, their property, their progeny, and the milestones of their personal lives, there was a problem with exactly who might be the intended viewer. As John Tagg observes, "At the level of spatial zoning, the city itself—at least, the respectable city of middle class life—was structured around the differentiation of a feminized private and domestic sphere from a masculinized public domain." Being seen in even the most respectable places outside the home would expose a woman to "the predatory public gaze of the male" and put her "in consequent peril of confusion with that other, unspeakable order of womanhood, which entered the public arena only as the brazen object of an exchange and desire that were decently

The World as Image

repressed in the closeted spaces of domesticity."[48] As if to underscore their difference from the people who inhabited public spaces, some people of taste considered members of the respectable classes unfit subjects for photographic representation. Photography was said to capture only the grosser features of the face, to attend to the details of an object rather than to its general design, and to prove incapable of capturing the natural landscape.[49] Where a Gainsborough "painted a soul as well as a face" and so endowed his subjects with the inner life that made them who they were, according to one Victorian critic, photography was not the medium in which to represent a fine-featured woman with a fair complexion, the architecture of a well-proportioned home, or the subtle effects of landscape. As another critic of photography explains, "a good photograph has a truth of its own, . . . and the truth has become idiomatic in our language, that a truthful transcript of a thing is 'photographic' in its resemblance. A good photograph often possesses a subtlety of resemblance which brings out characteristics of race or mental capacity scarcely seen in the original, but which undoubtedly exist."[50] Individuals who displayed such picturesque qualities generally had rough-hewn faces, and their bodies were often disfigured from the harsh conditions in which they lived. Photography could produce a curious opacity that seemed to racialize these figures, as it turned them into objects fit for exhibition. This could explain why A. J. Munby and Hannah Cullwick found it erotically gratifying to drag her image back and forth across the ontological divide separating the image of a woman of the street or scullery from that of her respectable counterparts.[51] Munby not only delighted in having Hannah scrub the scullery floor while he was entertaining his friends in fine style just a room away, he also enjoyed parading her as his fashionably attired wife. That he began this peculiarly Victorian relationship by hiring her as a photographic model for a repertoire of poses, including those of a slave, a working woman, and a respectable lady, suggests that his was no common thrill of domination. It was specifically the power of the image to determine essence that he loved.

But the abode of the observer ultimately required object status as well as a specific genre of photography in order to secure for itself a prominent position within the visual order. Photographs of private life sought to reintroduce nature as the source of value in an urban milieu from which the other genres of photography conspired to banish it. In the guise of nature, the signs of economic difference assumed a feminine form under the protection of bourgeois masculinity, whether the male is figured explicitly or not. During the 1860s, Lady Clementina Hawarden produced especially memorable scenes of the posh interiors of fashionable London homes and the women confined therein, out of the public view (Figure 2.11). Such photographs were often staged near a window or some other natural light source that not only ensured their characteristic luminosity, but usually placed a membrane or barrier between inside and outside as well. Lady Hawarden's better-known contemporary, Julia Margaret Cameron, similarly sought, in the words of Gerhard Joseph, "to materialize in the camera what her great-niece later metaphorized as 'a room of one's own,' a female space within which woman might realize her potential by making explicit the terms of her own interior discourse."[52] Indeed, to carry the analogy further, both Hawarden and Cameron charge this space with signs of pent-up subjectivity.

Cameron is perhaps best known for photographs that use upper-middle-class individuals to represent scenes from the Bible, classical mythology, and Arthurian romance, thereby producing a purely aesthetic aristocracy.[53] These photographs circumvented the problem of visually representing private people of some consequence by using their figures to represent, not the individuals themselves, but abstractions from legend and romance. Despite her tendency to use her friends and family metaphorically, Cameron never failed to inflect their images with gender according to an utterly familiar visual code that simultaneously assigned them a race and a class as well. To see how gender does all this work even when an individual is not posing as himself or herself, we might contrast a pair of Cameron's images with Thomson's photographs of the chimney sweep and crawlers, respectively. Cameron's famous men are distinguished by their opacity and cragginess, picturesque features which we might be tempted

FIGURE 2.11   Photographic study (c. 1860). Clementina,
Lady Hawarden.

to say they share with both of Thomson's East Enders. Turning to an
example of Cameron's well-bred women, however, one sees why it is
folly to believe a photograph can capture some element of humanity
that cuts across the boundaries of class. Their semi-transparent
otherworldliness naturalizes the social identity of such female faces

FIGURE 2.12   *Three King's Daughters Fair* (1873). Julia Margaret Cameron.

(Figure 2.12). Even when we fail to recognize the features of, say, her niece, Julia (later to be the mother of Virginia Woolf), some member of Cameron's social circle, or one of her maids, that body's transparency does not indicate obsolescence. Clearly representing the irreplaceable members of a middle-class family, a family of which each member has his or her own name and unique features, these bodies hardly wear the anonymous faces of Annan's city dwellers. Transparency cloaked in literary dress indicates "soul," in the Victorian sense of the term, or what might simply be called interiority. Under these circumstances, transparency in a woman is the sign of individualism, the transformation of her body into a sign of the moral and emotional qualities contained within that body. The same is true of Cameron's men. Their craggy picturesqueness builds on the individualism always implicit in the name attached to their portraits. Instead of a type, these men represent only themselves; each is one of a kind (Figure 2.13). As these portrayals of Victorian aristocracy (Cameron's Arthurian allegories make that term appropriate) equate class with the absence of racial marking, a pure or transcendent humanity, they also appropriate the picturesque exterior of working-class physiognomy for the tormented masculinity of the Victorian intellectual.

I want to stress the fact that Cameron's are not typical family portraits whose name recognition and distinctive features indicate a unique interiority known only to their intimate social group. As an aesthetic transformation of the family portrait, however, Cameron's men and women not only play by the rules of the genre, they also do so hyperbolically.[54] One can observe how qualities of interiority appear as features of the body to naturalize the economic power distinguishing those who commissioned photographs from those who were either paid to model or whose photographs could simply be "taken." Thus it is fair, I believe, to regard the kind of family portraits that became a fixture in every middle-class home as both prototypes and appropriations of these efforts to turn photography into an artistic medium (Figure 2.14). Such photographs tend to use objects to indicate the value of the bodies within the photographic frame, whereas Hawarden and Cameron had relied on distinctive facial expressions, literary allusion, or sheer radiance to do so. Nature seems to flourish in an artificially illuminated interior, blossoming in the folds of rich clothing and gauzy curtains, bursting out in organic carvings on a piano front, and peering down from the chinoiserie poised near the top of the frame. Where Hawarden's use of space

FIGURE 2.13 *Thomas Carlyle* (1867). Julia Margaret Cameron.

and light and Cameron's blurred focus obscured the kind of detail-
ing associated with the picturesque, the more conventional family
portrait tries to capture individuals and the objects surrounding
them as precisely as possible. These photographs were originally circulated among members of the family and their acquaintances, providing a private historical record of a closed social group. Looking
back at the preceding decade from the perspective of the 1860s, a
popular Victorian journal notes that "whilst no one was guilty of the
vulgarity of leaving a portrait as a visiting card, everybody sat for a

FIGURE 2.14   *The Music Lesson* (1857).

picture in the new style, and a system of portrait exchange and portrait collection was initiated, which has no precedent in pictorial art."[55] At the same time, these photographs convey very little sense of the "trespassing voyeurism" generated by artistically more ambitious examples of the medium, where, as Bryan Lukacher explains, "the internal fiction of the tableau often implied the simultaneous negation of the camera's observing and recording presence."[56] Though destined for those who already knew and recognized the people being photographed, the conventional photograph obviously displays them, not as they really were, but as they wished to be seen by the camera.

Only when we appreciate the number of family photos, of *faux* family photos, and of other nineteenth-century versions of the city pastoral, can we understand how an image of the respectable family affected countless lives that had not been so mapped out in terms of the opposition between the streets and bourgeois interiority. We know that the popularity of photography increased at a rate unprecedented among the arts and sciences, with the result that virtually no moderately well-appointed home would have been without numerous examples of the new scientific art by the last decade of the nineteenth century. Any number of essays in Victorian periodicals testify to the rapid spread of the medium in hyperbolic terms, but two should suffice to indicate the flavor of such testimony. In 1857, Lady Eastlake remarked on how recently photography was invented and how unprecedented its growth in popularity had been in relation to the other arts:

> Since then, photography has become a household word and a household want; it is used alike by art and science, by love, business, and justice; is found in the most sumptuous saloon, and in the dingiest attic—in the solitude of the Highland cottage, and in the glare of the London gin-palace—in the pocket of the detective, in the cell of the convict, in the folio of the painter and architect, among the papers and patterns of the millowner and manufacturer, and on the cold brave breast on the battlefield.[57]

For rather similar reasons, another commentator found photography equally exceptional among scientific discoveries, including the telegraph, with which it was frequently compared:

> Men of all tastes, habits, and stations seemed smitten as with a mania, but which, unlike older manias, such as the Dutch tulip rage, did not die out in a short time, but has rather gone increasingly. Never was a taste so catholic as that which has united in the bonds of brotherhood the disciples of the new iconolatry. Several priests of the Church of Rome have

The World as Image

been amongst the most active contributors to the new art-science. An archbishop of the English Church is one of its zealous devotees.[58]

Certain changes in the city accompanied what might be called the rise of photography. The mid-nineteenth century saw a massive reorganization of urban space itself, as various groups presumably strove to reproduce idealized images of private life in their living spaces.[59] After the 1850s there was a steady march of the so-called "stink industries" to the East End of London. As new thoroughfares and railways cut through the old city, those who lived in its narrow alleyways and crowded tenements had to go where rent was cheapest, which was also where air was unwholesome, space cramped, and drainage nearly impossible. Those who could afford to pay higher rents or buy property migrated to the West End, where townhouses sat comfortably along tree-lined streets. At first, we can assume, life within such exclusive neighborhoods provided the material for urban pastoralism. By the time photography was less than two decades old, however, photographs depicting the gratification of private life were everywhere and seemed to offer that gratification to everyone. In the manner Mitchell ascribes to exotic exhibitions, these visual representations sent increasing numbers of people in search of the signs of private life on the assumption that a certain emotional reality came with them.[60] Photographs of a generic family defined the inside of the house as both a metaphor and a refuge for people who felt in danger of being caught in the flow of commercial traffic, wandering in the perilously dark and twisted passageways of the old city, or suffering the degradation of the laboring body as depicted by topographic, gothic, and picturesque photography respectively. The home was pictured as a space where the body's difference, and thus individuality itself, was secure.[61] By the 1890s, as a result, economic differences within the city had taken on a metaphysical life that could be represented and grasped as a single image.

Perhaps an advertisement for a housing development in the London suburbs provides the best example of this transformation of the

FIGURE 2.15   Poster (1908).

cultural behavior of images (Figure 2.15). Rather than adhering to some original, one copy (namely, the photograph) begat another in the form of this poster featuring a house that has not been built and a social space that has not yet been inhabited. The picture addresses an observer who thinks of housing as the encasement for the kind of interior that had been reproduced and circulated in photographic images—a spot of artificial nature that could contain and give comfort to a single family. At the point where topography began to recapitulate photography, the gap between image and object began to close, and it must have become rather difficult to distinguish that way of seeing the city from the city that one saw. Photography was certainly not the only cultural means of reproducing, expanding, and hierarchizing ontologically hostile kinds of urban space, but it certainly collaborated to produce this effect with exhibitions, museums, and all the machinery of spectacle for which the Victorian period is known. Moreover, photography alone brought the production of visual field to an unprecedented level of efficiency and made it suddenly and radically portable.

For the Love of Things Themselves

Like the exhibition, however, the advent of the photograph made viewers yearn for the very things that photos were displacing—not only for the remnants of an earlier England that had crumbled before the construction of modern thoroughfares, but also for contact with whatever the camera had identified as real. Put another way, photography instilled in those very middle-class people a desire to see the sorts of people, places, and things that modernization marginalizes and ultimately eliminates. Out of this form of nostalgia, modern iconophobia was born. Having some sense of the iconophilia that fueled and was fueled by photographic images, we should be prepared to examine the ambivalence that colors nineteenth-century realism—ambivalence produced by a decisive gesture of disavowal, which I will briefly describe here and will elaborate at some length in Chapter 6.

Let us recall that Marx was writing *Capital* during the same period when photographic images were flooding the market alongside commodities from all over the empire. Thanks to a sequence of innovations that made them relatively cheap to make and easy to reproduce, by the 1860s these photographs could arrive at one's home on the front of postcards. They filled photo albums, hung on the walls of respectable parlors, and were displayed in public galleries and exhibitions. In the words of a commentator writing in 1867,

> The rapid growth of new and special industries is a fact so characteristic of the present day, that the statistics of photography can scarcely be regarded as wonderful, viewed merely as a question of economics. Nevertheless, some of the facts are sufficiently startling. Twenty years ago, one person claimed the sole right to practise photography professionally in this country. According to the census of 1861, the number of persons who entered their names as [professional] photographers was 2,534.[62]

For the people who had incorporated photographs so completely into the fabric of their lives and their very being, all this imaging was a sign of the advance of civilization, and it was doing the new technology no disservice to compare it with the advance of industrial capitalism. In an essay that begins by promising to "take stock" of its practical value, Dickens links photography to the commodification process in a way that Karl Marx would no doubt have understood. Dickens observes that certain manufacturing firms presently "furnish their travelers with specimens of their best and most novel productions. These specimens are carried from shop to shop, and from town to town, and are given away at last to the best customers." How much easier, he imagines, if "the traveler would take these pictures or [stereoscopic] couplets with him . . . and convey to [his customers] a notion of the appearance of the choice ware of his firms."[63]

We can read Marx's analysis of "The Commodity Fetish and Its Secret" as both a response to this situation and a recapitulation of the paradox of realism I have been sketching here. As these mendacious objects proliferate, he predicted, the signs of things will begin to replace things themselves. Objects will no longer acknowledge the fact they are the products of human labor; they will begin to behave in the manner of a "fetish," religious "figure," or "social hieroglyphic."[64] Marx uses the language of necromancy to indicate the nature of a second inversion that would, he warned, ensue from the inversion of image and object, were that inversion to occur on a sufficiently wide scale. Soon people would not even realize that signs had replaced objects, and once images took control of the way objects circulated, those same objects would acquire an occult power over the subjects who produced and consumed them.

I have reduced this foundational analysis of late capitalism to a tale of two inversions: the inversion, first, of images over objects and, second, of objects over the people who made and used them. My point is to stress the importance Marx assigns to the visual component of objects. He bases his prediction of a gothic future at least in part on his sense that people were already losing contact with one another and with the things that were supposed to mediate between them, and he attributed this loss of affect to a loss of visibility; there is something about the commodity that keeps us from *seeing* what is real. His explanation observes the logic of the camera obscura: "In the act of seeing, light is really transmitted from one thing, the external object, to another thing, the eye. [Seeing] is a physical relation between physical things" (165). By way of contrast, "the commodity-form has absolutely no connection with the physical nature of the object itself" (165). When we look at a commodity, we do not really see it, according to his argument, because the traces of its production become invisible to us whenever the product becomes a commodity: we cannot know how, by whom, or for what purpose it was made. In the process of commodification, the human relations that arise from making and exchanging products consequently acquire "the fantastic form of a relation among things" (165). The commodity effaces the difference between image and object and creates an object whose value—often whose very existence—depends on its position within a differential system of visual signs. In a world of such objects, it is impossible to distinguish original from copy.

According to the cultural logic implicit in the camera obscura as well as in Gilpin's description of the picturesque experience, the human eye could directly encounter an object and make a copy that more or less accurately represented the thing itself. The advent of the photograph made such a theory of unmediated vision impossible. The lesson of the world-as-exhibition is that people can see only what has already been put on display for them to see in certain ways. What we see is the thing already transformed into the object of the gaze, transformed so as to reflect the way in which it has been seen by other people. At the same time, the object has been encrusted with gritty details, expansively dilated, or surrounded by a luminous cloud to constitute a visual field in which the glance can wander seemingly at will. "Something is forever intruding between the object and our grasp," as Elizabeth Ermarth puts it, "so that our knowledge, always distanced from direct apprehension, is always mediate rather than immediate."[65] Is there any wonder such a strong sense of loss arises out of Marx's assumption that seeing is believing and pervades his argument? He obviously felt that the time when one could really see things was fast coming to an end. This same nostalgia still manifests itself in the love on the part of critical theorists for things real intertwined with a sharp antagonism toward the veil of images that seems to come between the individual observer and the world of objects. Marx's essay on the secret of the commodity fetish might be called the first theoretical articulation of this iconophobia.

Marx tells us that what fuels aversion to commodities also triggers the longing for things themselves—namely, the loss of one's ability to see them. In doing so, he reveals the contradiction that not only shapes his argument but accounts for its peculiar affect. To imagine a world in which social relationships could be natural, self-evident, or gratifying, Marx has to posit a world prior to mediation, a world, what is more, that is rapidly and irretrievably vanishing: "All the relations between Robinson [Crusoe] and these objects that form his self-created wealth are here so *simple and transparent* that even Mr Sedley Taylor could understand them. And yet those relations contain all the essential determinants of value" (170; italics mine). An understanding of the world-as-photograph suggests that this world of things as they once were, in all their pristine honesty, is nothing other than the good image, or the alluringly exalted other side of the degraded image. Thus, in Marx's description of the secret of the commodity fetish, the commodity form is a bad image because, as he puts it, that form has "absolutely nothing to do with the physical nature of the object itself," which can be seen directly with the human eye (165). From this, it necessarily follows that the so-called "object itself" is something that we see. The very things that Marx considers to be most real are, in this sense, already images.

If the difference between products and commodities boils down to a difference between objects and images, and if "the object itself" is in fact nothing more than the visible traces of that thing, or what can be seen with the eye, then the difference between object and image is not a difference between real things and false images. To make historical sense of Marx's aversion to images, one must understand that the difference between objects and images whose collapse he laments is actually a difference between good images and bad ones. For Marx, the good image puts people in touch with things, while the bad image obstructs the kind of social truth that he is seeking. His discovery that mass-produced objects necessarily subsume and so conceal the labor that went into making them only increases his desire to see. Thus the gap between image and object does not challenge the relationship between seeing and knowing in his account but, quite the contrary, that gap makes seeing that object seem more desirable than ever and identifies "simple and transparent" images as the means of doing so.

Marx's analysis of commodities, then, perfectly articulates the paradox of realism, as it reveals how the desire to get beyond the image intensified the love of images and increased image-dependency. To generalize from his example, we might say that Victorian iconophilia fostered disappointment with things themselves, which in turn produced a market for more subtle and comprehensive forms of visual representation. Writing at the dawn of mass visuality, Marx built his lament for the loss of visibility around this contradiction, which we inherit along with his definition of materialism. Having examined, however briefly, some of the changes that sudden and mass imaging wrought upon the object world, I want to shift attention to the subject and to those aspects of Marx's essay that suggest that something on the order of commodification was happening to people too. Marx understood that producers were affected differently from consumers by the subsumption of their labor into an abstract differential system where that labor acquired value as commodities. He is quite specific about the way in which objects acquire certain aspects of their makers as so many features of the objects themselves. As I have tried to demonstrate, however, Marx is perhaps most explicit about the way in which the substitution of an abstract image-object for a particular product of human labor conceals the intellectual component of the labor actually shaping that object.

In concluding this chapter, I want to stress the second half of the process whereby objects, once detached from those who made them, not only came to represent interior qualities of the consumer—his or her taste, his or her familial affection—but also became the psychological property of people who looked a certain way themselves—namely, members of the affluent middle classes. The result of this transformation of certain goods into personal property was a sumptuary code that was every bit as elaborate in its rigid hierarchies of dress, food, friends, education, art, and iconographic environment as the sumptuary codes that once maintained aristocratic hierarchies. This code was all the more powerful because, though purely artificial, its features were subsumed in images which represented those features as so many physical properties of its subject matter. Thus, as countless photographs systematically, if half-unconsciously, followed the rules of self-presentation, class became visible on the body, and the body became a transparent image revealing class distinctions.

✃ CHAPTER THREE ✃

Foundational Photographs:
The Importance of Being Esther

JANE AUSTEN OCCASIONALLY CALLS ATTENTION TO THE WHOLE person, as when she brings the heroine of *Pride and Prejudice* face to face with a portrait of her lover handsomely displayed in his well-managed manor house. Austen may even point synecdochally to that heroine's own fine pair of eyes, but she will not ask her readers to *see* these features. For all her acclaimed attention to detail, Austen rarely asks us to infer the truth of a character from his or her visible attributes. Fiction written during the second half of the nineteenth century, however, tells quite a different story. Charlotte Brontë's heroines hate to be seen. Yet Brontë repeatedly subjects them to scrutiny by friends and foes alike, and her narratives consequently abound in visual description. On the basis of this kind of information, we can place them within the same visual order in which they, as narrators, locate all other characters. Anyone who resists such placement is suspect. The snobbish members of the Ingram party chalk up Jane Eyre's desire for social invisibility to the stealth of those women who hire themselves out as governesses, and even we, as readers, are forced to consider whether the heroine of Brontë's later novel, *Villette,* is less than straightforward in representing others simply because she is so averse to being seen by them herself. Compelled though she may be to remain invisible, the fact is that Lucy Snowe cannot perform her supervisory duties in a Belgian girls' school, much less place herself in something approximating an English home of her own, unless she too has been seen, and seen with relative accuracy. These retiring heroines are extreme cases of what I will try to describe as a much more general condition.

After the mid-century mark, an individual had to have an identity that could be seen in one of a number of predictable ways, if that individual presumed to have any identity at all. Accordingly, novels written in the second half of the nineteenth century observe the same principle put forth by Brontë's contemporary Elizabeth Eastlake. In a journalistic piece on physiognomy, Lady Eastlake claims that "no single object presented to our senses . . . engrosses so large a share of our thoughts, emotions, and associations as that small portion of flesh and blood as the hand may cover, which constitutes the human face."[1] Given the author's lifelong fascination with phrenology, reading faces was destined to be a necessary skill for Charlotte Brontë's characters, narrators, and readers. If Lucy Snowe's application of this skill seems always to be verging on pathology, it is not because she is less consistent than a Dickens narrator in supplying us with the visual information we need to negotiate the modern metropolis. To interpret this information, however, she does not rely on the distinctions among popular stereotypes. She prefers to scrutinize the surface of particular bodies for signs of the subject who dwells within. For this she uses a systematically inductive method that Victorian readers would have expected from a scientist, not from a young woman interested in finding a companionable husband.[2] Faces were an obsession not only for illustrators and novelists, but also for scientists and social scientists who pursued the experimental method. But of these two general kinds of endeavor, I would argue, the illustrators and novelists were the ones to take advantage of the propensity of visual appearance to *bestow* an identity on an individual which they claimed to discover in the person, place, or thing itself. At a certain point in his career, we find that Dickens was ready and willing to abandon any pretense of resemblance between image and object in favor of assigning his characters a place within a system of visual differences.

With the development of photography, a significant number of physiognomists looked to the new technology, as did Francis Galton, to provide a scientific basis for reading faces. To their regular disappointment, these scientists of human nature discovered that "it was infinitely easier to illustrate physiognomic works with engravings of artist's impressions" than "to seek out suitable photographs."[3] Frustrated by photography's failure to prove empirically that the precise nature of a mental condition could be read on the subject's face, some doctored their evidence; to get the desired result, they used composite photographs, photographed plaster masks, and electrically stimulated the subject's face.[4] As I argued in the Introduction, this failure is itself instructive. Here was a culture predisposed to consider photography as the ultimate mimetic technology, a process capable of making an exact copy of actual things and people, a copy for which the referent could be sought and named well after the photograph had been taken. Yet one could not depend on a photograph to reveal its referent except in the most self-evident way. Photography failed to provide an adequate basis for induction. In taking the place of an object, it did just that: it replaced the object with a visual representation. While it could not reveal all that much about the object represented, a photograph was uniquely capable of distinguishing itself—and only by implication its object—from all others of its type.

In locating the decisive shift in the basis for individual identity from resemblance to difference during the 1850s, I am attributing effects to photography a decade or so before there were very many of these images in circulation. As preceding chapters argue, however, the history of photography implicitly challenges supply-side theories of culture that assume cultural production comes first, elicits a response, and thereby creates a demand for more of its kind. There is abundant evidence to suggest that, on the contrary, authors and presumably their readers were predisposed to think photographically before there were many photographs to substantiate the kind of visual description we now associate with literary realism. It is indeed fair to say that not only the technology for making these images but also the kind of image produced were as much the result as the fuel for a desire to convert the world into specific kinds of visual information.[5] A. A. E. Disdéri's rise from bankruptcy in 1855 to prosperity and international fame in 1859 can, for example, be attributed to the enormous demand for *cartes de visite.* In support of this explanation for the change in the fortunes of a studio photographer, Elizabeth Anne McCauley offers this 1856 testimony from Julie Bonaparte, a cousin of the emperor: "Now it's the fashion to have your portrait made small in a hundred copies: it only costs fifty francs and it's very handy to give to your friends and to have their images constantly at hand."[6] But Disdéri's ability to move as a photographer from the status of magician, or master of illusion, to that of professional and artist within such a short period of time also had a great deal to do with the fact that a pictorial tradition had prepared the way in France for the *cartes de visite* of which he was one of the great impresarios. During the 1830s and 1840s, McCauley explains, a French public familiar with an aristocratic tradition of painted portraits "grew accustomed to viewing full-length, black-and-white portrayals of middle- or lower-class figures as physiological specimens displaying characteristic costumes, facial features, and stances."[7] Given that a vigorous market in *cartes* emerged just as suddenly in England and offered a similar breadth of subject matter, there can be little question that readers were as predisposed to receive this kind of visual representation in England as they were in France.

By the late 1850s, the traffic in *cartes de visite* in England indicates an English readership willing and able to determine at a glance whether an individual complied with or fell short of a visual norm. A photograph mounted on a two and a half by four-inch card, the *carte de visite* could portray any number of things, including family members, celebrities, native peoples, animals, landscapes, artifacts, buildings, monuments, and important events. The rage, sometimes known as "cartomania," not only to collect such portraits but also to print one's own portrait and those of one's family members on these cards offers a good example of the degree to which pictorial thinking had by that time already saturated the lives of ordinary people. As one scholar writes, "In England alone 300 to 400 million *cartes* were sold every year from 1861 to 1867." *Cartes de visite* were small, sturdy, cheap, novel, and diverse, "but the most significant feature was their purpose or function, to provide visual information. Despite the name, they were seldom used as visiting cards."[8] Indeed, the new medium achieved such iconographic power that Victoria and Albert broke with tradition and became the first British royalty to allow their photographs to circulate freely. When in 1861 the Prince Consort died, the Queen personally took over the late Albert's supervision of their collection of photographs. Frances Dimond implies a superior sensitivity on the Queen's part to the cultural power that inhered in the new system of faces: "Queen Victoria was less interested in fine art than in people and places. She continued her collection of family portraits and was soon able to obtain photographs of many more distinguished and remarkable people than had previously been possible. At the same time, she allowed increasing numbers of herself and her family to be sold."[9] Given Victoria's insistence that she and her consort were not simply the Royal couple, but also the ideal domestic couple, it seems perfectly in keeping with her manipulation of that ideal that she understood the importance of putting her photograph along with Albert's at the top of the emergent classification system—as the face cards, one could say, of a new social iconography.[10]

In contrast with any previous reproduction of the human face and figure, the viewing of the photographic image could not be restricted to a specific place or occasion. In 1863, a commentator for a weekly magazine observed that window displays in photographic studios were drawing many viewers away from the miniature room at the Royal Academy, which "used to be mobbed by fair women, bent either upon criticising their friends or furtively admiring their own portraits." But with the discovery of the collodion process, "the occupation of the miniature painter was gone."[11] This commentary suggests that in offering a new way of displaying likenesses of face and figure, photography also reclassified those likenesses. Portraits were no longer reserved for people of birth, wealth, or prominence. By the 1860s, images of such individuals had been incorporated into a more comprehensive system—organized, most obviously, by differences of race and gender—that naturalized a way of seeing specific to the modern middle classes. In contrast with "the old exclusionary governmental principle" that had determined which images would be hung in the National Portrait Gallery, this so-called "street portrait gallery," according to another commentator, seemed blatantly egalitarian:

> No committee of selection decide on the propriety of hanging certain portraits. Here, on the contrary, social equality is carried to its utmost limit, and Tom Sayers is found cheek-by-jowl with Lord Derby, or Mrs. Fry is hung as a pendant to Agnes Willoughby. The only principle governing the selection of the *carte de visite* portraits is their commercial value, and that depends on the notability of the person represented.[12]

Also put on display and circulated were photographs of architecture, monuments, battlefields, plant and animal specimens, political cartoons, sentimental illustrations, and classic works of art. The seemingly arbitrary and open-ended character of this classification system was particularly advantageous, for who could suspect it of being any less than democratic and all-inclusive? These images, after all, had their origins in popular culture.

Rather than inspiring a proliferation of photographic types and genres, however, the increasing demand for new faces and exotic costumes fueled a countertendency to portray all new visual information in one of several familiar ways, among them, family portraiture, celebrity portraiture, mug shots, picturesque types, and native peoples of the world. As photographic subject matter increased in scope and variety, the kind of shot that was used acquired greater predictability. The distinction between the portrait of a loved one and that of a criminal became just as obvious as that differentiating either a celebrity from a native or a sentimental illustration from a political cartoon. In each case, the one portrait offered a normative image and the other, some disfigurement of a specific face and figure of respectability. In this way, a constant influx of new visual material reproduced, revitalized, and revised a whole range of subdivisions within both respectable culture and its outcast counterpart. By the sheer force of repetition, moreover, these categories established not only how objects and people were supposed to look but also what would happen to their appearance, were they to violate the norms of reason and respectability.

Where phrenology and physiognomy continued to rely on the principle of resemblance to determine an individual's identity, photography banked on difference.[13] Charlotte Brontë's Lucy Snowe consequently strikes us as an eccentric reader of human topography, because she relies on a phrenological system based on the resemblance of image to object represented. When *cartes de visite* burst upon the scene, their instant popularity should suggest that, contrary to Lucy's practice, the majority of readers had already left it to science to discover what kernel of identity might rest in the object itself, so content were they to read an image in terms of its difference from others.[14] In addition to popular appeal, there was an ideological advantage in doing so. If the repetitive capacity of photographic shots and poses substantiated the visual genres and stereotypes already circulating in fiction, then the details that necessarily crept into each new photograph subtly renewed, updated, qualified, and even criticized the very category it reproduced. As photography offered readers visual proof that the categories in terms of which they looked at the world were categories of that world and capable of explaining all things and people in it, photographic differences displaced traditional codes of visual representation whose meaning depended on their resemblance to the object represented.[15]

Before Realism Was Resemblance

Critics generally attribute Dickens's realism to his first-hand experience of reality itself—a boyhood stretch in the blacking factory, years as a reporter at criminal court, a tormented sex life and an even unhappier marriage. Realism invites us to assume that fiction mediates between such a person and his social environment. Realism therefore asks us to believe that novels represent the author's relation to his or her time. To mediate, according to the epistemology of realism, fiction ideally records the interaction between the individual and his or her social-historical milieu without significantly modifying either one. To this day, many readers are convinced that writing does exactly this when it offers a detailed picture of the world specific to an individual at the moment he or she confronts it.[16] Were this indeed the case, we could expect Dickens's early fiction to represent such conflicts more vividly than his later work, since the unstable economic circumstances of his early years forced him to confront a reality impervious to his every wish and ambition. In fact, just the opposite is true. It is only in his so-called mature fiction that Dickens begins to incorporate the excessive forms of visual description for which he would ultimately become so famous. There is no lack of wit in an early novel like *Oliver Twist*, no lack of biting contempt for England's social institutions, no lack of ingenuity expended in giving the plot first a comic spin, then turning it into a gothic story with extraordinary melodramatic moments along the way. But in *Oliver Twist*, Dickens exercises his wit, vents his contempt, and cranks up the melodramatic gears of his plot through means other than the visual disfiguration to which he subjects even the sentimental heroine in *Bleak House*. Indeed, on this basis alone it is plausible to read *Oliver*, a novel published in serial form in 1837, as a pre-photographic version of *Bleak House*, which first appeared in 1852–53.[17]

Both novels explore the question of how one acquires an identity in the modern urban world if one has not been born into a fixed position there. In both cases, a resolution to the question of identity depends on who a child's mother is and under what circumstances she gave birth to that individual, as if knowing his origin would tell us who that child resembled and thus what kind of person that child is. Oliver's visual resemblance to his mother is established both early on and heavy-handedly. Convalescing from the trauma of his collision with criminal culture, Oliver fixes on a portrait of a woman. "What a beautiful, mild face that lady's is!" he remarks to the housekeeper. "Ah," said she, "painters always make ladies out prettier than they are, or they wouldn't get any custom, child. The man who invented the machine for taking likenesses might have known *that* would never succeed; it's a deal too honest." [18] From this, the reader is to gather that portraits necessarily falsify; they are in fact designed to violate photographic accuracy. When, however, Mr. Brownlow first interrogates Oliver concerning his role in the pocket-picking episode that brought the child to his house, "the old idea of the resemblance between his features and some familiar face came upon him so strongly, that he could not withdraw his gaze" (72). Oliver's location just below his mother's portrait is such that this resemblance is no longer one between his face and "some familiar face" but a resemblance between his and hers: Brownlow "pointed to the picture above Oliver's head; and then to the boy's face. There was its living copy. The eyes, the head, the mouth; every feature was the same" (72). Though beautiful, the reader must infer, the portrait is not so different from a mechanical reproduction after all. The fact that both the mimetic tradition of painting and the mechanically reproduced image would refer to Oliver in approximately the same way ultimately makes little difference in a novel where copies of any kind end up playing a relatively minor part in determining who the protagonist is. We must wait for other information to reveal Oliver's true identity.

Only after Brownlow establishes a more primary link between the portrait and the woman behind it can he decipher Oliver's resemblance to the portrait correctly. We learn, first, that some years ago a distraught friend of Mr. Brownlow "left with [him], among some other things, a picture—a portrait painted by himself—a likeness of this poor girl—which he did not wish to leave behind, and could not carry forward on his hasty journey" (334). Having been snatched from the clutches of the police, Oliver "lay recovering from sickness in [Brownlow's] house." There, as Brownlow later recalls the scene, "his strong resemblance to this picture . . . struck me with astonishment. Even when I first saw him in all his dirt and misery, there was a lingering expression in his face that came upon me like a glimpse of some old friend flashing on one in a vivid dream. I need not tell you he was snared away before I knew his history—" (335). To decipher the resemblance between the boy and the portrait of a woman who turns out to be his own mother, Brownlow must reroute that image back through his memory to Oliver's father, the long-lost friend who entrusted him with a portrait he himself had painted of the woman whom he loved. Then, and only after Brownlow establishes the paternal origins of the painting, can he explain Oliver's resemblance to it. Visual appearance is not the basis for identity in this novel but the conduit to more authentic memories, on the one hand, and to more authoritative forms of social legitimacy, on the other.

That Dickens himself was thinking in terms of a theory of memory that links people and things to one another by bonds of natural sympathy becomes particularly clear as Brownlow describes how the truth of the boy's identity "came upon me like a glimpse of some old friend flashing on one in a vivid dream" (335). Oliver's half-brother Monks is intent on finding the boy and ending the threat he poses to Monks's inheritance. In much the same way as Brownlow comes to recognize the child, Monks's "suspicions were first awakened by his resemblance to his father" (336).[19] It should be noted, moreover, that "resemblance" in both cases is strictly a natural resemblance, or what might be described as a relation between a copy and the original in which Oliver's father consistently plays the latter. Such a natural resemblance clearly upholds an older system of family relations in which the father's position determined that of the son, and the son quite literally embodies the position he was born to occupy. Within such a system of identification, resemblance can carry all this cultural-semantic weight only after the more primary blood relationship between original and copy has been established. Though moral antagonists, Brownlow and Monks agree that the "proof" of identity resides in verbal rather than visual documentation. "There was a will," Brownlow claims, "which your [Monks's] mother destroyed, leaving the secret and the gain to you at her own death . . . These proofs were destroyed by you, and now, in your own words to your accomplice the Jew, '*the only proofs of the boy's identity lie at the bottom of the river, and the old hag that received them from the mother is rotting in her coffin*'" (Dickens's italics, 336). To keep Oliver from sliding off the social map and into oblivion along with his identity papers, Mr. Brownlow must bully Monks into setting "your hand to a statement of truth and facts, and repeat it before witnesses" (337). The protagonist's physical appearance seems to play little part in securing him a position within respectable society. Only written certification will do.

Nor does Dickens make much effort to classify his protagonist in visual terms. The following is the most developed physical description we receive: "Oliver Twist's ninth birth-day found him a pale thin child, somewhat diminutive in stature, and decidedly small in circumference. But nature or inheritance had implanted a good sturdy spirit in Oliver's breast. It had had plenty of room to expand, thanks to the spare diet of the establishment" (5). Identity resides within this child, waiting for material circumstances to afford it opportunity to expand and assume its natural position. Indeed, of all the characters—sentimental, gothic, and picturesque—who populate the city in this particular novel, only Fagin receives much in the way of pictorial elaboration:

> In a frying pan which was on the fire, and which was secured to the mantelshelf by a string, some sausages were cooking; and standing over them, with a toasting-fork in his hand, was a very old shrivelled Jew, whose villainous-looking and repulsive face was obscured by a quantity of matted red hair. He was dressed in a greasy flannel gown, with his throat bare, and seemed to be dividing his attention between the frying-pan and a clothes-horse: over which a great number of silk handkerchiefs were hanging. (50)

There is just enough visual detail in this passage to call up the traditional figure of the Jew, relocate that figure at the infernal center of the nineteenth-century slum, and give its satanic features a perversely maternal spin; to assert his resemblance to a type requires but a few select details. Hired to eradicate Oliver's unblemished character, his last claim to a position in polite society, Fagin serves as a "bad mother" who reproduces English subjects, not in his image, we should note, but as the criminal agents of his illicit business practices. Significantly, his tenure as one of Fagin's boys does nothing to alter Oliver's appearance. The Cruikshank illustrations for the novel operate in a supplementary relationship to Dickens's prose in lending the characters of the urban underworld the picturesque qualities that belong, at this point in cultural history, strictly to the domain of popular illustration and cartoon. Throughout the novel, according to these illustrations, the protagonist retains the finely chiseled blandness denoting the kind of upper-middle-class interiority that defies a picturesque description.

In *Bleak House*, too, Dickens's investigation of the protagonist's identity involves a sexual scandal, false identities, lost documents, disguises, and murder. So intricate and pervasive is the intrigue that its reverberations are felt at all levels of the social order. As I have suggested, *Oliver Twist* similarly naturalizes identity. But if Oliver embodies himself and thus *is* his identity, then the heroine of *Bleak House* must be described as *having* an identity; there is nothing *in* that individual that cannot change with transformations of its visible surface and position in the visual order. My aim in reading *Bleak House* is to demonstrate that the primacy of images in forming identities makes a profound difference in how the game of identity plays out. In moving from *Oliver Twist* (1838) to *Bleak House* (1852–53), we leave a novel whose protagonist achieves identity when he arrives at the position already indicated by his appearance and conduct, and we enter a novel whose protagonist exactly inverts those priorities. In *Bleak House*, that is to say, identity is one and the same as the position an individual occupies within a differential system of images.[20] Position is not determined by the body, because the body's legibility—the kind of body that one has—is determined by its position within that system.[21]

A change in the relationship between word and image registers this inversion of the mimetic dependence of body-image on body within the Dickens corpus. In a monograph on the relation between Dickens's narration and Cruikshank's drawings in *Sketches by Boz* and *Oliver Twist,* J. Hillis Miller argues that while "Dickens . . . kept the upper hand with his 'illustrious' illustrator" in these early works, "it is also evident that he wrote *Oliver Twist* in order that it might be illustrated by Cruikshank."[22] Cruikshank in turn represented London, not as he saw it, but as Dickens had described it. The result of this collaboration of two different media between the covers of a Dickens text was, according to Miller, a change in the operation of the literary sign itself:

> Illustrations in a work of fiction displace the sign-referent relationship assumed in a mimetic reading and replace it by a complex and problematic reference between two radically different kinds of sign, the linguistic and the graphic. Illustrations establish a relation between elements within the work which shortcircuits the apparent reference of the literary text to some real world outside.[23]

Thus words set the stage for images, in that we know who is doing what to whom before we see it, and images confirm words by affirming the presence and appearance of those character types. While I entirely agree with this analysis, I also believe there is a good reason why writing and not images finally determines what place the protagonist occupies. This reason becomes apparent when we turn from the *Oliver* illustrations to those Dickens commissioned for *Bleak House.* In striking contrast to the Cruikshank illustrations, a glance at what Hablot Browne designed for *Bleak House* reveals how little information he offered that Dickens had not already provided.

To mark the turning points in the career-long collaboration between Dickens and Browne, who briefly identified himself as N.E.M.O. and acquired his reputation as an illustrator under the pseudonym of "Phiz," Michael Steig identifies two major shifts in the prevailing winds of illustration. During the early Victorian period, Browne resembled Cruikshank and Thackeray in his reliance on the emblematic "techniques of Hogarth and his followers in the 'lower' graphic art."[24] Then in the early 1840s there was a pronounced shift away from what Steig calls "the old emblematic modes" to the "simpler and clearer style" practiced by John Leech and the other artists and illustrators associated with *Punch* (10). While Cruikshank had trouble finding work in this new semiotic environment, Browne managed to adapt and remained active through the 1850s, when what Steig calls "the quasi-caricatural way of drawing characters" gave way to a "blander, rather idealized style, and emblem and allusion disappeared almost totally" (11). The fortunes of Cruikshank and Browne correspond rather directly, I would argue, not only with a change in popular visual taste but also with a change in the relationship between the verbal and visual dimensions of the illustrated text, or, in the case of fiction, between narration and experience narrated.

In an article devoted to Dickens's illustrators, Q. D. Leavis expresses her keen disappointment with Browne's illustrations for *Bleak House,* on grounds that the author "does nothing to actualize the Chancery fog," and "there is little in the way of background and almost no interesting detail."[25] Leavis only half-blames Browne for this problem, however. It was just "the habit of having illustrations" that made them seem necessary, she reasons, for at this point in his work Dickens had virtually become his own illustrator. If in writing *Bleak House* Dickens incorporated into his writing the kinds of visual details it had been Cruikshank's business to supply in *Oliver Twist,* then this would indeed destroy the stereoscopic triangulation of verbal narration and narrated image that Miller admires, creating a basis for Leavis's disappointment. Though an energetic apologist for Browne, Steig too allows that the illustrations for *Bleak House* are "far more uneven in quality than those for the three preceding novels."

While the comic plates are "weak, even sloppy," those featuring Esther Summerson "are relatively uninteresting, though usually done
with care" (131). The major source of unevenness comes not from a
sudden decline in the quality of the images compared with those he
had done for *Pickwick*, *Nickleby*, *Chuzzlewit*, and *Dombey*, but from
Browne's decision to switch over to a "wet-plate process" that resembles mezzotinting halfway through *Bleak House* (Figure 3.1). In
changing to a different technology of illustration, Browne also chose
to abandon detailed representation of the human face and figure in
favor of the subtle interaction of light and shadow. In making this
decision, Browne did not forsake a relationship of visual to verbal
representation that strove for a stereoscopic effect. On the contrary,
he turned to a method of illustration that further enhanced this
effect.

It is with this shift that Browne's illustrations cease to observe
older physiognomic or caricatural codes borrowed from Hogarth,
political cartoons, and any number of popular sources. But what the
dark plates do instead is gesture toward the same gothic city that
Dickens is referencing in his city novels. The novelist's and illustrator's respective ways of representing the city come to seem all but
redundant as fiction and illustration begin to point outside themselves to pieces of the contemporary world whose appearance defies
the older iconographic tradition. If the dark plates that constitute
most of the illustrations in the second half of *Bleak House*—images
designed to accompany Lady Dedlock's progress from the height of
Chesney Wold to the depth of Tom-all-alone's—appear uniquely de-
void of particularized human characters, it is because Browne is figuring out how to reference the various social spaces that had begun to
frame and define the individuals who inhabited them. Details could
no longer carry an iconic meaning in and of themselves, as they do
within the physiognomic tradition, but instead receive their meaning
from the visual context which inflects them. In *Little Dorrit*, a novel of
the late 1850s where this trend apparently continues, Steig notes that
the details that had marked the illustrations of the 1830s "have virtually disappeared." Consequently, "as a group, the *Little Dorrit* illustra-

FIGURE 3.1   *Tom-all-alone's* (1853). Hablôt K. Browne ("Phiz").

tions seem less necessary than those for *Bleak House,* and yet some enhance the novel, making its 'dark' feeling visible, and underlining some of its themes by means of familiar iconographic techniques" (158). Browne's drawings may appear more subservient to the written text, but in fact both fiction, in its increased visual detail, and

Foundational Photographs

FIGURE 3.2   *The Little Old Lady* (1853).
Hablôt K. Browne ("Phiz").

illustration, in its atmospheric patches of light and shadow, participate in a collaborative structure resembling that of the twin images in
a stereograph.

Certain of Browne's illustrations for the first half of *Bleak House*
suggest that this loss in physiognomic detail was accompanied by a
new awareness of what it meant to withhold certain kinds of information from visibility. In contrast to the *Dombey* illustrations, where the

FIGURE 3.3 *Oliver claimed by his affectionate friends* (1838).
George Cruikshank.

heroine's face announces itself as such whenever she is pictured, Browne not only refuses to allow us to see Esther, but also makes that refusal impossible to overlook (Figure 3.2). To offer the reader a view of the back of her respectable bonnet, as this image does, is to conspire with the novel in concealing the face she shares with her mother, and thus in withholding the basis for imagining how illness will graphically disfigure that face later on. The same gesture of withholding also indicates that Esther is more than and presumably

FIGURE 3.4   *Rose Maylie and Oliver* (1838). George Cruikshank.

different from the type she shares with Ada Clare, whose pleasant face the illustration does expose fully to the reader's view. Yet more to the point, such a gesture indicates that to know what makes her herself, we have to see her. Cruikshank's portrayal of Oliver is contrastingly redundant. It strives to create through repetition the idea that, despite Oliver's misplacements within the social order, some principle within him maintains his continuity with himself and therefore with his father (Figures 3.3, 3.4). Browne renounces this kind of repetition for another kind, as he enters into a mutually mirroring relationship with Dickens's prose whereby both media refer to a world that either had been or could be photographed.

The Difference That Realism Makes

That *Oliver Twist* does *not* refer to a world in which truth takes a visual form is apparent in the protagonist's first view of the city:

> A dirtier or more wretched place he had never seen. The street was very narrow and muddy; and the air was impregnated with filthy odours. There were a good many small shops; but the only stock in trade appeared to be heaps of children, who, even at that time of night, were crawling in and out at the doors, or screaming from the inside. The sole places that seemed to prosper, amid the general blight of the place, were the public-houses; and in them the lowest orders of Irish were wrangling with might and main. Covered ways and yards, which here and there diverged from the main street, disclosed little knots of houses, where drunken men and women were positively wallowing in the filth; and from several of the doorways, great ill-looking fellows were cautiously emerging: bound, to all appearance, on no very well disposed or harmless errands. (49)

Everything in this city is identical to its type. Indeed, it is by means of the continuity ensured by repetition of the type that things and people come to have identity as such, as Dickens here compresses the kind of information available in treatises on the moral condition of the working classes for his reader's benefit. This passage offers as much auditory and olfactory information as visual description, as if one kind of information ("filthy odours") can do as well as any other ("heaps of children . . . crawling in and out at the doors, or screaming from the inside"). This description is not, in other words, particularly visual. Although he easily conjures up a picture, Dickens feels no inclination to supply colors, textures, or shades of light and dark. If there is more to see than a verbal description thus grounded in other verbal descriptions can supply, then it is up to an illustrator such as Cruikshank to provide that information.

By way of contrast, in *Bleak House* our introduction to the city abandons all such conventional pictures in order to present us with a landscape virtually the same in content as the one we encounter in *Oliver*, but one that cannot be known for what it is when represented in terms of conventional verbal description:

> As much mud in the streets as if the waters had but newly retired from the face of the earth, and it would not be wonderful to meet a Megalosaurus, forty feet long or so, waddling like an elephantine lizard up Holborn Hill. Smoke lowering down from chimney-pots, making a soft black drizzle, with flakes of soot in it as big as full-grown snowflakes— gone into mourning, one might imagine, for the death of the sun. Dogs, indistinguishable in mire. Horses scarcely better; splashed to their very blinkers. Foot passengers . . . losing their foot-hold at street-corners, where tens of thousands of other foot passengers have been slipping and sliding since the day broke . . . adding new deposits to the crust of mud, sticking at those points tenaciously to the pavement, and accumulating at compound interest.[26]

Dickens's description moves detail by surface detail from drizzle into mud and from mud into smog, allowing the timeless cycle of condensation and evaporation to spread from its urban source across the countryside and down to the docks, where it instantaneously renews itself in filthy water. To see is to see nothing but an obfuscating film, a homogeneous emulsion of dark and light revealing only that it conceals a more primary reality beneath. This film turns London into a filthy if fascinating surface, a visual framework that obscures the particularities that would allow us to distinguish one thing from another, animate from inanimate nature, culture from nature, present from past. When does such visual mediation resemble "compound interest"? When its accumulation creates an opacity that conceals the true meaning of the world it represents, just as too much paper currency misrepresents the value of the gold for which it is a substitute. And what of the megalosaurus that is as much at home on this terrain as any other object? As a signifier without a home, it represents all other signifiers in a field where differences cannot be accurately discerned. To get the picture we would have to see the difference between light and dark. The presence of the megalosaurus in modern London equates the overwhelming accumulation of information in the modern city with the primal slime of a time before there were such differences, much less a place for every person and thing or a grammar regulating the interaction of such categories.

We might regard the opening to *Bleak House* as Dickens's declaration that to know the city is no longer to know how it looks and smells. Nor is to know the city to receive a catalogue of the objects it contains. While such a self-obscuring image might seem to support the simple hypothesis that to see would be to know the things themselves, this passage actually mounts a far more complicated epistemological argument that to see requires us to know what exists on the other side of mediation to be seen. The very mud that covers them creates a need to know the boundaries distinguishing inside from outside, high from low, beautiful from ugly, good from bad, animal from object from human being—those differences, in other words, that give something a visual identity. Thus the film with which Dickens coats the city produces a double reality: a bad copy that refuses to locate its object within such a visual order, and a good copy that does so. Throughout this particular novel, the two work in tandem, the opaque surface that makes for wandering signifiers lending to its pure and transparent partner a strange and historically new allure.

What I am saying about the doubled image in a Dickens novel gives it certain rhetorical effects in common with what D. A. Miller has called "the secret."[27] Drawing on Foucault's concept of "the repressive hypothesis," Miller argues that a novel has to indicate the presence of unrevealed information if it wants to add the promise of erotic pleasure to the power of surveillance. So too in offering the city to the reader's view, Dickens indicates there is much more to it than meets the eye. Like the megalosaurus, most of his urban dwellers initially come before us as mysterious bits of visual information, whose "nature" or "truth," should they happen to have any, await our discovery of the differences that identify their rightful places in the city. For the most interesting characters in the novel, this is often the last bit of visual information we receive. Such truth remains unseen only so long as it is in the wrong place and therefore cannot be identified for what it really is, the secret of Lady Dedlock's identity being the case in point. As if in search of a purloined letter, the narrative sorts through a surplus of such images, until there is no question as to what is out of place. By promising a visual revelation he ultimately withholds, Dickens creates an appetite for images or, perhaps more accurately, a wish that more and more social phenomena could be converted into objects which can in turn be located within the visual order.

What we have seen when we have seen it all consequently remains many little patches of light and color amid pervasive darkness. These bits of visual information stubbornly resist every traditional attempt at linear narration and obey instead the formal principle perhaps best exemplified by "combination printing," a popular technique for turning photography into a bourgeois parlor art. Along with Oscar Rejlander, Henry Peach Robinson was one of those Victorian photographers who sought to fulfill their artistic ambitions for the medium by perfecting the printing process which combined shots of different subjects, at different times, and in entirely different places into a single, seamless print. In a sentence that mimics his procedures for making combination prints in that it offers a seemingly endless number of equivalent details all of which aspire to cohabit in this one conceptual unit, Robinson explains the virtues of his method as one

> which enables the photographer to represent objects in different planes in proper focus, to keep the true atmospheric and linear relation of varying distances, and by which a picture can be divided into separate portions for execution, the parts to be afterwards printed together on one paper, thus

enabling the operator [of the camera] to devote all his attention to a single figure or sub-group at a time, so that if any part be imperfect from any cause, it can be substituted by another without the loss of the whole picture as would be the case if taken at one operation.[28]

The advantage of the method was, in other words, to suppress the relations among the various elements supplying the photographer's subject matter and to resituate them in a relationship determined by the sense and symmetry among their photographs. This relationship may appear exceedingly democratic in that it grants to all things an equal exactness of detail. As demonstrated by the combination print that Oscar Rejlander titled *The Two Ways of Life*, however, the effect of detaching images from the social relations governing their subject matter was to create a new set of distinctions between light and shadow, foreground and background, high and low, nature and culture. Inequities among and between the various subgroups of Victorian society were reinforced as they were turned into visual information and accordingly assigned to one of several social spaces (see Figure 2.10).

While insisting there is no sleight of hand to photography, Robinson also insists that those who would use his method must keep the illusion intact: "It is certain (and this I will put in italics, to impress it more strongly on the memory) that *a photograph produced by combination printing must be deeply studied in every particular, so that no departure from the truth of nature shall be discovered by the closest scrutiny.*"[29] The Dickens world so-called does not even try to represent what was actually there any more than such combination prints do, even though both produce a remarkable density of visual detail to indicate that we are in the presence of something real. What does achieve hypostasis, though, thanks to the artificial framework shared by city novels and combination prints, is a set of categories for classifying visual information. When such images repeat themselves, they become what Francis Galton described as "real generalisations," the "blur" of whose outlines, "which is never great in truly generic composites, except in unimportant details," measures "the tendency of individuals to deviate from the central type."[30] These categories determine the locations at which the multiplicity of urban phenomena will become visible for what they truly are.

Within the desultory spaces of the rich, we find Lady Dedlock, wearing the very kind of face that readers saw not only in portraits (indeed, her portrait hangs among those of her husband's noble ancestors), but also in the art photography of Julia Margaret Cameron and Clementina Hawarden (Figure 3.5; also see Figures 2.11, 2.12). "Where the throng is thickest, where the lights are brightest, where all the senses are ministered to with the greatest delicacy and refinement," Dickens tells us, "[there] Lady Dedlock is" (572). Such a face operates as both index and icon. Its location in the social order is also its place in the universe of being, a place in polar opposition to that occupied by the virtually placeless figures haunting the slums in Gustave Doré's illustrations and in photographic images of those sections of the old city slated for demolition (see Figures 2.2, 2.3). Dickens makes the incompatibility of the spaces inhabited by rich and poor even more incompatible by adding the element of sludge that seems to dissolve the individual bodies of the poor as it obscures their images, leaving them unrecognizable as such.[31]

In order for the novel to suppress and yet reveal the dirty little secret of its protagonist's identity, Lady Dedlock must leave the hallowed halls of Dedlock, slip into the modern city, and there transform her identity. The novel prepares us for her transformation thus: "She hurriedly addresses these lines to her husband, seals, and leaves them on her table: she veils and dresses quickly, leaves all her jewels and her money, listens, goes downstairs at a moment when the hall is empty, opens and shuts the great door, flutters away in the shrill frosty air" (667). One might be inclined to imagine this woman losing substance as she "flutters away in the shrill frosty air," but her lightness of being means simply that she ceases to exist within that particular frame of reference. Indeed, to retrace her steps along with

FIGURE 3.5   *Portrait of a Young Lady*
(1888). Frederick Hollyer.

Esther Summerson is to learn that, should she want to divest herself
of that identity, a person of Lady Dedlock's high position had only to
look like the women who occupied a lower social position. Lady
Dedlock chose one that reduced her to the all-but-invisible status of
those other denizens of city ooze that populate both Dickens's fiction
and John Thomson's photography. Victorian image lovers enjoyed

Foundational Photographs

photographs of women who frequented the city streets for the roughly hewn surfaces that located them at the other end of town and social spectrum from fine-featured respectability (Figure 3.6).

By giving her another dress, the novel disengages Lady Dedlock from the interiority that once smoldered beneath her sleek exterior and sets her on the road to becoming an object. "Traversing this deserted blighted spot," Dickens tells us, "there is a lonely figure with the sad world to itself, pelted by the snow and cast out, it would seem, from all companionship. It is the figure of a woman too; but it is miserably dressed, and no such clothes ever came through the hall, and out at the great door, of the Dedlock mansion" (674). By moving Lady Dedlock across the same kind of landscape with which he opened *Bleak House,* Dickens reduces her to a visual surface barely distinguishable from the physical elements with which he pelts her. Thus he renders her virtually indistinguishable from the generic type with whom she has exchanged clothing. As Mrs. Snagsby's nervous maid-servant explains to a Detective Bucket hot on the trail of what he calls "the dress," "I found a common-looking person, all wet and muddy, looking up at our house" (711). Dickens lets this much interiority look out of such a "common-looking person" in order to let us know that the former Lady Dedlock now embodies an entirely different gaze, one for which interiority scarcely matters.

Thus the changes wrought upon her face quite literally amount to a loss of face that redefines Lady Dedlock's earlier social ascendancy as moral decline. In so transforming her, however, the novel sets the stage for her aesthetic elevation. This paradox deserves some attention. To escape the lofty social position on which she is bound to heap disgrace, Lady Dedlock dons a dress which magically obscures her distinguished face. This is all it takes to transform herself into a "lonely figure" and "common-looking woman." But the moment she vacates that position and undergoes such defacement, paradoxically, her face is sorely missed and begins to acquire enormous sentimental value. Indeed, once the body bearing that face has been discovered, it is plucked from the pauper's graveyard and enshrined in the Dedlock family mausoleum according to the same logic authorizing Victorian photography to empty certain women of all desire and aesthetically enshrine them (Figure 3.7).[32] Much like Poe's purloined letter, then, this face of hers is both the sign of the woman and the woman herself. Such a signifier plays upon what Lacan calls "the realist's imbecility," by which he means that nothing hidden, no matter how deeply or cleverly, is in fact hidden in the usual sense of the term.[33] Contrary to what he considers the naive tenets of realism, Lacan argues that what is hidden is neither buried nor concealed from view but simply out of place.

FIGURE 3.7   *The Lady of Shalott* (1860–1861). Henry Peach Robinson.

To describe the path of such a signifier in Poe's story, according to Lacan, one has to realize that "we are quite simply dealing with a letter that has been diverted from its path; one whose course has been prolonged." It is this displacement of the signifier, he continues, "that determines the subjects in their acts, in their destiny, in their refusals, in their blindnesses, in their end and in their fate."[34] Thus far the analogy between Poe's parable and the way narrative behaves in *Bleak House* holds up. To make it work, however, I have had to emphasize the graphic character of the letter in Poe's story, on the one hand, and of Lady Dedlock, on the other. It is the distinctive image of her face that gets diverted on the way to its destination, as if, in some brutally literal way, that face and her fate were one and the same. Much like Poe's story of the missing letter, Dickens's story of the errant woman is propelled by a graphic sign that has detached itself from a written message that apparently contains a sexual secret. Although the graphic copy cannot reveal that secret, it nevertheless indicates that such a secret does exist and has been diverted on its way from sender to receiver.

But the displacements in *Bleak House* are obviously much more complex than those we encounter in Poe. We soon discover there is more than the one copy, Esther Summerson's mother in disguise as Lady Dedlock: there is Esther herself, the murderous Hortense, the humble Jenny, and the noble portrait that consoles Sir Leicester once the original has been sealed within his family crypt. Moreover, a surplus of letters follows in the wake of the image: Nemo's letters, those and whatever other documentation the lawyer Tulkinghorn holds over Lady Dedlock, Hortense's false testimony, as well as the letters in Lady Dedlock's own hand meant for her husband and daughter. It is almost as if the novel were trying and failed to capture that face and give it a caption. We cannot, however, read this paper trail as another version of the larger legal snarl in which the supplicants at Chancery Court are caught. True, the structural qualities by which both written records render themselves contagiously unintelligible create an important bond of similarity between the surreptitious record and the letter of the law.[35] Caught in a chain of displacements and unable to change its direction, however, the letter is what remains after the face itself has disappeared.

In *Bleak House* the letter exists in much the same relation to the image as does the inside of Poe's purloined letter in relation to the page folded, sealed, delicately inscribed with an address, and yet absolutely empty. At the same time, and by virtue of its disappearance in advance of the letter, the face acquires the thickness and density of a referent as it resurfaces at various locations throughout the city. Ronald Thomas argues that what the predatory Guppy sees in looking at her portrait hanging austerely in Dedlock manor is in fact "a mug shot, a wanted poster that silently announces Lady Dedlock's dark past." "*This* visual representation," Thomas concludes, "is, then, more threatening to her station than the much dramatized fear surrounding the discovery of her handwriting and signature as they appear in the lost letters" to Esther's father.[36] Reading Dickens in terms of the relationship between his fiction and photography thus suggests that realism refers neither to things in themselves nor to the writing that records their vicissitudes as such, but to things as they might be captured and reproduced within the photographic frame. Guppy is simply good at adjusting that frame to accommodate another way of seeing.

Given that Dickens was known to have visited the Court on several occasions to research his novel, those who believe that realism resides in his allusions to Chancery personnel and procedures may want to question the primacy I am granting to visual images. It is important to note, however, the terms in which he translated that experience into fiction. This, says the narrator of *Bleak House,* "is the Court of Chancery; which has its decaying houses and its blighted lands in every shire; which has its worn-out lunatic in every madhouse, and its dead in every churchyard; which has its ruined suitor, with his slipshod heels and threadbare dress, borrowing and begging through the round of every man's acquaintance" (5–6). This description embodies Chancery Court in the individuals who pass through its bureaucratic machinery and come out visibly wasted and maimed as a result. As for the law itself, incarnate in "JARNDYCE AND JARNDYCE (the cause at hand)," it remains an abstraction: "The scarecrow of a suit has in course of time, become so complicated, that no man alive knows what it means" (7). Abstraction turns to obfuscating metaphor as the influence of legal discourse spreads like an ethical equivalent of the slime that obscures the life of the city, "and even those who have contemplated its history from the outermost circle of such evil, have been insensibly tempted into a loose belief that if the world go wrong, it was, in some off-hand manner, never meant to go right. Thus in the midst of the mud and at the heart of the fog, sits the Lord High Chancellor in his High Court of Chancery" (9).

Face Off

Having left Esther to find her way in the world on some basis other than her good looks, more than halfway through the novel Dickens suddenly devotes a number of episodes to the process of scarring her.

The critical tradition offers many ingenious explanations as to why Dickens felt so compelled, and the sheer number of reasons why this gesture should make sense to us has proved, if nothing else, how baffling his act of disfiguration actually is. The author must have expended at least as much ingenuity working this episode into his plot as his critics have subsequently devoted to figuring out what made him do so. When a narrative has to labor so self-consciously, in apparent contradiction to the logic of the genre itself, we have cause to read those signs of labor as indications that something in the culture is calling for a shifting of narrative gears in midplot. The author's figural contortions may even indicate that the novel is hauling out and significantly modernizing an earlier way of making sense. Such, I believe, is the situation we encounter in *Bleak House* and the reason why this change takes place through the disfiguration of Esther's face.

If before the onset of mass visuality, origins mattered most and writing testified to those origins, then after people began to think of their relationship to others in photographic terms, visual clues assumed primary importance in determining who someone was. To be an individual, a person's visual features had to distinguish him or her in a meaningful way from every other individual. We have already seen that attempts to capture the essence of the criminal population by photographing their faces proved futile. This failure to capture the individual displaying precisely the features expected of his or her type indicates that photographic portraits in and of themselves could not provide a meaningful way of distinguishing one person from another so long as an earlier set of physiognomic codes was in place. Photographers quickly borrowed, adapted, and created genres— formulaic combinations of pose, lighting, backdrop, costume, and angle—to detach these codes from specific kinds of bodies and redirect them to specific kinds of images instead. Thus the photographic portrait automatically classified one according to type. At the same time, a photograph also contested its type by supplying more details than either the eye could see at a glance or the painter could incorporate in his painting without ruining the very resemblance he was striving to create. The photographic portrait was uniquely suited for a culture that felt compelled both to type all individuals and to individuate some of them.[37] To achieve identity within such a culture, the protagonist of a novel had to become one of a kind and, at the same time, reproduce the type from which he or she was notably different. It is the mission of literary realism, I believe, to authorize a rather primitive classification system of visual types while endowing certain exemplary members of the dominant group with uniquely complex identities.

The proof of this hypothesis is the elaborate process by which Dickens suddenly revises the question that generates all of Oliver's story and the first half of Esther's. Although Brownlow early on notices Oliver's resemblance to the painting of a woman in his home, to uncover the secret of the boy's identity he must first recall the man who painted the portrait and how he identified the woman he portrayed. At the origin of the image resides the secret of resemblance that will give the wandering signifier a home. In *Bleak House,* by way of contrast, resemblances tend to threaten identity rather than secure it. So long as Esther resembles her mother, the facts of her ignominious birth and fabricated death are in danger of being exposed. Exposing the secret of Esther's origins will not only shatter the resemblance between Lady Dedlock and her noble portrait but also inflict on Esther a kind of social death. Instead of simply asking *where* does the individual fit in, arguably a question that all novels ask, *Bleak House* suddenly turns that question on its ear and asks *how* or on what basis does that individual fit in. For this reason, it becomes just as vital for Esther to get rid of her heritage as it is for Oliver to recover his. As if the principle of difference itself were at stake, Dickens decides that his novel's first order of business is to differentiate a protagonist, reared in "secrecy," from her mother whose "face" she had never seen after "a few hours of my birth" (452). Dickens went to such lengths to efface the daughter's resemblance to her mother before their meeting that we must assume what he wanted the two to encounter when they finally met was their essential difference from each other.

Dickens, then, is not only changing the rules by which a woman could acquire a place in the middle-class world, he also wanted readers to experience this change as a kind of defacement quite comparable to that performed in revising a manuscript.[38] Having infected her with smallpox, he has Esther's caretaker remove the looking glass from her room and then put the newly recovered woman through a painful confrontation with her altered image: "I was very much changed—O very, very much changed. At first my face was so strange to me, that I should have put my hands before it and started back" (445). But once she understands the finality of this change—that the recovery of her health does not entail the recovery of her image—Esther quickly accepts this other image as her own. She finds, in gazing at her face in the mirror, that "very soon it became more familiar, and then I knew the extent of the alteration in it even better than I had done at first" (445). It is clearly an understatement to say that Dickens is hard on Esther, first abandoning her in the hands of an unloving relative, then visiting the plague on her, then forcing her to undergo the trauma of confronting her altered face in the mirror, and finally putting her through a surprise reunion with her mother after a lifetime of complete separation. But if Dickens was as hard on his heroine as I am making him out to be, then why, we must ask, does he refuse to let her mourn the loss of her beauty in the form of the face she had presumably shared with Lady Dedlock? An examination of this episode will reveal that Dickens never actually allowed Esther to enjoy her good looks before he destroyed them. Despite the face that Dickens elsewhere suggests she does share with Lady Dedlock, Esther confesses she had "never been a beauty" or "thought herself one" before her illness; she had simply *"been very different from this"* (my italics, 445). That good girls must have a pretty face is, in other words, one of a number of narrative propositions that Dickens deliberately sacrifices to the principle of photographic realism.

A third near-death experience testifies to the importance of Esther's having differentiated her image from that of her illustrious mother. Perilous as the negation of their resemblance had been, it is what maintains Esther's ontological status as an individual during the still more perilous meeting of the two. Upon confronting her mother face to face for the first time since birth, Esther undergoes a loss of boundaries implying something on the order of maternal engulfment: "I looked at her; but I could not see her, I could not hear her, I could not draw my breath. The beating of my heart was so violent and wild, that I felt as if my life were breaking from me" (449). But while she undergoes this subsumption to the mother type in psychological terms, it cannot happen in fact. As Esther explains, "I felt, through all my tumult of emotion, a burst of gratitude to the providence of God that I was so changed as that I never could disgrace her [Lady Dedlock] by any trace of likeness; as that nobody could ever now look at me, and look at her, and remotely think of any near tie between us" (449). If Esther emerges as an individual when she acknowledges her scars, then Lady Dedlock renders herself less than real by struggling to preserve the conventional codes of physiognomy. "If you hear of Lady Dedlock, brilliant, prosperous, and flattered," she tells Esther, "think of your wretched mother, conscience-stricken, underneath that mask!" (452). Her portrait remains where it was, hanging among the images of Sir Leicester's noble ancestors, unblemished by the telltale signs that might have transformed it into a mug shot before Guppy's de-idealizing gaze. In putting her to rest among Sir Leicester's ancestors, Dickens not only allowed Lady Dedlock to remain Lady Dedlock, a type unmarked by signs of her being in the world, he also reassigned Esther her mother's role as protagonist—as if to say her defaced image is more appropriate for that position. As the mantle of heroine shifts from mother to daughter, the novel also records and authorizes the displacement of portrait painting (which Brownlow's housekeeper criticizes for representing "ladies as prettier than they are") by mechanical reproduction (which she claims to be "a deal too honest").

Why must the novel labor to perform this inversion of mother and daughter, if doing so is simply a matter of exchanging the one kind of image for the other? I think it is because the rhetoric of realism requires just this kind of layering to thicken the type and lend it something that passes for the substantiality of flesh.[39] Only when Dickens has shuffled and redealt the cards of identity several times over do some few of his characters acquire the thickness required to ground his so-called "world" in the world of objects that his readership equated with reality itself. To understand the consequences of rejecting such closure, we might briefly compare the complex process of differentiation by which Esther comes to inhabit a category of social being with the process that prevents Dorian Gray from achieving any closure of self with self-image.

The Bad Copy

The Picture of Dorian Gray provides an instructive retrospective on the pervasive and irreversible triumph of photographic realism. Wilde invokes the protagonists of Dickens when he gives Dorian a mother with a story that reads like a glib synopsis of Shakespeare's *Romeo and Juliet:* "They say Kelso [Dorian's grandfather] got some rascally adventurer, some Belgian brute to insult his son-in-law in public; paid him, sir, to do it, paid him; and that the fellow spitted this man as if he had been a pigeon . . . Oh, yes, it was a bad business. The girl died too; died within a year."[40] Wilde tosses this morsel of family history to his reader in order to dismiss any natural definition of individual origins and posit another, purely cultural and primarily visual basis for personal identity. In exposing realism's secret, as it were, Wilde is not a modernist, I want to insist, and to regard him as one would be to miss the point completely. He is realism's inversion. Contrary to both realism and modernism, Wilde refuses to ground either image or word in a domain on the other side of mediation. Instead he inverts the relation between copy and original and mobilizes a simple but devastating syllogism that goes something like this: one is originally a type; he or she acquires individual particularity only by virtue of eye-catching deviations from that type; and realism therefore depends upon an exchange of positions between copy and original. For Wilde, all copies are bad copies in that they do not arise inductively from the material facts of the body. On the contrary, they operate deductively upon the body so that its material facts authorize the dominant system of visual types. Wilde refuses, in other words, to resolve the conflict between type and individual implicit in the relationship between the longstanding tradition of portrait painting and the differential system created by the market in photographic images.

When Dorian confesses he is "not the same" as he was before his portrait was painted, Lord Henry correctly contradicts him: "Yes, you are the same . . . Don't spoil it with renunciations. At present you are a perfect type. Don't make yourself incomplete" (237). So long as Dorian regards his portrait as a copy and understands the changes wrought upon it as corruptions of the original type, he can enjoy everything the modern city has to offer and still retain the purity of his image—a duality, let us not forget, that he initially relished:[41]

> . . . there would be a real pleasure in watching it. He would be able to follow his mind into its secret places. This portrait would be to him the most magical of mirrors. As it had revealed to him his own body, so it would reveal to him his own soul. And when winter came upon it, he would still be standing where spring trembles on the verge of summer. When the blood crept from its face, and left behind a pallid mask of chalk with leaden eyes, he would keep the glamour of boyhood. Not one blossom of his loveliness would ever fade. Not one pulse of his life would ever weaken. Like the gods of the Greeks, he would be strong, fleet, and joyous. What did it matter what happened to the coloured image on the canvas? He would be safe. That was everything. (118)

Entrapped within the epistemology of realism, however, other observers would assume they knew the true Dorian simply by looking at his outward appearance. Wilde clearly believes that social identity depends far less on anything approximating a quality of "soul," to use his word for it, than on visual features one possesses as an object and the style in which these features are displayed. As if to prove this very point, he has Dorian's portrait undergo the kind of disfiguration that would afflict the young man's body, were this a work of realism. The portrait thus provides the original Dorian and, as such, continues to provide the mirror-image in relation to which he, as copy, can be said to "have" his own identity.

Upon viewing the transformations that have been wrought upon the portrait he painted many years before, Basil Hallward confronts this fundamental truth:

> Good heavens! it was Dorian Gray's own face that he was looking at! the horror, whatever it was, had not yet entirely spoiled that marvellous beauty. There was still some gold in the thinning hair and some scarlet on the sensual mouth. The sodden eyes had kept something of the loveliness of their blue, the noble curves had not yet completely passed away from chiselled nostrils and from plastic throat. Yes, it was Dorian himself. (171)

Basil also recognizes his complicity, as the painter and lover of types, in producing the monstrous gap between object and image that actually determines who Dorian is: "In the left hand corner was his own name, traced in long letters of bright vermilion" (171). In acknowledging that the image is, as Dorian claims, his "own handiwork," Basil experiences a vertiginous loss of autonomy comparable to Esther's, which suggests that, with the destabilization of Dorian's type, the painter-observer's identity is equally in doubt. In contrast with this pair of modern individuals, we might note that the equally distraught Sir Leicester still has his heritage, as represented by the portraits of his ancestors to prop up his identity, even after he has wearied of occupying that position. That this moment of vertigo precedes Basil's death suggests, further, that having lost the objectification of the difference that propped up his sense of self, the painter has nowhere else to ground his identity. If, by remaining beautiful, Lady Dedlock preserves the difference on which Esther depends for her identity, then, by desecrating the portrait of Basil's masculine ideal, Dorian punctures the illusion of difference and takes revenge on his creator. In Wilde's novel, there is quite literally nobody once the image one has idolatrized is gone.

Thus Wilde proceeds according to the same logic that Dickens follows, one completely hostile to the inductive logic of physiognomy. Wilde stops, however, where the work of realism must close the gap between the logic governing the market in *cartes de visite* and an older cultural logic justifying the claim that such images reflect a truth manifest in the object rather than the image itself. Realism must do so, as I have argued, by constituting an object behind the visible surface, a foundation in the object prior to its reproduction, an original unsullied by its copy. This is what Basil learns from viewing the portrait in the attic. Not to be confused with the world outside its frame, a world dominated by types, the portrait observes the laws of realism as Dickens carried them out on Lady Dedlock. Struggle as he might to find a material cause for the disfiguration of the image to which he bears witness, what Basil sees there is a mixture of types, one image canceling out certain signs of another in a manner that calls into question the empirical distinctions among types and thus the resemblance between types and bodies.[42]

This is the same recognition that prompted Wilde's contemporary, Max Nordau, to deliver his protracted diatribe against the degeneration of the modern urban upper classes. In their obsessive concern with how they look, he complains, the men of these classes have begun to look curiously the same: "They are preserved from excessive oddity through fear of the Philistine's laugh, or through some remains of sanity in taste, and, with the exception of the red dress-coat with meal buttons, and knee-breeches with silk stockings, . . . present little deviation from the ruling canon of the masculine attire of the day."[43] This unnatural sameness in their external appearance marks them, for Nordau, as manifestations of an aberrant psychological type:

> The common feature in all these male specimens is that they do not express their real idiosyncrasies, but try to present themselves as something that they are not. They are not content to show their natural figures, nor even to supplement it by legitimate accessories, in harmony with the type to which they approximate, but they seek to model themselves after

some artistic pattern which has no affinity with their own nature, or is even antithetical to it. Nor do they for the most part limit themselves to one pattern, but several at once, which jar one with another. Thus we get heads set on shoulders not belonging to them, costumes the elements of which are as disconnected as though they belonged to a dream, colours that seem to have been matched in the dark. The impression is that of a masked festival, where all are in disguises, and with heads too in character.[44]

Like Wilde, Nordau is acknowledging the collapse of the distinction between images and objects. For Nordau, this collapse will surely render the world illegible: How can we know who a person really is, if his image has no grounding in the body, much less in his qualities of mind and soul? The idea of an autonomous system of types arbitrarily connected to bodies and faces, or worse, the idea that types can be broken up and recombined, fails to inspire in Wilde any of the horror of disfiguration that so unnerves Nordau.

Quite the contrary, Wilde obviously accepted the fact that any individual is easily subsumed in types, of which inner qualities become as so many visible features. He knew that one achieves individuality only by virtue of differences from that type and that this is the precondition for being in a culture compelled to type virtually everyone on the basis of how he or she looks.[45] Unless the visual features that give one a place in the prevailing system of types are effaced, moreover, the world will become repetitive—and boring. A desire for difference is not only the source of Dorian's fascination with his portrait, but the whole appeal of realism as well:

From cell to cell of his brain crept this one thought; and the wild desire to live, most terrible of all man's appetites, quickened into force each trembling nerve and fibre. Ugliness that had once been hateful to him because it made things real, became dear to him now for that very reason. Ugliness was the one reality. The coarse brawl, the loathsome den, the crude violence of disordered life, the very vileness of thief

Foundational Photographs

163

and outcast, were more vivid, in their intense actuality of impression, than all the gracious shapes of Art, the dreamy shadows of Song. (204)

Both Dorian and Basil ultimately die, as had Sibyl Vane before them, because each failed to appreciate fully the fact that what he considered most himself—features that appeared excessive, atavistic, fragmentary, cruel, or abject in relation to the type—was simply another image. The most secret recesses of the observer are part of the visual order too.

Wilde is equally instructive when it comes to understanding where writing figures into the modern system of identity formation. Although Esther's place within the social order can be construed as relatively image-dependent in comparison with Oliver's, writing still plays an important role in Dickens's fiction—often threatening the position one occupies by virtue of his or her appearance. The documents read into the Chancery Court record represent this threat on a society-wide basis. Family history establishes the body's natural continuity from one generation to another, uses that body to determine social position, and assumes that words transmit interiority. This older system of identity persists into the modern age and invariably disrupts the presentism that lends stability to the visual order. Words seem to threaten personal history in Wilde's novel as well. When, for example, Dorian encounters Sibyl Vane as pure spectacle, he is completely enraptured with her. Upon taking his older, more worldly-wise companions to see her perform *Romeo and Juliet,* however, he is forced to measure her according to a verbal standard:

She over-emphasized everything she had to say. The beautiful passage . . . was declaimed with the painful precision of a schoolgirl who has been taught to recite by some second-rate professor of elocution. When she leaned over the balcony and came to those wonderful lines . . ., she spoke the words as they conveyed no meaning to her. It was not nervousness. Indeed, so far from being nervous, she was absolutely self-contained. It was simply bad art. She was a complete failure. (93–94)

Following close on the heels of this head-on collision between words and images is a notice in the paper announcing Sibyl's "death by misadventure," which initiates the defacing of the portrait and lends Dorian his first complexity of character (138). If these instances of writing open the gap between the protagonist and his portrait, then a little yellow book Lord Henry sends him sets the two reeling on entirely different courses that finally place them in different—indeed, incompatible—genres of visual representation:

> It was the strangest book that he had ever read. It seemed to him that in exquisite raiment, and to the delicate sound of flutes, the sins of the world were passing in dumb show before him. Things that he had dimly dreamed of were suddenly made real to him. Things of which he had never dreamed were gradually revealed . . . It was a poisonous book. The heavy odour of incense seemed to cling about its pages and to trouble the brain. The mere cadence of the sentences, the subtle monotony of their music, so full as it was of complex refrains and movements elaborately repeated, produced in the mind of the lad, as he passed from chapter to chapter, a form of reverie, a malady of dreaming that made him unconscious of the falling day and creeping shadows. (139)

The encroachment of this more satisfying sensorium on the visual order, as the passage openly admits, is the beginning of interiority. If the idealized type that inscribes itself on Dorian's body originated in Basil's painting, then the secret self whose experiences inscribe themselves on that painting has a cultural origin as well. Lord Henry's poisonous little book demystifies what Dickens, as the author of a work of realism, represented as the plague: the force that rescued Esther from the extinction/banality awaiting all those who are mere repetitions of a type and gave her face the marks of individual difference.

Whereas Dickens was unwilling to describe those features in visual detail and had his illustrator turn Esther's face from the reader, Wilde reproduces the effect of the book as a portrait, so that we may see its development into the visual type of the degenerate, the gentleman who masquerades as a type. This type is as pure in its grotesqueness as that of the perfect gentleman was in its beauty.[46] As the concluding lines of the novel explain, "When they entered they found, hanging on the wall, a splendid portrait of their master as they had last seen him, in all the wonder of his exquisite youth and beauty. Lying on the floor was a dead man, in evening dress, with a knife in his heart. He was withered, wrinkled, and loathsome of visage. It was not till they had examined the rings that they recognized who it was" (246).

There is no mistaking Wilde's intention. His inversion of body and portrait will not let us read the body's surface as the outward and visible signs of a psycho-biological condition. Instead, he forces the reader to see that this way of reading is but one more means by which Victorian culture reproduces human nature in its own image. Or to put it another way, if resemblance is always a resemblance to type, as it is, for example, in *Oliver Twist,* then difference is resemblance to type as well, albeit resemblance to a contrary type. All copies are bad copies in this respect, and copies are in fact what we are. Thus Wilde refuses to resolve the implicit contradiction between opposing theories of identity, one based on identification with or repetition of an original object, the other on the negative principle of repetition that differentiates one particular version of the type from every other copy. Under these circumstances, closure is simply the interaction of cultural types as they inscribe themselves on the individual body, in this way constituting for themselves a bio-essentialist source. Realism is the triangulation producing such an entity—the common referent of word and image.

CHAPTER FOUR

Race in the Age of Realism: Heathcliff's Obsolescence

IT IS A PARADOX OF LITERARY HISTORY THAT WHILE FEW SCHOL ars would object to my characterizing the Victorian period as the age of realism, most would have trouble naming more than a handful of novels that consistently display the referential transparency associated with that term. By using *Bleak House* to examine the workings of realism in Chapter 3, I placed noticeable strain on the conventional definition. Framing one of Charles Dickens's three big city novels with what I have characterized as a pre-photographic novel, *Oliver Twist*, on the one side, and Oscar Wilde's cheeky account of identity formation in *The Picture of Dorian Gray*, on the other, was my way of easing that strain. Although literary critical tradition tends to think of the high Victorian period as the age of realism and the mid-Victorian novel as the preferred vehicle of realistic representation, the fact is that few nineteenth-century novels can be described in terms of realism, as it is commonly understood. As if in inadvertent acknowledgment of this fact, literary criticism has proliferated an impressive number of thematically defined subgenres of the Victorian novel, including the Romantic novel, the sensation novel, the gothic novel, the historical novel, the industrial novel, the colonial novel, the imperial gothic novel, the detective novel, the domestic novel, and the boy's adventure novel. As a result, few Victorian novels qualify as realism pure and simple. When the subspecies of a genre grow more plentiful and fascinating to scholars and critics than the genre itself, it is clearly time to rethink the umbrella category. I am no more willing to throw out the term "realism," however, than to pretend that most, or even many, Victorian novels—including the industrial novel—strove for an accurate picture of actual social conditions at the various levels of English society.[1]

I call realism any representation that establishes and maintains the priority of the same social categories that an individual could or could not actually occupy. Realism so defined can be distinguished from writing that reflects or refers to people and things themselves.[2] While knowledge of an individual made it possible to identify his or her image when one saw it, that image rarely if ever gave one access to that individual's character, mind, or soul. There was, in this crucial sense, no such thing as a perfect copy. During the same period when science was discovering to its dismay that even photographs could not guarantee a one-to-one relationship between image and object, fiction was insisting that images did in fact provide an accurate map of the world. If you could transform something into visual information, Dickens seemed to say, you could assign it a place in the visual order; to do so was not only to know that person or thing, but also to feel that you somehow controlled it.

In contrast to the notion of realism I am pursuing, literary realism in the simple and restrictive sense is writing that refers to the categories of the visual order *as if* those categories were indeed the things and people they label. Among those works of literature we consider worth reading today there is hardly a one that displays this manifest naiveté. Even Friedrich Engels's effort to document his journey through the slums of Manchester plays the game of classification and occasionally succumbs to the very categorical divisions that the author set out to debunk; thus when he arrives at the center of his nineteenth-century inferno where Irish workers are housed, he finds, true to prevailing stereotypes, the proverbial pig in the hovel and dirt obscuring the boundary between house and street—implicitly, then, between human and animal. Realism that refers to the world as things (for example, the kind of realism we find in the scientific literature of the period) was an entirely different kind of writing and much less important to literary production than the kind of realism that refers to the world as image. While very few novels attempted anything like the consistent fidelity to the object world for which Engels strove, every genre of Victorian fiction made frequent reference to the world as image. Even the most romantic love story carries on the work of Victorian realism by declaring itself unrealistic. By opening the Thornfield section of her fictional autobiography with indications to this effect, Jane Eyre, for example, lets her reader know the standard of realism is in place even though she is about to violate it. Indeed, it could be argued, such novels carry on the work of realism all the more effectively by virtue of their departures from it. Hence the proliferation of fantastic subgenres during a period known for realism. Subspecies of the Victorian novel often make themselves more memorable, as do the more fanciful moments in Dickens, precisely because they refer to the world of images as if it were independent of the world of objects. When information that exceeds or contradicts the visual order is either pronounced unreal (as, for example, in *Wuthering Heights*) or finally finds a home and folds into a type (as it does in *Jane Eyre*), the categories we identify with realism per se acquire the authority of the real.[3] As he is reduced from a Byronic hero down to the size of a Victorian father, Rochester, significantly, must learn to see all over again before regaining his eyesight. Thus even the most fantastic of these novels cements the bond between the map established by Victorian photography and the social spaces of the modern city proper. What compels them to do so?

Foucault identified the Victorian era as the moment that gave rise to modern institutions: prisons, sanitariums, factories, colonial bureaucracies, museums, schoolrooms, and families—all those institutions, in other words, that materialized and enforced the categorical differences organizing a complex modern culture.[4] Foucault also identified this as the moment when normal people retired from the discursive scene and Western culture began its century-long preoccupation with the sexual behavior of women, children, the mentally disturbed, masturbators, homosexuals, paupers, natives, regional types, and immigrants.[5] So extensive was the proliferation of literature on questions of deviance, and so intense the debate over its causes and consequences, that Victorian readers were virtually forced to reformulate their sense of who they were as English men and women, from identities based on their resemblance to one another, to identities based on how they differed from deviant individuals and peripheral groups of people. This shift in the means and model of cultural reproduction might be compared with a shift within contemporary theories of identity formation from one emphasizing positive identification and repetition to one emphasizing negative identification and repetition with a difference. Where the first model would have individuation begin with the recognition that one is male or female, for example, and proceed with attempts to maintain and adapt that identity to meet the demands of changing circumstances, the second model assumes that the individual begins in a mixed condition and abjects those attributes and behaviors that threaten his or her proper category.[6] According to this second theory, it is the negative stereotype that holds the self together, allowing a person to enact a wide range of individual characteristics so long as he or she maintained the difference between self and symptom.

In this chapter and the next I will offer readings of three Victorian subgenres that gave body to theories of identity which seem to have little to do with Dickens's London or Gaskell's Manchester. Despite the generic differences between these novels, Emily Brontë's *Wuthering Heights,* Lewis Carroll's *Alice's Adventures in Wonderland,* and H. Rider Haggard's *King Solomon's Mines* situate themselves at the opposite pole from realism by virtue of their palpable disdain for the complexities of modern urban life. But while these novels are unquestionably *un*realistic in crucial respects, they are not *anti*realistic in the same way I insisted that *The Picture of Dorian Gray* was. Indeed, Brontë anticipates the form most fantastic fiction would take later in the century, when she makes it clear that the rules of realism can be suspended only within the frame defined by fiction, dream, or legend. Everywhere else, as these departures from the protocols of realism invariably indicate, realism writes the rules that determine human identity, and realism dominates because it is more directly in touch with the world beyond the text than any other version of reality. Given that such fiction ultimately concedes, if not entirely welcomes, this one-to-one relationship between narrative possibilities and the constraints of social positioning, why did so many alternatives to the possibilities allowed by realism per se come into being and flourish during this epoch? I shall try to demonstrate that Victorian fantasy of whatever stripe did something for realism that realism could not accomplish within the limits it placed on itself. Victorian fantasy displayed the fragility, the pure and often clumsy artifice of the very categories in which realism in the narrow sense had inscribed the faces, bodies, and behavior of modern human beings.[7] Such fiction fostered a desire to play with these same categories and see how things might look from the position of the peripheral subject.[8] The varieties of fiction that concern me here thus added the ingredients of play and risk to the process of acquiring and maintaining a social identity. They opened up the visual order where realism seemed bent on closing it down, but they ultimately resolve any ambivalence and attendant anxiety in favor of the prevailing visual order.

It is part of the game fantasy plays with realism to exclude from its field of vision things and people that loomed large in the historical world beyond the novel. Thus, for example, the effects of industrialization are notoriously absent from Brontë's *Wuthering Heights*, forcing critics either to divorce her work from its historical moment, or else to take the bait and render visible what she chose to leave unmentioned.[9] Heathcliff drops out of the novel and then reappears, miraculously transformed, we presume, by the effects of capitalism. At the same time, things that have no existence outside the text can assume spectacular proportions within it, as is the case in *Alice*. In either and all cases, the element of fantasy insists on the fundamental illegibility of the material world, indicating that all is not already seen, because visual categories are far too limited to encompass all of reality. The more extravagant the package in which such epistemological uncertainty arrives, the stronger is our sense of utter dependence on those differences that do remain visible even from a peripheral perspective. Victorian fiction at its most fantastic proves, if nothing else, that all differences are not equal, that certain boundaries cannot be crossed, and that the most intransigent of these are always drawn in terms of race.[10] This is not to say that race either motivated or shaped the categories of identity that I have associated with realism. That would be putting the cart before the horse. Racism as we know it followed rather than preceded the extensive visual objectification of colonial subjects throughout Africa and Asia.[11] The effort to mark indelibly those whose inclusion would compromise the very coherence of the emergent social order began significantly closer to home.

The period of Victoria's reign saw the entrenchment of the modern middle class and established the way they would deal with an organizing urban proletariat. During this period, English people were already reconceptualizing their relationship as a race to the colonial populations. Historical scholarship has given us two separate narratives to account for these changes in the semiotic behavior of class and race respectively. One narrative describes the class struggle that took place within England as the nation underwent industrialization, and the other tells of Western Europe's attempt to dominate the rest of the world.[12] What falls through the crack between the two accounts is the process by which Great Britain was reconceptualized as a modern urban core with a Celtic, or ethnic, periphery.[13] During the first half of the nineteenth century, a variety of authors, artists, and intellectuals collaborated with the British government to create a geographical difference between one kind of British subject and another.[14] The line was drawn in terms of culture—how did these people use the land, how did they live, what were their sexual proclivities—but the end result was a difference between two peoples so profound that when both groups occupied the same territory, they could not intermarry. Thus we find that while Heathcliff's emotional similarity to Catherine Earnshaw makes them too endogamous to become husband and wife, his difference from Isabel Linton makes them too exogamous for anything permanent to come of that admixture; it kills both Isabel and her son by Heathcliff. Race provided a way of distinguishing modern from pre-modern individuals as the people inhabiting core and periphery acquired incompatible ontologies.

It is important to understand that Britain's Celtic folk were not racialized in quite the same way as its African and Asian subjects were. Again in collaboration with printed news, government policy, developments in the human sciences as well as medicine and law, colonial fiction, and expeditionary photography reproduced on an international scale much the same cultural geography that was enabling readers to imagine Britain as an English core and a Celtic periphery. Having positioned themselves at the center of a nation ringed with a brand of primitives indigenous to their nation, it was perhaps not that much of a stretch for readers to see themselves at the center of a nation ringed with the exotic peoples of Africa, Asia, the Middle East, and the South Pacific. As it redoubled itself on a global scale, however, the imaginary relation of core and periphery underwent an important change, one that wed race to disfigurations of the body image that distinguished European men and women from what they came to consider "the rest of the world." Race began to indicate a human excess of some kind that manifested itself in visible terms. Bodies inscribed with the signs of such excesses were by definition also lacking—lacking in the categorical distinctions that made them legible. Sara Suleri reads the aggression of the English colonizer in the face of such "unreadability" as "a symptom of terror rather than of possession."[15] In response to their homegrown savages, I would argue, aggression on the part of literate Englishmen was a response to both terror and possession. Denoting an excess of appetites, race in turn reinforced the relationship between core and periphery at home, linking the physical differences of colonial subjects to the apparent indigence and wild ways of regional folk in Great Britain, and vice versa.[16]

Inverse Transparency

The critical tradition has used Emily Brontë's only novel, *Wuthering Heights,* to exemplify a range of literary phenomena—from popular romance, to high Romantic lyricism, to the *sui generis* product of a delusional woman—but it has never, to my knowledge, read this novel as one that observes the protocols of realism. *Wuthering Heights* did in fact carry out the work of realism, however, in collaboration with the burgeoning industry of Victorian folklore and the precocious art of regional photography, as it demonstrates the consequences of abandoning realistic protocols. In this respect, it is more akin to a historical novel like Walter Scott's *Waverly* than to Mary Shelley's *Frankenstein.* To explain how Brontë's novel fits into this overlooked chapter of modern cultural history, I find it helpful to turn to a popular Victorian genre called spirit photography.

Any photograph, Roland Barthes reminds us, provides a memorial or relic of the person or thing whose image it preserves.[17] To look at a photograph is to know that the figure and ground within the image no longer exist outside its frame. Because object and image parted ways and began to pursue entirely different histories the moment the photograph was taken, the photographic subject can no longer exist as it was represented. Only certain details remain to link the image to the historical world that used to live outside the photograph and therefore to the story of its production. To make a spirit photograph, the photographer exploited this situation. He arranged his subject—usually a woman—in a potentially otherworldly pose and dress and had her step outside the field of vision while the negative was still underexposed. The woman's image remained transparent, stripped of the accidental details that would tie that image to a specific person, place, or time. But while her underinscribed body remained transparent, her surroundings developed the detailed sub-stantiality within the photographic frame that is ordinarily conveyed by an image's opacity.

To understand the historical impact of folklore and photography, we must resist the silent instructions that link opacity with substance. If a photograph memorializes something by substituting its image for the object in question, then the image's opacity would indicate that this person or that thing is, in this specific sense, dead. Instead of death, then, the transparency of the woman's image in the spirit photograph tells us she has detached herself from that image and gone on with life outside the frame. Transparency is, in this sense, a vital sign. In contrast to a photograph that is merely bad, the spirit photograph overturns the logic of realism or, in other words, the assumption that the image depends upon things which can be seen with the eye. Indeed, the spirit photograph flaunts photography's ability to produce an object that could not otherwise be seen, be-cause that object has no existence outside the image. The ghost could be said to thematize this semiotic behavior; it turns something old (a body) into something entirely new (the spirit body) by repre-senting that thing (or body) as something that is no longer there (namely, a real human being). In this chapter I will argue that fiction, folklore, and photography together brought the same power to bear on the native people and customs of the British Isles that spirit pho-tography used to dematerialize women.

The Nostalgia of the Latter-Day Tourist

During the 1830s and 1840s, a substantial number of relatively well-to-do British tourists took to touring the more remote regions of Great Britain in search of quaint customs and rugged landscapes. Along the way, they began to take notes on the local folklore, sketch choice patches of scenery, and capture segments of rural life in pho-tographs. By circulating this information among their families, friends, and colleagues, this particular wave of tourists succeeded in portraying what was then the majority of the British population as remnants of a primitive past that remained on the fringes of the modern nation. When cast in forms that could be mass-produced—namely, travelogue, fiction, and photography—this cultural information apparently created a prodigious appetite for more. The consequences were swift and brutal. If in the early decades of the nineteenth century the expanse of untrammeled countryside seemed limitless, then by the close of the century, the tourist had difficulty finding any traces of an authentic Britain. One frustrated photographer complained that he could discover but "few villages and hamlets which seem to belong to past centuries—fresh looking plaster and stucco are there unknown; fashion has not quite ousted primitive dress, nor has the din of factories disturbed the sleepy aspect of the surroundings."[18]

How can this veneration for the countryside and the ways of rural people be reconciled with the devastating effects of tourism and its attendant methods of memorialization on indigenous cultures? Renato Rosaldo's thumbnail description of the phenomenon he calls "imperialist nostalgia" can set us on a path to an answer. "Curiously enough," he observes,

> agents of colonialism—officials, constabulary officers, missionaries, and other figures from whom anthropologists ritually dissociate themselves—often display nostalgia for the colonized culture as it was "traditionally" (that is, when they first encountered it). The peculiarity of their yearning, of course, is that agents of colonialism long for the very forms of life they intentionally altered or destroyed.[19]

If one applies this statement to the photographer's lament for the passing of a more natural Britain, striking parallels emerge. The photographer has completely ignored the fact that his quest for an originary landscape is what destroyed the very thing he sought. Like the "agents of colonialism," the photographer requires the traces of a premodern Britain "both to capture people's imaginations and to conceal [his] complicity with often brutal domination."[20] Indeed, as Rosaldo explains further, "much of imperialist nostalgia's force resides in its association with (indeed, its disguise as) more genuinely innocent tender recollections of what is at once an earlier epoch and a previous phase of life."[21] What Rosaldo fails to acknowledge, however, is that nostalgic representations not only exculpate those who recollect a former phase of cultural history with such yearning, these representations also participate in the annihilation in which the tourist and the photographer, like the ethnographer himself, deny complicity. I am suggesting that the words and images that memorialized "the folk" throughout Great Britain also rendered obsolete the local forms of labor that had long held those communities together.[22]

As one-sided as this form of internal colonialism may now appear to be, the transformation was not free of consequences for those who produced and consumed such words and images. In the manner of the spirit photograph, the wholesale transformation of indigenous culture into information that could be distributed on a mass basis created an entirely new world of primitive people, places, and things in relation to which members of the literate elite were positioned as observers.[23] The curious form of *Wuthering Heights* was shaped by the double meaning I am attributing to "internal colonialism."[24] Brontë's novel not only dramatizes how certain textualizing procedures created what appeared to be a premodern periphery within Great Britain and subordinated that periphery to a modern metropolitan core, the novel also shows how those same procedures changed the identity of readers whom it situated at the core. With the help of such works of fiction, readers could understand that precisely those features branding other people as peripheral were also the means by which those readers distinguished their elemental selves from the superficial appearances and mannerisms that identified their place within the visual order. Novels also indicated that the readership's authority to master others rested on their sometimes shaky ability to master the same primitive element in themselves.

Brontë's treatment of her genteel narrator produces an unbridgeable cultural gap between the educated observer and an entire territory of English life. His mastery of the same region that was home to the Brontë family depends on his incorporation of local differences through a process that strips the culture of those details and then reclassifies members of that culture according to their conformity with or deviance from a modern familial norm. By depriving people of the local names and habitations that situated them within the regional geography of early nineteenth-century England, however, internal colonization transformed respectable English culture into one haunted at the core by possible violations of that family model. Lockwood himself fails to meet that standard. His venture into the north of England both dramatizes the limits of modern stereotyping and challenges the visual order those stereotypes uphold.

To trace the lineaments of such a struggle in *Wuthering Heights*, it is necessary for me to begin transforming the novel from an object of literary analysis into what might be called an object of cultural studies. Brontë scholars tend to look at the novel as a series of enclosures within enclosures, a structure they regard as symptomatic of a female author who withdrew from adult sexuality into the sanctuary of her family, fantasy life, and finally death. Tenacious as this reading of *Wuthering Heights* may prove to be, it is not all that difficult to rethink the novel's self-enclosure in terms of the sweeping displacement of local kinship systems by a mass classification system grounded on visual differences. All enclosures within the novel are violated. No spatial boundary remains intact—neither Heights, nor Grange, nor bedroom, nor body, nor book, nor dream, nor burial ground. Everyone in the novel crosses at least one threshold unbidden and ravishes some sacred ground. We might recall, for example, the moment when Lockwood first approaches the portals of Wuthering Heights and is attacked by one of the Earnshaw dogs. Or when Catherine and Heathcliff peer in the window of Thrushcross Grange, only to have Catherine seized by one of the Linton dogs. Or when Linton separates Catherine from Heathcliff and then speeds her decline and death by childbirth. Or when her daughter scales the wall between the Heights and the Grange for the purpose of nursing her sickly cousin. Or when Heathcliff takes over the Heights, elopes with Isabel Linton, takes custody of their son, and forcibly marries him off to

Catherine's daughter. It is as if the narrative itself is a sequence of boundary violations, each of which makes an entire classification system shudder at the blow and change in some profound way to account for the intrusion. Each territorial invasion happens strictly according to the law, and yet each is described as if it were an act of rape, pedophilia, necrophilia, or all of the above.[25]

One scene in particular—at the kernel of Lockwood's dream—can be read as a condensation of these episodes. To recover from his traumatic encounter with a household dog, Lockwood retires to a chamber where, he tells us, Heathcliff "never let anyone lodge willingly" (25). Inside the chamber there is "a singular sort of old-fashioned couch . . . [that] formed a little closet" (25). Once secured within this second chamber, Lockwood enters yet another enclosure: "It was a testament, in lean type, and smelling dreadfully musty: a fly-leaf bore the inscription—'Catherine Earnshaw, her book' and a date some quarter of a century back" (26). To this point, the novel extends the empire of the educated observer into the private sanctuary of another person, a woman who died some years ago. But the pleasure of looking is vexed to nightmare as Lockwood reads the notes she had scribbled in the book's margins. The more the place invades his sleep, the more he struggles to regain the power of a bedroom tourist, and this depends on reestablishing the boundaries between inside and outside—between himself, that is, and the rest of the world. To this end, he identifies the source of violence as

. . . the branch of a fir tree that touched my lattice, as the blast wailed by, and rattled its dry cones against the panes!

I listened doubtingly an instant; detected the disturber, then turned and dozed, and dreamt again; if possible, still more disagreeably than before.

This time, I remembered I was lying in the oak closet, and I heard distinctly the gusty wind, and the driving of the snow; I heard, also, the fir-bough repeat its teasing sound, and [I] ascribed it to the right cause; but it annoyed me so much, that I resolved to silence it, if possible . . .

"I must stop it . . .!" I muttered, knocking my knuckles through the glass, and stretching an arm out to seize the . . . branch: instead of which, my fingers closed on the fingers of a little ice-cold hand! . . .

"Catherine Linton," it replied, shiveringly . . . "I'm come home, I'd lost my way on the moor!"

As it spoke, I discerned, obscurely, a child's face looking through the window. Terror made me cruel; and, finding it useless to attempt shaking the creature off, I pulled its wrist on to the broken pane, and rubbed it to and fro till the blood ran down and soaked the bed-clothes: still it wailed, "Let me in" and maintained its tenacious grip, almost maddening me with fear. (29–30)

I have written about this scene more than once, and still it eludes me. How can one say with any sense of certainty whether this account of a dream expands or limits the narrator's consciousness? Does it ask us to make palpable something that someone like Lockwood can never feel or know, because the categories he brings to the act of reading are too limited for the culture he encounters in the north of England? Or does the dream carry us from the moors, house, bed, and book into hitherto unacknowledged recesses of Lockwood's fantasy life? This just may be that rare moment in canonical literature when we can see exactly how contending ways of making meaning once struggled for possession of the same cultural material.

The ghost is symptomatic of this struggle. It simultaneously acknowledges and conceals the nature of the conflict between local and mass-mediated cultures. It prevents the two from posing an open contradiction that would destroy the unity of "Britain" by translating what is in fact a spatial conflict into a conflict between two moments in time, one of which is over: Yorkshire supposedly belongs to the past. The ghost identifies this earlier moment in time with women and children and, by so doing, provides a spectacle of interiority that incorporates the other culture within modern consciousness, as something that has been forgotten or repressed. To examine this process in more detail and suggest in more precise terms what its political impact might have been, I will turn to a discussion of folklore, another kind of classificatory activity that had gained what would prove an irreversible momentum by the time Brontë began to write her novel. From there, I will move into a brief description of the regional photography that along with British folklore and *Wuthering Heights* became extremely popular as the Victorian age wore on.

The People as Folk

By the 1840s when Emily Brontë was writing *Wuthering Heights,* a substantial number of literate, mostly middle-class people had been collecting stories, superstitions, cures, and arcane practices from every out-of-the-way place in the nation and writing them down for weekly and monthly publications. Interest in this activity had been increasing since the early decades of the nineteenth century. By 1846, the influential collector William Thoms acknowledged the substantial accumulation of such information when he coined the term "folklore" to describe "a vast body of 'traditionary lore' floating among our peasantry."[26] As consolidated by Thoms and his fellow collectors, the project always assumed, in the words of Richard Dorson, that "a rude and primitive peasantry fitted naturally into the landscape and intrigued the traveller with their superstitious rites and ceremonies."[27] Turning back to this rather substantial body of writing for an account of rural life in the early nineteenth century, the modern scholar finds remarkably little that qualifies as the genuine article, despite the ample supply of place names, local variations of some demon or cure, and the specific conditions under which such magic was supposed to work. Nevertheless, through their exchanges in letters and newsletters, and by collecting their information in anthologies and what were called Every-Day Books, nineteenth-century folklorists systematically reclassified ordinary life in most regions of Great Britain as both primitive and obsolete. They broke down working symbolic systems into representative details. Then they rearranged those details, regardless of local origin and function, under such abstract headings as "costume" or "superstition," which reclassified all such information as signs of cultural backwardness, on the one hand, and of picturesque charm, on the other.

Like the collections and Every-Day Books, Thoms's 1846 "Folk-Lore" column in *The Athenaeum* gradually converted the symbolic economies of different regions into a coin of exchange among literate men of leisure. From eighteenth-century antiquarians these men had inherited the idea that native customs indicated something much more insidious than the mere lack of elite manners and education. Writing in 1777, for example, John Brand regarded British folkways as the relics of pre-Reformation England. This was a time, he claimed, when "a Profusion of childish Rites, Pageants and Ceremonies diverted the Attention of the People from the consideration of their real State, and kept them in humour, if it did not sometimes make them in love with their slavish Modes of Worship."[28] Nineteenth-century folklorists often saw local customs as pernicious in much the same way, and could be quite forthright about wishing to stamp them out. "Those who mix much amongst the lower orders," wrote William Henderson in his *Notes on the Folk Lore of the Northern Counties and Border* (1866), "will find in these remote places,—nay, even in our towns and villages,—a vast mass of superstition holding its ground most tenaciously."[29] In such statements, however, the rationale for combating folkways no longer rested on linking them with the practices of Catholic Europe; nineteenth-century folklore identified the folk as foreign in a distinctively nineteenth-century way. Regional people did not constitute a competing subculture with whom the folklorist, as a representative of mass-mediated culture, engaged in a struggle for meaning. Rather, folklorists represented the struggle as one that was over by the time it actually began. They identified indigenous cultures as an earlier stage in the development of modern English culture, since those cultures sanctified precisely the excessive, frivolous, or nasty behaviors that educated English adults had outgrown.

A second and far more positive view of folk culture existed side by side with the view that justified wiping it out. Thomas Keightley's *Tales and Popular Fictions* (1834) regarded its object of study as a rare and fragile thing that—like anything whose value was not evident to the ordinary run of readers—was destined to pass into oblivion. Keightley situated himself as the lone witness to such primitive beauty: "Yet, though thus despised by the narrow-minded and intolerant disciples of utility, popular fiction [by which he means "folklore."] has attractions for those whose views are more enlarged, and who love to behold Philosophy extending her dominion over all the regions of the Human Mind."[30] This statement invites us to think of folklore as a precursor of modern literature that affords privileged insight into what was often designated geographically as the more remote regions of the human mind.[31] The statement also suggests that, by reclassifying the primitive folk as charmingly archaic versions of themselves, educated Englishmen could enjoy dominion over them.

The argument that primitive cultures should be regarded as the idyllic childhood of the modern nation proved to be an effective way of actually destroying the very thing that men such as Keightley longed for. In the second half of the nineteenth century, folklore defined its mission as preserving an authentic, pre-industrial Britain.[32] It translated all hostility toward the groups it was busily describing into an appreciation—even reverence—for what was obsolete. Folklore did not restrict this method of description to cultures that had in fact stopped working; it also regarded thriving local cultures with nostalgia. In this way, it can be argued, folklore sought to write many viable forms of livelihood out of practical existence.

A book-length account of gypsy life in Great Britain encapsulates the logic concealed within this paradox. Entitled *Lavengro: The Scholar—The Gypsy—The Priest,* the book was written between 1842 and 1844 and first published in 1851, the year after the second edition of *Wuthering Heights* appeared. Like Brontë's novel, this peculiar mix of travel literature, folklore, and fiction initially outraged certain readers by exalting gypsies at the expense of more respectable people. But eventually it, too, enjoyed immense popularity. The author, George Borrow, suggested the reason for such a turnabout in popularity when he prefaced the account of his travels through rural Britain with these remarks:

> In the following pages I have endeavored to describe a dream, partly of study, partly adventure, in which will be found copious notices of books, and many descriptions of life and manners, sonic in very unusual form. The scenes of action lie in the British Islands. Pray, do not be displeased, gentle reader, if perchance thou hast imagined that I was about to conduct thee to distant lands, and didst promise thyself much instruction and entertainment from what I might tell thee of them. I do assure thee that thou hast no reason to be displeased, inasmuch as there are no countries in the world less known by the British than these selfsame British Islands, or where more strange things are every day occurring, whether in road or street, house or dingle.[33]

Thus the author warns his readership that his traversing of the countryside will resemble an account of foreign travel. He will show British readers that much of their nation is a foreign country in the double sense that it is both unknown to them and inhabited by a people (personified by "The Gypsy") with whom the literate population neither shares beliefs nor observes common customs. Yet, in contrast to Catholic Europe ("The Priest" named in Borrow's title), this same nation within the nation is an integral part of Great Britain and paradoxically resembles what is most authentic in respectable English readers themselves. If *Lavengro* portrays "the nation" as a cultural landscape littered with a heterogeneous population of foreigners, this strange account also classifies those strangers and quite literally puts them safely in their place. By means of his inquisitive eye, facility for languages, and sure-handed pen, the tourist-ethnographer-author of *Lavengro* reorganizes all manner of other cultures into types that he can personally see, hear, and master intellectually, types presumably unfamiliar to the reader's relatively untutored eye.

Modern Britain's incorporation of such a stranger was not without its problems, however. Native people and their cultures did not always agree that their moment in history was over. Nor did they often substantiate the enchanting stereotypes in terms of which the reader was encouraged to imagine them. While it can be argued that many traditional ways of making a living from land and sea were in fact rendered obsolete by Victorian culture, the Brontës' fiction also indicates that local cultures continued to govern personal life throughout much of England. The old ways of observing feast days, habits of courtship and kinship, and methods of caring for the body remained to challenge the norms of the novel-reading public well after the economies and political hierarchies specific to a given region had been dismantled.[34] We can regard Lockwood's dream as a product of the conflict that occurs when the cultural past refuses to die and continues to govern the production of meaning at the local level. The child's ghost brings cultural conflict to life within the contemporary moment, where it exists as something that eludes more modern categories. If the ghost places regional culture in the past, then it also translates that time back into cultural space, albeit a fictional space, so that the moment reproduced in Catherine's book can challenge Lockwood's protocols for reading Yorkshire culture and its people.

What is at stake in Lockwood's dream, if one thinks of it in these terms? The dream represents two kinds of violence, the violence of enclosing identity and confining it to the individuated body, on the one hand, and the violence of violating this very kind of self-enclosure, on the other. Lockwood commits violence in the first sense when he insists on severing the bond of common humanity that links him to the place and to its history, as represented by the phantom child. But the ghost causes violence of another kind: It allows the dead to permeate the place, the book, and the name. Larger than the body of the woman that was supposed to contain it, the essential Catherine enjoys a sinister afterlife in things. What is more, the voice and appearance that once belonged to her tend to enter other people's thoughts and field of vision. Heathcliff blames Lockwood for cutting off and shutting out the child. In so doing, urban man performs a violent act of self-enclosure. Such people are shallow, heartless, and unreal—"dolls," the gypsy calls them. From Lockwood's point of view, however, the violence was done when Catherine infiltrated his dream and compromised his self-enclosure. Readers tend to think that Brontë tips the scales of meaning in favor of the ghost.

Lockwood encounters the regional landscape as a tourist, converting that landscape and its occupants into a private aesthetic experience. He takes secret satisfaction in prying into out-of-the-way places with his eyes. It would be easy to identify Lockwood with the folklorist, were it not for the fact that he is enticed by the possibility of crossing over from image to object and becoming involved with his subject matter. Moreover, he is sorely traumatized by the discovery of how vastly the rustic north of England differs from the stereotypes in which he sees it. Brontë prepares us for his penchant for optical pleasure and his incapacity for any other relationship when she has Lockwood confess why he came to the north of England in the first place. "While enjoying a month of fine weather at the sea-coast," he explains, "I was thrown into the company of a most fascinating creature, a real goddess in my eyes, as long as she took no notice of me . . . [But] she understood me at last, and looked a return—the sweetest of all imaginable looks. And what did I do? I confess it with shame—shrunk icily into myself like a snail" (15). Lockwood plays out the same exchange of glances at least two more times, once with Catherine Earnshaw and then with her daughter. Such repetition makes it clear that he not only wants the pornographic thrill of fixing an object with his gaze, but also expects the objects he encounters to *be* nothing more than what he sees. By having the audacity to look back, the women in this novel challenge his way of seeing and define his categories as inadequate to scan and contain them.

If the thrill of looking indicates that looking confers power on the observing subject, then one would think that returning such a look ought to shift power back onto the object observed. But resistance on the part of a subject so objectified does not result in the political emergence or even recognition of that subject's position. Quite the contrary, the novel's way of revealing the political nature of this conflict becomes a way of incorporating the conflict itself within modern culture, where such conflicts register as assaults on reason and sentimentality and tend to be regarded as a threat to Lockwood's masculinity. That is to say, the materials of his dream may resist his best attempts to internalize and rationalize the ghost, but the novel, being a novel, allows one to read this indigestible lump of cultural information as Lockwood's nightmare—a peripheral territory within the educated mind.

Untimely Images

For more than a decade before *Wuthering Heights* appeared and caused a minor sensation, a number of individuals in England and France had been developing the technology for mechanically reproducing the countryside and making these photographs available to urban viewers. Regional photographs put the observer in touch with a countryside that was primitive and yet utterly passive to view. These images also separated the observer from this countryside by an unbridgeable gap in time. The image of a cottage doorway from *The Pencil of Nature,* the first volume of English calotypes by Henry Fox Talbot, demonstrates how one of the earliest photographs transformed cultural space into historical time (Figure 4.1). Talbot's process detaches the object from the symbolic economy in which it had a practical role to play. As an image, the object could be valued for its flaws, signs of decay, indications that it is on the verge of perishing.[35] Having cut the image free from the object and infused it with aesthetic value, Talbot then placed it in an album alongside the crumbling facade of Queen's College Oxford, shelves of well-worn books, statues from antiquity, a piece of old lace, a leaf, and a haystack with a ladder. The volume appeared at bookshops in six paper-covered installments between June 1844 and April 1846 and was a huge suc-

FIGURE 4.1   *The Open Door* (1844). William Henry Fox Talbot.

cess. *The Pencil of Nature* appeared to imitate the act of seeing. In fact, however, it presented viewers with an array of objects that they could not have seen without Talbot's process. His calotypes operated as synecdoches, broken off and standing in for a whole system of natural, social, or economic relationships. Much like the ghost, they allowed one to see people, places, and things that were no longer really there and certainly never coexisted with one another in this particular way.

Photographers especially liked to perform this vanishing act on the very forms of labor that sustained most of the rural population. Regional photography did to working people what Talbot's did to fragile objects: it stripped them of local meaning and utilitarian value; it transformed their means of livelihood along with the setting, their clothing, and their bodies into details indicating rudeness and obsolescence. Individuals thus appear before us in these photographs, not as individuals, but as curious survivors from an earlier

FIGURE 4.2   *Reverend James Fairbairn and Newhaven Fishwives* (c. 1845).
Robert Adamson and David Octavius Hill.

time. The calotype and daguerreotype techniques were invented during the late 1830s, and by the early 1850s both were available for use by professionals as well as amateurs. A historical sequence of such "folk" images reveals what happened to the image of regional people as the method underwent professionalization. The photographs of David Octavius Hill and Robert Adamson display a conscious selection of the details of dress, body, and labor to create a regional type and set that type apart from similar types as well as from the people who made and consumed these photographs. To create the impression that the local people in the photograph belonged to another time frame, regional photographers tended to keep themselves out of the picture. Adamson and Hill could achieve the same effect by inserting a modern individual inside the photographic frame of reference (Figure 4.2). These images thematized what remains implicit in the genre when they cast the literate urban individual in the role

FIGURE 4.3   Scottish fisher girl (1880). Studio
setting. Moir & Halkett, Edinburgh.

of father and mentor to compliant subjects, completely obfuscating
the fact that *he* was intruding in their household, not they in his.

By the 1860s, the camera and its subject matter had moved from
the countryside into the studio, and many of the same shots taken by
amateur photographers were restaged by professionals against artificial backdrops. A photograph from 1880 of a Scottish fisher girl
shows how the new setting seeped into the image and transformed
the regional subject (Figure 4.3). This woman appears to be just any
young woman, not necessarily even Scottish, and probably someone
who needed to earn a model's fee. Her clothes are treated as a
costume and her baskets as ornamental objects. She consequently
presents the viewer not with a relic of a passing way of life so much as

FIGURE 4.4 *Eily O'Connor, the Coleen Bawm*
(c. 1870).

with the memorial of something that was already gone by the time the photograph was taken. A photograph from the 1870s entitled *Eily O'Connor, the Coleen Bawm* exhibits the same streak of sensationalism readers found in *Wuthering Heights* (Figure 4.4). It glamorizes a woman otherwise unattractive by Victorian standards. As legend has it, "the Coleen Bawm," meaning "the White Girl," refers to a sixteen-year-old Irish girl named Ellen Harley who was murdered in 1819 by a local squire and his servant. A story about the fatal beauty of a rural woman was evidently just the sort to inspire several plays and books before providing a title for this photograph. As the image of such a woman came to illustrate a sensational narrative, that image completely detached itself from the history of the woman in the photo-

Race in the Age of Realism

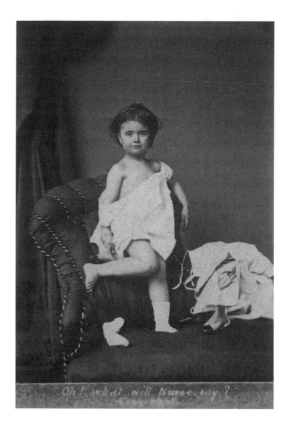

FIGURE 4.5   "Oh! What will Nurse Say"
(1865). *Carte-de-visite.* Leopold F. Manley,
London.

graph; she ceased to testify to the condition of Irish peasant culture
and became an object of modern sexual desire instead. Thus re-
named, framed, and titled, the migration of this image from a local
culture into the marketplace of reproduced and reproducible images
demonstrates the power of a photograph to fix a meaning and value
to the human body, regardless of whose it was and how it might have
been regarded in previous frames of reference.

Along with *The Coleen Bawn,* I want to consider an extremely
popular genre of Victorian photography that Asa Briggs calls "slightly
risqué material" (Figure 4.5).[36] By eroticizing the image, the photo-

graph calls attention to the same constellation of visual features that coalesces in Lockwood's dream. In these peculiarly suggestive portraits, excluded humanity steps forward and presents itself to the public gaze in the form of a nameless, placeless child. It is important to note how the photograph taints this child, making her more exotic than pristinely primitive. A different order of details suddenly beckons to the viewer, telling him to reclassify this image. In contrast to the kind of ethnographic information that the photographs of Newhaven fisher women provide, the exotic girl is interesting for the body beneath her costume, as indicated by the missing shoes in *The Coleen Bawm* and, even more obtrusively, by the appearance of one foot from which the little girl has yet to remove her shoe in the process of undressing.[37] Given that it does not seem right for us to see her in this state, this half-clothed child forces us to ask how she entered our field of vision. Moreover, the girls in these photographs return the viewer's look. By refusing to become intransitive objects, they embarrass those who can afford the privilege of looking, and much like the ghostly child in Lockwood's dream, they shatter the sentimental frame. In thus returning from the past to confront the viewer within his own historical milieu, these girls cross over from the primitive to become exotic. They intrude into the world dominated by the tourist and reveal what his voracious appetite for images is really all about.

Regionalism

Along with folklore and photography, *Wuthering Heights* performs the task of miniaturization. Folklore divided rural Britain into small communities that could be represented synecdochally by a couple of curious practices. Photography did the same thing and then reduced its object in size. Seeking out the odd detail, it too had a way of putting local people in awkward positions. When staged in this way, those people resembled children who survived from a more primitive time into a modern industrial present. At the same time, one knows the miniature is nothing but a copy. Photography's object is at once out there and already gone. It is by thus triumphing over the facts of nature, as Susan Stewart tells us, that the miniature offers its consumer a fantasy of omnipotence in which art and technology appear to conquer even death itself.[38] To move outside the frames of fiction and photography and insert those frames themselves in history, however, one must push the logic of miniaturization one step more.

A long tradition of British travel literature testifies to the fact that British people had always fixed themselves on a cultural map. But the period during which folklore flourished saw the development of new technologies for reorganizing and reproducing this information for a mass audience. As a result, this particular remapping of regional Britain had a strikingly different impact than earlier efforts. No matter where a person went throughout Great Britain, he or she was either in the core or at the periphery. Whether you felt at home or out of place on either terrain depended entirely on the kind of person you were. Were you someone who consumed fiction, leafed through photograph albums, and savored the accounts of local people and their customs written by the early folklorists? If not, according to the emerging classification system, then you were probably the kind of person who provided the subject matter for such leisure-time activities. Fiction, folklore, and photography automatically set regional people apart from the educated people who amused themselves by learning all about their primitive counterparts.[39]

Fiction, folklore, and photography also asked the reader to imagine regional people as having racially different bodies, even though those bodies were not often explicitly identified as such. In contrast with the people of Africa and Asia, these people were British; they were just not truly English. Their flesh may be described as swarthier in folklore and travel accounts, as indeed Heathcliff's is, but primitive cultural practices were regarded as the important cause and symptom of their exclusion from the modern social order. Ethnic flesh was never half so responsive to self-restraint and education as it was to curious superstitions, arcane cures, and incomprehensible desires. The cultural map that shaped the way Victorian readers conceptualized and, indeed, acted out their relationship to other British people

FIGURE 4.6   *Lady M. Campbell Argyle as Red
Riding Hood* (c. 1865). *Carte-de-visite.*
James Ross, Edinburgh.

automatically placed those people within another time frame: they
belonged to an archaic and benighted past that existed in precise
contrast to the enlightened, progressive culture of people who could
read novels, take photographs, and study the relics of an earlier
British culture.

Geography designated one's place on a psychosexual landscape
that linked the place where one worked to the kind of work he or she
did. The fiction, folklore, and photography I have discussed characteristically ask us to imagine peripheral people in terms of the labor
peculiar to their geographical location. These texts rendered their

FIGURE 4.7 Group of children at the seashore (c. 1885). Studio setting. T. A. Grut, Guernsey.

tools primitive and the end products themselves hardly worth the trouble. Detail by detail, the genres that began to flourish in the 1830s and 1840s revised the whole concept of work. Forms of labor that had stood the test of time and natural conditions capitulated to the printing press and the camera. Turned into something to look at, these forms of labor were set in opposition to mechanized production and defined as significantly lacking in the kind of practicality that translated into money.

To become a modern imperial nation, according to the materials I have been examining, Great Britain underwent an internal division that would only be exaggerated with the spread and even the collapse of British imperialism. This cultural division of labor established the dialect, religion, clothing, skills, and appearance of a privileged minority of men and women as those who have inherited Great Britain itself. By the end of *Wuthering Heights,* we might recall, such people have taken over both the Heights and the Grange—in other words, both of the cultures competing to define the landscape and determine the identity of those who live there. Anyone who cannot assume a role within the modern nuclear family has passed or will soon pass away. Let us take a brief look, then, at what the camera—having spirited indigenous British culture away—saw fit to offer in its place. In a photograph entitled *Lady M. Campbell Argyle as Red Riding Hood,* the effects of miniaturization are immediately apparent in the child's fanciful appropriation of the dress formerly associated with the women of British fishing villages (Figure 4.6). Other family photographs staged in the studio transform the landscape and labor of regional Britain into a patently artificial backdrop for the bourgeois family. Children pose where local people used to be, tools are reduced to toys, and pets occupy the space once reserved for the livestock on which most regional families depended for survival (Figure 4.7). These forms of miniaturization turn regional culture into the childhood of urban man and the countryside into his place of recreation.

Emily's Ghost

Once we see the novel in relation to a process of internal colonialism that marginalized most of regional England, we can place Brontë herself in this process by means of the same cultural logic that I abstracted from the technology of the spirit photograph. In a well-known photograph of the parsonage at Haworth taken at about the time Emily Brontë wrote the novel that would make her name immortal, one can see that visitors to the surrounding cemetery did not come there simply to pay their respects to the dead (Figure 4.8). The well-heeled tourists are too busy looking at something. The garden of

mingled tombstones and heather surrounding a place that was reputedly home to a family of poets, madmen, dying women, and their preacher-poet father was evidently something of a spectacle. Surviving into the present time, the town and parsonage themselves appear as reduced in size as the traces of girls afflicted at birth by an illness that stunted their growth and limited their lifetime. The parsonage exists as a tourist attraction on the Yorkshire moors to this day, its objects riddled through with captions, signs, and relics pointing to lives that resemble fiction more than history. In short, a text of the very kind I have been describing.

Having examined *Wuthering Heights* in terms of the upsurge of interest in local folklore and the development of photography, we can now see what binds them together in a single project. When reviewers greeted *Wuthering Heights* with suspicion and even outrage, Charlotte Brontë used the same framing procedures in the Preface to the second edition to describe her late sister as the author who transformed "the outlying hills and hamlets in the West-Riding of

Yorkshire" into "things alien and unfamiliar."[40] To identify the novel with the region it represented, Charlotte's Preface reframed the novel's landscape, much as the studio matting reframed *The Coleen Bawm,* as something "rustic all through. It is moorish, and wild, and knotty as a root of heath." Having called up a people not only primitive but also "moorish," a term with obvious Orientalist connotations, Charlotte promptly arrogated those qualities to Emily: "Nor was it natural that it should be otherwise; the author being a native and a nursling of the moors."[41] Once the preface to the 1850 edition had situated the author of *Wuthering Heights* within the landscape of her own creation, something on the order of a cult began to develop around Emily Brontë, and a perspective not that much different from the one frozen in the snapshot of Haworth parsonage determined the way in which literary criticism approached her ever after.

Like Heathcliff, Emily Brontë belongs to regional culture. Like this culture, too, the author's way of life and especially her way of writing were tragically out of date, as evidenced by her novel's departure from realism. Her hero and heroine demonstrated that such people could not be confined to bed, to bodies, or to books because their identities eluded such forms of incarnation. The modern literary tradition has made it very difficult to distinguish the author's traces from the characters of her fiction. Bonding Emily to her book to form an object of intense nostalgia, literary criticism has followed Charlotte's example and done unto Emily precisely what the spirit photographer did to his female subjects when he stripped away the details that would attach them to a place in history. But in a spirit photograph, we might recall, transparency is actually the vital sign that links the traces of the woman to her specific place in time and should be read as such. In similar fashion, Emily's transparency records the moment of her departure from a world in which the role of the observer was rapidly changing. *Wuthering Heights* demonstrates that those who cannot be placed within the system of differences organizing the metropolitan city will soon have no identity at all. If realism is the mode of representation that observes those categories, this novel tells us, then what happens on the Celtic periphery is not something that can be described realistically. Primitive cultures require another mode of storytelling. By thus distinguishing the north of England from the world that realism describes, Emily Brontë nevertheless participated in the same project with such relatively worldly-wise novelists as Walter Scott and Maria Edgeworth. She helped to render herself as well as her region obsolete in fact, as she immortalized them in literature.

CHAPTER FIVE

Sexuality in the Age of Racism: Hungry Alice

BOTH LEWIS CARROLL'S EXPLORATIONS OF THE INTERIORITY OF a little girl and H. Rider Haggard's equally fantastic colonial adventure stories for boys acknowledge the dullness of a world bound to realism's categories. They do so, however, only to demonstrate that a world lacking such differences is terrifying. Violation of the visible distinctions between the races of humankind is especially so. It can be enjoyed only in and as a fiction, and then only at the cost of gender and implicitly at the cost of class as well. If we compare *Alice's Adventures in Wonderland* with *King Solomon's Mines*, we are likely to notice that both embark on their respective investigations of the perilous alternatives to realism when an image gets out of hand. A white rabbit streaks across Alice's field of vision sporting a pocket watch, and the band of brothers who provide the composite hero of Haggard's story stumble on a map to a territory from which the mapmaker failed to return alive. These images draw the girl and boy protagonists of each adventure story into a big, dark hole in the earth, where boys are especially at risk of being swallowed up. As in the female victims of Bram Stoker's Dracula, however, being consumed by another manifests itself in Carroll's girl protagonist as a penchant for consuming others. For her to "go native" in this way would obviously remove her from modern culture as surely as being swallowed up by the earth. Where Haggard pits his English men against an African sorceress capable of turning them to inert lumps of physical nature, Carroll pits his girl protagonist against an equally fantastic brand of matriarchy. Every bit as dangerous as the female landscape of Haggard's Africa, the contrastingly domestic terrain of Wonderland threatens to send Alice in the other direction—toward unbridled agency and the murderous exercise of will. Their respective departures from humdrum realism thus put both protagonists at the mercy of a ravenous woman who, as I will explain, was the product of an unwitting cultural collaboration as pervasive as that among the photographers, folklorists, and novelists who at once produced the folk of Great Britain and rendered them obsolete.

In this chapter I will explore the relationship between British colonialism and the fear of engulfment embodied in a racially marked woman. This fantasy of self-dissolution can be read as a way of dealing with the circulation of information and objects from the colonies, into English homes, and out again into the colonies where national identity was undergoing perpetual redefinition as new territories and peoples were incorporated into European empires. This fantasy of engulfment not only made certain categorical differences seem absolutely essential to one's very being, it also provided the means of maintaining the differences on which European realism itself depends.

During the second half of the nineteenth century, photographers and fiction writers took up the same ethnographic project that occupied many a nineteenth-century anthropologist, the quest to discover whether human beings were bound together as a single species. This common ground was especially difficult to chart in situations where both the customs and the physical features of the populations under observation made them appear so different from those making the observations as to suggest that those differences arose from different species.[1] The effort to identify a common humanity across lines made visible as race would profoundly change how readers imagined their relation to the various Asian and African populations newly incorporated into the British Empire. It was incumbent on those readers to imagine the Empire as a single human population engaged in reciprocal—indeed, even familial—relations. But it was also necessary for the British to think of themselves as different from other people by virtue of a Britishness that positioned them above people of Asia and Africa in the evolutionary tree.[2] In this respect, Britain's understanding of itself as the core of an Empire ringed by colonies might seem, at first glance, to reproduce externally the same cultural difference and internal colonialism that asked readers to reconceptualize the nation as an English core with a Celtic periphery.

It is, however, a matter of some debate as to whether the Eurocentrism that developed with colonial expansion can be seen as either a reproduction of or a model for the ethnocentrism that maintained the Celtic periphery. To make a clear distinction between the two very different literary manifestations of racism, we do not have to understand race in terms of the physical properties of the populations in question. Étienne Balibar contends that the difference between the two kinds of racism has nothing to do with the populations so subjected. The difference is a matter of a shift in European perspective. He sees the racism associated with internal colonialism as a means of justifying the marginalization of "an internal minority which is not merely 'assimilated,' but constitutes an integral part of the culture and economy" of the European nations from their beginning. It might appear, he argues, that in comparison "colonial racism constitutes the prime example of external racism—an extreme variant of xenophobia combining fear and scorn—perpetuated by the awareness the colonizers have always had, in spite of the claim to have founded a durable order, that that order rested on a reversible relation of forces."[3]

Balibar regards this distinction as much too simple to be true. Just as "internal colonialism" has an externalizing function, so "external colonialism"—those practices we tend to associate with nineteenth-century colonialism proper—has an internalizing dimension.

Racism confirms the marginalization of assimilated minorities within the nation, in the first case, and the subordinated inclusion of "native" populations—by such means, for example, as forced labor and sexual exploitation—in the internal structure of the colony, in the second. Assigning them a racial difference is one way of explaining the exclusion of certain assimilated groups from the privileges enjoyed by the dominant ethnicity. Just so, the fundamental "interiority" of the colonial population is responsible, in Balibar's estimation, for both a European "ambivalence" toward "natives" and the "way in which the subhuman nature attributed to the colonized comes to determine the self-image developed within the colonized nationalism in the period when the world was being divided up." Colonialism is, he concludes, "a fluctuating combination of continued interiorization and 'internal exclusion.'"[4]

V. Y. Mudimbe uses a similar notion of cultural oscillation to define the so-called colonial periphery as neither purely a "premodern" or "underdeveloped" space nor a cultural space where the premodern had been successfully appropriated and transformed in European terms; the periphery is wherever something like this "fluctuating combination" between modern and premodern is taking place.[5] To explain the cultural conditions creating and maintaining such a relationship between European and African, Mudimbe offers a just-so story about the production of Hans Bergmair's painting *Exotic Tribe* (1508):

> Let us imagine the painter at work. He has just read Springer's description of his voyage and, possibly on the basis of some sketches, he is trying to create an image of blacks in "Gennea." Perhaps he has to use a model, presumably white but strongly built. The painter is staring at the pale body, imagining schemes to transform it into a black entity. The model has become a mirror through which the painter evaluates how the norms of similitude and his own creativity would impart both a human identity and a racial difference to his canvas.[6]

If Europeans had long envisioned Africans as Europeans blackened and stripped of their cultural uniqueness, we should not be surprised to find the differences between one culture and another threatening to collapse centuries later under the pressure of a modern form of imperialism that incorporated other peoples and sought to dominate them culturally. Under these circumstances, the African might on occasion appear before the European displaying all the ontological difference denoted by race, but the relationship between colonizer and colonized was actually much more complex than any such visual binary could suggest.

The primitivism of the "good native" had the capacity to meld with its evil twin, degeneracy, whenever natives could be read as blackened versions of the white European. So perceived, difference was no longer difference so much as the pure negation of whatever made Europeans modern and guaranteed their superiority as such. Where the primitiveness of the "good native" called for the kind of acculturation and education a child required from a parent, the so-called degenerate native had to suffer complete exclusion. We might say that Conrad's Kurtz flipped from the one perceptual grid to the other when he simultaneously went native and madly scrawled "Exterminate the brutes!" across the page of his reformist tract. The equation of racial differences with natural facts of the body, because it changed the implications of assimilating so-called "natives" into the same human community with Western man, also changed the relationship of core to periphery.[7]

In Chapter 4, I read *Wuthering Heights* as a record of internal colonialism, wherein two factors mitigated the kind of conflict normally resulting from racial mixture in English fiction. First, insofar as the periphery represents an earlier moment in history, certain individuals and even some folkways—the knowledge preserved by the Earnshaw housekeeper, for example—survive into the present tense and invigorate modern culture by doing so. Contrastingly primitive and urbane versions of British men and women thus appear to exist along the same ontological continuum, where the one can presumably develop into the other. Second, those who—like Heathcliff—

bear visible racial markings do not survive into the future. Their legacy is neither biological nor cultural but is confined to disruptions of the past that clear the way for modernization.

To imagine the African as a biologically earlier version of the European is to preclude the possibility of individuals breaking out of a peripheral position and assimilating to the core in any other than the most degraded of positions. When enacted on a global scale, the differentiation of core from periphery cannot constitute two different moments of the same cultural history, as they do in *Wuthering Heights*. Indeed, biological racism inevitably comes to the fore and distinguishes two different moments of a natural history that has already transpired. Nineteenth-century natural history supported Victorian anthropology's belief that so-called primitive peoples reached their natural maturity as the Victorians now saw them—as both primitive and degenerate versions of themselves—while Europeans continued to evolve. From this perspective, the relation of periphery to core cannot be understood as a relation of past to present, not if those who inhabit the periphery represent a historical cul-de-sac which modern man avoided. Though enmeshed in a single political history, the two belong to distinct and irreconcilable moments of natural history. For an individual to break free from a periphery with such arrested natural and cultural development and enter the culture of the core would necessarily change the very status of the core as such. Movement across the racial timeline was therefore virtually impossible.

According to the same cultural logic, however, the idea of a human continuum held up in the other direction; it was entirely possible for modern man to slide down the evolutionary slope into the abyss of primitivism, where he would become just one more among many peripheral peoples. It is helpful to think of this later mapping of the core-periphery relationship as a reversal of the logic according to which Europeans exalted the unsullied state of nature they had modernized. Confronting their own image in that of an African body inscribed with signs of degeneracy, Victorian intellectuals phobically disavowed the African in themselves and sought to modernize what could not successfully be repressed or marginalized.[8] The European not only projected his body onto the African or Asian; he subsequently introjected the bad desires he had inscribed in that body and sought to subdue them internally, or so late Victorian literature would suggest.[9] Thus the desire to achieve continuity with the native as the embodiment of a more original and pure brand of humanity led inevitably to the demonization, repression, and abjection of signs of that same primitivism as the symptom on which depends the identity of the modern individual as such. The reflux of both Africanness and Asianness into European culture and consciousness threatened to dissolve racial distinctions into an imaginary field of equivalencies, where modern man appeared to be just another variety of a common mankind rather than the most direct line of descent to the endpoint and zenith of natural history. [10] This, it could be argued, is the way with symptoms.

In order to maintain its identity, a class may externalize all those features one cannot have and behaviors one cannot enact and still belong to modern European culture. But this fantasmagoric embodiment will not permanently maintain the boundaries between what belongs inside and what outside that culture. As both Balibar and Mudimbe suggest, peripheral phenomena always flow two ways, both in and out of an equally imaginary core. The initial gesture of externalization, or abjection, is destined to be repeated, because the gesture is one that necessarily fails to fix a boundary between self and non-self. I will be emphasizing this reflexive dimension of the colonial project as I read Lewis Carroll's girl's book and II. Rider Haggard's boy's adventure story. This reading will trace the complex process by which Victorian culture reversed the threat posed by Great Britain's incorporation of other peoples and refigured that threat as a voracious woman.

Natives and Prostitutes

My account begins with a highly contested bit of domestic legislation passed in 1864 and amended in 1866 and again in 1869. As Judith

Walkowitz made unforgettably clear in her classic study of Victorian prostitution, the Contagious Diseases Acts named prostitutes as the source of venereal disease and attempted to combat the problem of infection quite simply by confining it to the bodies of a specific group of women.[11] The new law required all women who were considered prostitutes to register and submit to regular pelvic examinations. It appointed surgeons to perform these examinations and empowered them to incarcerate infected women for up to six months. A full account of the medical procedures is beyond the scope of this discussion, but I do want to note the zealous efficiency with which such professional men as William Acton carried on this important work. Stalwart liberal, esteemed surgeon, and author of numerous medical books and treatises, Acton proudly claimed to have "assisted in the thorough examination of 58 women with the speculum . . . in the course of one hour and three-quarters."[12] One cannot read much of his protracted account, despite his good intentions, without understanding it as a record of how one class humiliated another by subjecting its women to involuntary pelvic exams.[13]

It becomes very clear that purification rites of exactly this nature were carried on in the name of national health when we consider what metaphors were used to describe infected women. With the exception of a few dissenting voices (that, for example, of John Stuart Mill), the cast of experts mobilized in defense of the Contagious Diseases Acts used the language of class to describe the women whom they had forced to register as prostitutes. These women were, in the words of one man of medicine,

> . . . dirty, clad in unwomanly rags, some appearing half-starved, covered with vermin, causing those near them to shun them with aversion; careless in matters of common decency, their conversation having mingled with it such words as made one shudder to listen to; wofully ignorant, they appeared, in their utter filth and depravity, lost to all the better qualities of human beings.[14]

Metaphors of pollution encouraged the most technical medical discussions to conclude that these women were in fact the cause of infection, or "poison," as it was more often called. Certain of their assumptions about the female body made it possible for the specialists in the disease to argue that a man had contracted the disease from a woman. This was true even when his symptoms were far more advanced than hers, because her body gave off poisonous fluids even under ordinary conditions. Thus one expert concluded that "uterine discharges are one of its constitutional manifestations, and I think that these discharges, at any rate, may be a vehicle of the virus."[15] Working-class women were still more likely to be infectious because, according to other testimony,

> at those particular times when a woman should retire from all sexual communication, in consequence of her natural monthly disturbance, it is well known that except in rare instances they do not so withdraw, on the contrary they afford intercourse to soldiers as usual, and the menstrual discharge in this class of women being exceedingly irritating, the production of urethritis, orchitis &c., is frequently the consequence.[16]

Though the effects of mercury were known to be extraordinarily toxic, especially when people were overworked and undernourished, the medical profession frequently classified it as "an antidote to [the] poison" that women naturally exude.[17]

Given that the official summary of reports on the effectiveness of the Contagious Diseases Act passed in 1864 admitted the Act neither decreased the number of prostitutes nor curtailed the spread of disease, it is particularly revealing that the same report is generally positive about the results of its implementation. The report claimed the Act had inadvertently produced two positive results. First, it generated a great deal of information about venereal disease that testified to "its prevalence among all classes of society, its insidious nature, the frequent failure of all but men of great experience to recognize it, and, moreover, to the most important fact, that the poisoned *foetus in utero* is no infrequent cause of miscarriage."[18] According to the summary, in other words, women of the lower classes had spread a poison throughout English society that directly assaulted motherhood. In this way, the report removed middle-class men from their position as the pernicious transmitters of the poison inside the bodies of the one class of women to the babies inside the bodies of the other. Moreover, the report identified those with specialized knowledge of the disease—again, middle-class men—as all that stood between unborn middle-class children and a disease aimed directly at them by working-class women.

Although their patients are described as poisonous, it is important to note that the same group of experts attributed maternal qualities to the institutions where these women were incarcerated. It was on grounds that the hospital provided a kindly nurse and a spiritual home to wayward women that the official summary of reports managed to portray the Contagious Diseases Act as a success, when it had actually failed to halt the spread of venereal disease: "The evidence shows that in [this] one most important point the Act has proved successful, . . . that which relates to the feelings of the unfortunate women with whom it has to deal; so far from opposing its operation, they appear to appreciate its value to themselves."[19] This transfer of the proper female function from inmate to institution is demonstrated in anecdotal evidence throughout the reports that follow. One doctor, for example, offered the following account to show "that a residence in the hospital, in some cases, has an extraordinary effect" on the prostitute:

> There was one house into which I went with the inspector of police lately. I heard a woman reading with a loud voice, when we got to the passage, I stopped to listen, and I found, to my astonishment, that she was reading from Bunyan's "Pilgrim's Progress." I went into the room and found no less than seven women sitting round a good looking woman of 25

who was reading from "Pilgrim's Progress," all paying the greatest attention.[20]

To conclude a string of observations that emphasize the degenerate features of working-class women who were less eager to seek redemption through literacy, the same man recommended that "fully one-half the class" of prostitutes be forcibly sent to a reformatory after their illness was cured. "It would," he claimed, "be a charity, as well as a mere precaution, to hide them from gratification of their sin for a year or two."[21]

Another cluster of legal measures was also aimed at coercive regulation of working-class sexuality. Beginning in 1859, a whole set of mutually reinforcing practices developed around motherhood to secure institutionally for infants what human nature had evidently failed to supply. The first infant protection societies appeared; safer adoption procedures were put in place; laws were passed to restrict baby farming, register midwives, and prosecute those who dropped newborns down public latrines. By 1874 the English Registration Act was passed as part of a concerted effort on the part of the state to register the birth and death of each child, whether bastard or still-born.[22] But despite all this legislation and the introduction of both the rubber nipple and the first manufactured baby food, it was not until the 1920s that the infant mortality rate decreased substantially in England.[23] The very fact that these measures failed as dismally as the Contagious Diseases Acts is significant. This failure implies that the public insisted so righteously on regulating working-class women, not because such regulation would curtail the spread of disease, but because their insistence on regulation itself solved a problem: The volumes devoted to the failure of working-class mothering relocated the cause of the deplorable physical condition of the working class in the moral condition of their women. All the discursive uproar concerning motherhood thus translated an insurmountable problem in the domain of production into an equally insurmountable problem in the domain of reproduction.

In turning from legal discourse to the new and flourishing social sciences, one can easily see how the female body developed into a text enabling literate people to establish moral differences between themselves and other social groups. During the second half of the nineteenth century, the madhouse population provided subjects for studies that identified women prone to mental illness. Prominent among experts in this area, Henry Maudsley claimed that women prone to inherited mental defects could be identified by such "'bodily and mental marks' as 'an irregular and unsymmetrical conformation of the head, a want of regularity and harmony of the features . . . malformations of the external ear . . . tics, grimaces . . . stammering and defects of pronunciation . . . peculiarities of the eyes,' and a predilection for puns."[24] Maudsley apparently advised men of the literate classes accordingly: they should inspect a prospective wife for "visible signs of inward and invisible faults which will have their influence in breeding."[25]

As Victorian intellectuals became increasingly absorbed in classifying, knowing, and controlling deviance, the female anatomy offered itself as a text whereon those deviant qualities of mind became especially legible. Social scientists discovered, for example, that a woman's moral condition could be read in certain details of her face and genitals. Indeed, they discovered that the genitals of prostitutes were typically enlarged by abscesses and tumors.[26] Others proved that the faces of these women characteristically bore protruding jaws, flat noses, misshapen foreheads, and attached earlobes. On the basis of such homologies, social scientists developed a set of analytical procedures which would determine the nature and behavior of one end of a woman by looking at the other. This logic of the body drove pioneers in anthropology to perform dissections on women of groups recently brought under European rule. These men discovered that Asian and African women normally bore the very features of face and genitals that characterized only prostitutes and madwomen in Europe.[27] To become familiar with these legal and scientific definitions of the body is to recognize a fearful symmetry that cut across

FIGURE 5.1   Untitled (1852). Hugh Diamond.

the visual media as well, which in turn made race something that was unmistakably inscribed on the surface of the body.[28]

During the 1860s, photographers broke away from aestheticized portrayals of madness that celebrated the individuality of human consciousness and began to capture the faces of madwomen, whores, and aborigines in a manner resembling the criminologists' use of photography (Figures 5.1, 5.2).[29] The point was not to capture the individuality of the deviant person but to classify deviance in a way that included very different cultural attitudes and behaviors within a

FIGURE 5.2 Female criminals (1886). Thomas Byrnes, *Professional Criminals of America.*

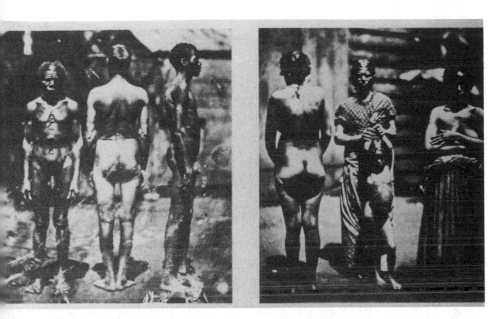

FIGURE 5.3   *Macuoa, Arab Indian, and black Creole from Reunion* (left);
Group of Negresses (right) (1863). Désiré Charnay.

single classification system where gender made all the difference. By
focusing on prostitutes, madwomen, and native women, this classification system identified forms of cultural difference with a lack of
femininity that took the form of female excesses. What began as a
difference between a culturally acquired gender and sexual nature
was well on its way to designating a difference between two different
natures which were embodied in modern women and their native
counterparts, respectively. Another example of scientific photography may help to explain why this style was so effective. It reveals the
quasi-pornographic quality that comes from subjecting the other's
body to the gaze. Taken from a collection of Désiré Charnay's expeditionary photography, these shots give the viewer a sense of seeing all
sides of the body and even penetrating into the body itself (Figure
5.3).[30] At the same time, the camera uses this power to strip the other
body of all national or ethnic specificity. The photograph of native
men bears the label *Macuoa, Arab Indian, and black Creole from Reun-*

FIGURE 5.4   *Sleep* (1866). Henry Peach Robinson.

ion, but the photograph itself arranges their bodies so that they seem to present different views of a single person. The other portrait is simply entitled *Group of Negresses,* suggesting that native women are even more generic than their male counterparts.

Coinciding with the production of this scientific body was the development of that equally stereotypical "salon" body that I have associated with the work of the Julia Margaret Cameron circle. Members of the circle used the camera to deify interiority in the manner of Pre-Raphaelite painting. Like the painters they admired, these photographers were attracted to women in the act of languishing or even leaving this world, but their work is also remembered for photographs of prepubescent children (Figure 5.4). Although the highly aestheticized female was the trademark of the group, they occasionally photographed common people, and when they did, they

FIGURE 5.5   *The Butcher's Visit* (c. 1863–1865).
Lord Somers (attributed)

adopted the documentary style. In a photograph titled *The Butcher's Visit* (Figure 5.5), the bodies of working man and servant women present a striking contrast to the otherworldly art body. Coupled with the title, the characteristic stockiness of these figures forges subtle links between the female servant and the masculine character of her labor. Nor can we overlook the racial difference suggested by a duskiness that sets her flesh apart from the near-translucent skin of an elite

FIGURE 5.6   *Alice Liddell as a Beggar Girl* (1859).
Lewis Carroll.

woman. Nineteenth-century photography established the difference
between the two classes as a difference of the body itself. A case in
point is one of Lewis Carroll's photographs of the girl for whom he
wrote the *Alice* books, entitled *Alice Liddell as a Beggar Girl* (Figure
5.6). Here, there is no mistaking Alice for a girl of the underclasses.
Given that he has named her, posed her against a pastoral backdrop,

and had her confront the observer eye to eye, we know this is no mere type but the portrait of a name-brand individual posing as such a type.

Ultimately, my point in stressing the contrast between these two ways of visualizing the female body is to establish the collusion between them. Though mutually exclusive, the two were born together and behaved as a single cultural formation, one always calling the other to mind.[31] By the 1870s, this double-bodied figure was shaping almost every aspect of Victorian culture. I have already called attention to her presence on the pages of scientific studies and the walls of art galleries. Add to this her regular appearance in daily newspapers, weekly magazines, and monthly and quarterly journals and reviews; then consider how she hung for years on tastefully decorated walls in sentimental line drawings and oil paintings, lay on tea tables in open photo albums, arrived in vestibules on postcards, animated advertisements for household products, and illustrated some of the most popular novels, travel narratives, and missionary accounts of the day.[32]

In some respects, this was the same image that had earlier identified womanhood itself with the women of the respectable classes. But something happened to her slim, white, and self-contained figure as it began to operate on an international scale, authorizing Englishmen to supervise members of less developed nations on grounds that non-European women were not really women even if they were unmistakably female. It may well have been that this way of depicting their relation to the colonizer made newly subordinated peoples more likely to misrecognize themselves as defective versions of middle-class Europe, but that is not my concern here. I am more interested in the fact that European intellectuals had trouble maintaining the idea that cultures with such women were childlike and feminine versions of themselves. It was through their reinscription of the differences between European self and racial other at the level of popular culture that the colonial venture had the greatest impact on respectable people back in England. For such people, sexuality was "normal" only in the abstract. It was then and still is now, I believe,

Sexuality in the Age of Racism

all-important to reject those specific appearances and behaviors that indicate an excess of sexuality at a given moment in time, for in so doing we maintain our status as "normal" people.

The Africanization of English Girlhood

Having indicated something of the proportions that the image of degenerate womanhood had assumed in nineteenth-century culture, I would like to consider how this negative representation of the subordinated gender changed the sexuality of the class who consumed photographic representations of her. Lewis Carroll's *Alice's Adventures in Wonderland* offers special insight into the relationship these representations established between middle-class women and their racially marked counterparts. Written and published during the same period as both the Contagious Diseases Acts and legislation to reduce infant mortality, Carroll's story carried many of these same textualizing procedures into a whole new arena of human experience. We can indeed observe the link between children's literature and the Victorian obsession with the bodies of madwomen and whores at the very beginning of the story, as Alice plummets down the rabbit hole:

> First, she tried to look down and make out what she was coming to, but it was too dark to see anything: then she looked at the sides of the well, and noticed that they were filled with cupboards and bookshelves: here and there she saw maps and pictures hung upon pegs. She took down a jar from one of the shelves as she passed: it was labeled "ORANGE MARMALADE," but to her great disappointment it was empty: she did not like to drop the jar, for fear of killing somebody underneath, so she managed to put it into one of the cupboards as she fell past it.[33]

In this passage, we bear witness to an event of no little historical significance. At the beginning of her fall (always a tip-off when women are concerned) the source of fear is located in the world outside her body.[34] Even so, Alice is strangely unconcerned about "what she was coming to," and for good reason. Halfway down the rabbit hole, she finds herself in a thoroughly domesticated interior.

Then, as appetites will, Alice's suddenly takes over her body. She grabs a jar marked "marmalade," and this empty sign of gratification mysteriously reverses the trajectory of her desire. Alice temporarily loses her interest in food. She grows anxious. Having disturbed domestic order, she wants nothing so much as to return the jar to its place. Appetite gives way to an equally compulsive desire for self-control, as Alice comes to understand herself as someone who endangers others. Or so Carroll writes: "she did not like to drop the jar, for fear of killing somebody underneath." Nowhere in the earlier fiction I have read—and there was a great deal written in England during the eighteenth and nineteenth centuries to tell girls how to be girls—can I recall anything like this: a girl in the act of falling, but a girl only vaguely curious about what would befall her. Then, within the space of a very few lines, an almost imperceptible danger outside her body gives way to a danger within, one capable of erupting at any moment. Alice consequently loses her fear of falling and becomes afraid of letting go.

Like those of working-class and native women, her body is potentially out of control and, by its very nature, in need of regulation. But where the problem with those other female bodies had a genital origin, the dangers contained in Alice's body begin and end with her mouth. With every act of ingestion comes certain loss of physical control. One such episode sends her shooting up in height through the branches of a tree exactly where an anxious pigeon has sought safety for her eggs beyond the reach of serpents. The following bit of their dialogue explains how eating destabilizes Alice's identity:

> "But I'm *not* a serpent, I tell you!" said Alice. "I'm a—I'm a—"
>
> "Well! *What* are you?" said the Pigeon. "I can see you're trying to invent something!"
>
> "I—I'm a little girl," said Alice, rather doubtfully, as she

remembered the number of changes she had gone through that day.

"A likely story indeed!" said the Pigeon, in a tone of the deepest contempt. "I've seen a good many little girls in my time, but never *one* with such a neck as that! No, no! You're a serpent; and there's no use denying it. I suppose you'll be telling me next that you never tasted an egg!" (54)

Carroll saw to it that Alice would have a problem controlling her mouth, when he gave her a prodigious appetite and put her in a world made of food. Wonderland contains such creatures as the mock turtle, the lobster, and all the little whitings who manage to swim with their backs well-coated with bread crumbs. Alice's situation, so defined, invites us to consider why Carroll animated a world by bringing the copious modern dinner table back to life, and why he had his heroine acquire her identity in relation to objects so strangely revitalized. The immediate and lasting popularity of his book suggests that we should look to the new consumer culture for the cultural link between the colonial venture and the appetite of a little girl.

It is now commonplace to say that fiction carried on a long-term intimate relationship with advertising. During the eighteenth century, argues Jennifer Wicke, fiction borrowed from advertising as a means of self-promotion. During the Victorian period, however, certain novels sought to distinguish themselves from the crass mass culture by criticizing authors and readers who were captivated by the values of the literary marketplace.[35] Novels, in other words, display an ambivalent relationship both with their own commercial success and with the class of people whose moral values provided the basis of literary authority. The 1860s was also the period when consumerism became part of mothering. Suddenly, shopping was something that women, rather than men, were supposed to do.[36] Moreover, department stores appeared in England and France to display the goods of empire in a setting that uniquely combined shopping with dining out and entertainment. In this way, the new mode of shopping associated the acquisition of objects with the pleasure of surveying and also literally consuming, or eating, them.[37] The locations for such pleasures were often described in terms of a wonderland. The enchantments of the Crystal Palace in 1851 and the solemnities of the Queen's Jubilee of 1887 carried over into the department store. In what appeared to be vast and illuminated museum-like displays of objects from many corners of the world, virtually any English man or woman could survey the wealth of Empire in the manner of the Queen.[38] But such democracy was also considered dangerous. Women might be seduced by the appeal of objects into purchasing what was beyond their budgets or beneath their station.[39] Such were the inducements to shop that kleptomania, a compulsion afflicting women of the respectable classes, became a problem for the first time in history.[40]

When one brings these insights to a reading of *Alice,* it becomes apparent that her tumble down the rabbit hole initiated a new moment in the history of desire. It is difficult to imagine one of Jane Austen's heroines so endangered by shopping. Indications that she was too attentive to the goods sold in town could indeed represent a minor flaw in such an otherwise goodhearted woman as Catherine Moreland's chaperone in *Northanger Abbey,* just as it could betray the malformed sensibility of an Augusta Elton in *Emma,* but neither a woman's eligibility for marriage nor the class status of her family hung in the balance when she shopped. Her relation to objects did not determine so much as reveal what kind of woman she was, and substantially more was revealed by the man to whom such a woman was attracted. That object choice determined what social position she would occupy.

Alice's problems with appetite tell us how the whole concept of desire changed as women became consumers in the world of the department store. Carroll's heroine feels anxious in a way that earlier generations simply could not have experienced: she is worried about fitting in. This anxiety produces a form of taste specifically formed to regulate the desire for food. It induces her to stop bolting down every consumable object she encounters and instead to nibble one side of a mushroom or another, in hopes of stabilizing the body that appetite repeatedly disfigures. Such control of consumption allows Alice to grow without ruining her figure in a way that invites her comparison to a serpent. For even though her size increases at the story's end, she retains the prepubescent shape that distinguishes her from all the other women in that story. As appetite assumes the central role within the child's body, then, it redefines sexual desire. The girl's ability to master appetite indicates whether or not she contains desires characterizing both men and unruly women. If so, she is destined never to fit in.[41]

As he made sexual desire contingent on the vicissitudes of a form of appetite present in childhood, Carroll also revised the role taste had to play in a world of beckoning objects. It is important to note how carefully he links the problem of appetite with another form of oral aggression. His wonderland is made of literature as well as food; both beast fable and dinner table supply its characters. Thus from the moment she reaches for the empty jar marked "Marmalade," words and food exist in a curiously interchangeable relationship for Alice. She is always in danger of letting it slip that she would not mind eating the very creatures with whom she converses, and perhaps she has. Along with a persistent hunger, Alice contains dissident voices that infiltrate and overturn the content of her speech performances. When requested to stand up and repeat "'*Tis the voice of the sluggard*," for instance, "her head was so full of the Lobster-Quadrille, that she hardly knew what she was saying; and the words came very queer indeed." When they do come, the words of the song are disfigured by her appetite: "'Tis the voice of the lobster [she says, substituting "lobster" for "sluggard"]: I heard him declare, / 'You have baked me too brown, I must sugar my hair'" (98). As she substitutes "lobster" for "sluggard," Alice also replaces the vice of laziness with an overconcern for food, demonstrating that appetite disfigures a girl's speech as surely as it does her body. Indeed, all the elements of the story conspire to convince us that appetite disfigures speech because speech, like appetite, originates within that body, while writing comes from the adult world of classrooms and books outside the body. Each lapse in her speech performances thus reconfirms the assumption that Alice could control her appetite if only she would stick to writing.

In the English society that Carroll offers up to girls' imaginations, objects behave much like transitional objects in British object relations theory. Both self and non-self, they represent the self as an object in the world. Thus when Alice suddenly grows farther than usual away from her feet, those feet behave as synecdoches of the body itself: "Oh, my poor little feet, I wonder who will put on your shoes and stockings for you now, dears? I'm sure I shan't be able! I shall be a great deal too far off to trouble myself about you" (14). This self-objectification seems to shatter Alice's autonomy in the very attempt to produce it: "'But I must be kind to them,' thought Alice, 'or perhaps they wo'n't walk the way I want to go!'" (14 15). In thus feigning mastery over the rules of her culture, however, Alice actually gains new mastery over herself, as she proceeds to cut a deal with her feet: "'Let me see. I'll give them a new pair of boots every Christmas.' And she went on planning to herself how she would manage it. 'They must go by carrier,' she thought; 'and how funny it'll seem, sending presents to one's own feet!'" (15). Childhood according to Carroll turns out to be the condition of lacking the very kind of power that subjects exercise over objects, the power to classify, to evaluate, to consume with discrimination. The acquisition of literacy is what empowers subjects to keep objects in their place. If Alice fails to distinguish herself from working-class and native women whenever she gives way to appetite, then she reestablishes that distinction in a more decisive way as she begins to crave this power more than she craves objects themselves.

In bringing us to this conclusion, however, Alice's misadventures bring us to the very heart of a contradiction. We must recall that objects in the story tend to come engraved with the invitation to consume them. "Eat me" or "drink me," they say. Her compulsive response to a marmalade label indicates that writing in fact creates the appetite that Alice must control through reading and recitation. How, then, can appetite originate inside her body if it originates in

FIGURE 5.7   *Royal procession to the garden* (1886). Lewis Carroll.

writing? *Alice's Adventures in Wonderland* defines the heroine's development as the acquisition of a peculiar kind of literacy that embraces
this self-contradiction. Put another way, Alice herself embodies the
fantasmagorical spiral of desire and restraint that women would soon
experience in relation to a world made of enticing objects. Alice's
tumble down the rabbit hole reveals an appetite for marmalade.
Because she has the literacy of the ruling class, however, Alice has
acquired an appetite for rules well before her adventures begin. And
even though something that seems more like an aversion to books
prompts her adventures in Wonderland, Alice's story is ultimately a
struggle to possess the kind of taste that comes with literacy. Like her
wish to enter the rose garden, her appetite for marmalade and
whitings is an expression of that taste.

In order for a woman to grow up within the spiral of desire that
constitutes such taste, objects must be inherently attractive. They
must present themselves to the consumer as things she must resist. In
Carroll's fantasy for little girls, there is neither a single form of appetite that does not require control, nor any gesture of control that

FIGURE 4.8   *Alice and the Queen of Hearts* (1866), John Tenniel

does not imply the presence of some appetite. Whether he knew it or not, it made sense for him to place his heroine in constant danger from her appetite, establishing a relationship between female subject and object that is essential to the modern consumer. Indeed, his story shows how fear of appetite became necessary to the production of the taste specific to women of the privileged classes. We can observe precisely this subtle but profound change coming over Alice during the course of her adventures; as she wanders back and forth

FIGURE 5.9   *The Duchess* (1866). John Tenniel.

between the poles of desire and self-restraint, all possibility for pleasure splits off from appetite and attaches itself to self-control.

In reading this account of childhood as a story about a struggle between words and appetite for the power to define the female body, I have tried to suggest how and why a work of children's literature came to reproduce the double-bodied figure that shaped very different territories of Victorian culture and linked them to one another. But nothing makes the point quite so well as the illustrations that appeared in the 1866 edition of the novel published by Macmillan. Studies of these illustrations have turned up several sources for the Duchess and probably for the Queen as well.[42] I must quickly add that this is not at all how Carroll himself envisioned these two powerful women when he sketched the designs for his illustrator, John Tenniel (Figure 5.7). In the original designs, the pair inhabit normal bodies.

FIGURE 5.10   *Alice in the pool of tears* (1886), Lewis Carroll (left);
Alice in the pool of tears (1866), John Tenniel (right).

It is likely that Tenniel, being more familiar than Carroll with the iconography of illustration, chose a body that would dissociate the two from Queen Victoria and link them to the women whom Victorian science portrayed as sexually defective (Figure 5.8). One of the most curious things about the memorable scene in which the Duchess peppers her baby is the fact that she obviously sports the same dubiously female face her cook does, even though one figure displays the profile and the other offers a frontal view (Figure 5.9). In this way, the scene where they nightmarishly confuse cooking food with feeding babies recalls the scientific positioning of natives in the photograph described earlier (see Figure 5.3). Their resemblance suggests, in other words, that the cook and the Duchess offer two views of a single disfigured body housing cannibalistic desires that cancel out maternal qualities.

In contrast with the other women in the novel, Tenniel drew Alice with the contours of a salon body, which he distorted whenever appetite seized control of her. Thus she could pass out of the original designs, where Carroll sketched her in a pose reminiscent of Ophelia, and into the Tenniel illustration without undergoing any such grotesque transformation (Figure 5.10). The Tenniel illustrations make it absolutely clear that there are only two kinds of women in Wonderland: women who control themselves and others who do not. This celebrated work of children's literature required children of the literate classes to imagine the body as something already out of control, something always in need of regulation. Thus *Alice* collaborated with many other Victorian genres to generate a fear of becoming someone or something else by which a culture indelibly brands subjects as its own.

Atavistic Objects

In Alice's memorable farewell to Wonderland, "'You're nothing but a pack of cards!'" Carroll's enchanting tale of childhood could be said to echo Marx's sentiments about the status of objects under the conditions of late capitalism in "The Fetishism of the Commodity and Its Secret." Here, Marx imagines a moment in the history of industrial cultures when the natural relation between people and things undergoes an inversion, and people are consequently dominated by the things they produce. Human desire ceases to determine what things are under these circumstances, and things determine what people want to buy. In this respect, his prediction of the mysterious power objects will acquire under conditions of late capitalism resembles their behavior in the fantasy Carroll attributes to a child. But while pointing out this resemblance may establish a historical relationship between the British obsession with childhood sexuality, especially that of little girls, and the new commodity culture, it does not link this peculiar turn in the history of sexuality with imperialism, at least not in an explicit way.[43]

Writing is the missing link. Arjun Appadurai offers one explanation for the relationship between Western insistence that words can dominate things, on the one hand, and our equally tenacious assumption that subjects have to dominate objects, on the other:

> Contemporary Western common sense, building on various historical traditions in philosophy, law, and natural science, has a strong tendency to oppose "words" and "things." Though this was not always the case even in the West, . . . the powerful contemporary tendency is to regard the world of things as inert and mute, set in motion and animated, indeed knowable, only by persons and their words.[44]

Subjects dominate objects through words. Words—presumably our words—endow the object with a name and thus a place in a differential system composed of such objects. Is it not the point of commodification to displace objects with the signs of those objects, signs that in turn endow them with an abstract relation value? Such inscription ought to set objects in motion and yet lend them complete legibility. Judging by both *Alice's Adventures in Wonderland* and Marx's description of the commodity fetish, however, quite the reverse proves to be true. In both accounts, objects elude human control and begin to manipulate the consumer. The problem, as Marx contended, lies not in any magical properties of the object but in the consumer's limited ability to read it. How such illegibility might arise at the very core of modern culture should become clear upon recalling a point from my previous chapter.

In the discussion of internal colonialism I emphasized the photograph's ability to reduce the dense semiotic texture of a local object or individual to a relatively predictable set of visual features, including the striped "peasant" dress, thick work shoes, and curious implements of labor. Stripped of utilitarian value, these objects did not go quietly into obsolescence but entered into the new commodities market with a noticeable jolt. Though removed from the symbolic economies in which their use gave them meaning and value, such objects nevertheless carried that history with them as they were taken up and reclassified within the metropolitan marketplace. As commodities, they circulated messages that turned the criteria for their own selection into a complicated game of prestige involving experts from the art world, scholars, and dealers, as well as women with money to spend and homes to decorate. According to Appadurai, most explanations of commodity culture stop with what "Baudrillard sees as the emergence of the 'object,' that is, as a thing that is no longer just a product or a commodity, but essentially a sign in a system of signs of status."[45] *Alice* is only one of several indications that such a system is far more complex and less stable than accounts of reification, simulation, or the society of spectacle generally allow.

To be sure, as things poured into the European metropolis from the four corners of the world, they were selected and arranged so as to maintain status distinctions peculiar to domestic Britain. Their placement within the categories of the well-appointed household did not, however, succeed in canceling out previous meanings embedded in those objects as they migrated from periphery to core, often with several stops along the way. Just because the commodification process tended to obscure that history, it could not prevent those objects from containing such a record as their material composition. Nor did commodification successfully prevent such objects from communicating something of that history. When one is unfamiliar with the kind of thinking that characterizes life at the periphery, commodification makes such information difficult to receive, and objects can seem illegible as a result. This at least seems to be the case of many of the objects Alice encounters in Wonderland. Carroll takes great delight in pushing the commodification process one step further, as he asks his reader to imagine familiar cultural objects as the creatures of an unfamiliar nature. As if born for the baking dish, whitings have their tails in their mouths, but they nevertheless manage to swim. Croquet balls roll when smacked with a mallet, only to turn into hedgehogs and scurry away. The Mock Turtle is simply a turtle who has been so subjected to mockery as to doubt his sense of identity as a turtle. Indeed, there is nothing in the British household that cannot undergo the inverse cultural logic that would relocate that object in an atavistic wonderland. This tendency of things to revert from nouns back into verbs and take on the agency reserved for human subjects is not so much Carroll's way of indicating Alice's immaturity as a reader as it is his way of demonstrating that the reigning domestic categories were barely able to contain the kind of information saturating the visual field around even this most coddled of readers.

Let us suppose a culture in which objects have to be kept under control. Let us suppose further that its ability to contain and classify objects is the basis for a culture's authority over those objects, thus over the people who make and consume them as well. What would happen, then, if occult objects began to flood into that culture from all over the Empire—if not strange objects, then parts of objects and new materials of which any object might be made, made perhaps by strange hands and in exotic places. These objects would no doubt appear to arrive at the household by way of the department store after a long, discontinuous, and apparently arbitrary process that succeeded in destabilizing all sense of the material value of things and of the labor it took to make them.[46] Under these particular circumstances, objects could suddenly acquire a mysterious value which one nevertheless had to translate into the status distinctions of polite society or else risk disruption of that status quo, much as Alice imagines she has done and must therefore trade places with the unfortunate Mable with her meager house and inferior education. Objects seemed to grow dangerous, in other words, as their value became increasingly legible as social currency. Alice's dream replicates this transformation of objects in the imperial marketplace. Thus, at the simplest level, Carroll's story offered an intricate language of objects for making class distinctions. Not only did it tell adults that such a language was the stuff of fantasy life requiring interventions on the part of literary realism—hence the frame tale that redefines Alice's adventures as children's fiction—the story also made that language available to successive generations of children.

If the story was indeed produced under the circumstances I have imagined, what, then, does it say about the relationship between such a little girl and British imperialism? For one thing, it tells us that the female body is in some sense the object of objects, the objectification of the code that regulates them all. For it is Alice's relation to her body that determines the relation of subjects to objects prevailing not only in Wonderland but presumably also in the household that will someday quite literally mirror her taste. Though contained within a framework marking it as make-believe, the story nevertheless implies that sense itself—the ability of words to dominate things—depends entirely on Alice's ability to dominate an appetite that seems to be the most direct expression of the body itself. As I have argued, the jar of marmalade is as much the sign of dangerous appetite as of the taste that controls it. For taste to exist, then, appetite must already be present, not in contradiction with taste but as another position along a single continuum of desire. Just as we know the Duchess and her cook cannot advance along that continuum and become a girl like Alice, we also know that Alice is capable of back-sliding and taking on features of their distorted figures.

It would appear that a whole range of cultural practices from nursery to department store worked in concert to produce a desire for objects that appeared irrational to the degree that those objects were illegible. As objects were cut off from the history of their production and exchange, taste became less tangible. And as taste became less apparent in things themselves, the quality of objects was transferred onto the consumer. Advertisers consequently began to market their products in terms of such qualities as the female consumer's "belonging, sex appeal, power, distinction, health, togetherness, camaraderie."[47] By a certain point in our own century, "she" had clearly become the object they were selling. Alice lets us in near the beginning of this process. She shows us that no desire for the goods of the Empire was ever free of danger, because that desire was located in women. There it took the form of an appetite capable of effacing gender, race, and class; it defined her body as one that could at any time undergo the loss of these distinctions. Any visual evidence of desire was thus destined to produce fear—not only fear in the body of a woman who aspired to middle-class taste, but fear of resembling other women who did not embody British self-control.

Eroticizing Africa

It might be possible to underestimate the negative effect of what had obviously become a free-floating image—one whose history was as obscure as those of the commodities among which it circulated—were my argument to remain within the domain of women and children. In order to see how both masculinity and political policy depended on this development in the feminine and psychological domain, it is useful to look briefly at H. Rider Haggard's *King Solomon's Mines*. "This novel came off the press in London in September 1885," William Minter tells us, "only six months after the European powers met in Berlin to set the rules for dividing up Africa. An instant success, it sold 31,000 copies in Britain and went through thirteen U.S. editions in the first year alone."[48] Dedicated "to all the big and little boys who read it," Haggard's novel helps to explain where men fit into the psychosexual formation I have been describing; it demonstrates exactly what kind of male is defined in relation to the double-bodied woman who shaped so much of Victorian culture.

To eat in Rider Haggard's Africa is to depend on a woman incapable of nurture. Even when the land yields the necessities of life, that food is also likely to poison Englishmen. It is in such terms that the narrator describes discovering a spring named the "pan of bad water" after days of parched existence in the desert:

> How it came to be in such a strange place we did not stop to inquire, nor did we hesitate at its black and uninviting appearance. It was water, or a good imitation of it, and that was enough for us. We gave a bound and a rush, and in another second were all down on our stomachs sucking up the uninviting fluid as if it were nectar fit for the gods.[49]

Even water is black in Africa. Consuming it simultaneously revitalizes and endangers the white adventurers, who grow at once more masculine and less European. As the narrator explains to his English readership, "You, my reader, who have only to turn on a couple of taps and summon 'hot' and 'cold' from an unseen vasty boiler, can have little idea of the luxury of that muddy wallow in brackish, tepid water" (288). Self-restraint makes all the difference, as Conrad would argue within fifteen years or so, in determining whether such moments of his (quite literal) incorporation of Africa will invigorate or corrupt the European.

This becomes particularly apparent when the heroes arrive at another moment of crisis while crossing the frozen mountain peaks that stand between them and the ancient road to Solomon's mines. With what strength remains to them before death by starvation, the Englishmen manage to kill "a great buck." Lacking the fuel with which to cook it, they have to eat raw meat or die. It is with some embarrassment that the narrator recalls this scene for the reader: "It sounds horrible enough, but, honestly, I never tasted anything so good as that raw meat" (296). He offers the fact of their renewal as proof that it was right for the Englishmen to consume this flesh: "In a quarter of an hour we were changed men. Our life and our vigor came back to us, our feeble pulses grew strong again, and the blood went coursing through our veins" (296). The scarcity of Africa may strike us as an antithetical condition to the surplus of consumable items that greets Alice in Wonderland. As one Englishman tells the others, "starving men must not be fanciful" (296). Nevertheless, unregulated eating can be fatal to the bodies of Englishmen in Africa as well. "Mindful of the results of over-feeding on starving stomachs," the narrator invokes the first principle of good taste that is also essential to self-preservation in Alice's world: "we were careful not to eat too much, stopping while we were still hungry" (296). To remain an English girl, Alice must master her own appetite. To remain English men, this band of buddies must not only squeeze a living from the barren landscape of Africa, they must also conquer a bloodthirsty woman. In contrast with Alice, their problem lies outside rather than within the English body.

Although the narrator, Quatermain, promises, "there is not a *petticoat* in the whole history" (243), this lack of petticoats does not mean an absence of women. For Haggard, the absence of petticoats simply means a lack of women who are properly clothed, a lack, that is, of proper Englishwomen. Indeed, the presence of another kind of woman permeates the entire story, and the villains of the tale bear the same female defects first discovered by the earliest social scientists and captured by nineteenth-century photographers. These are the terms in which the narrator recalls his initial impression of the witch, Gagoola, terms that elsewhere in the culture distinguished whores and madwomen from decent people. In a scene resembling Jane Eyre's first glimpse of Rochester's "mad, bad and embruted" wife, Quatermain

> observed the wizened, monkey-like figure creeping up from the shadow of the hut. It crept on all fours, but when it reached the place where the king sat it rose upon its feet, and, throwing the furry covering off its face, revealed a most extraordinary and weird countenance. It was (apparently) that of a woman of great age, so shrunken that in size it was no larger than that of a year-old child, and was made up of a collection of deep, yellow wrinkles. Set in the wrinkles was a sunken slit, that represented the mouth, beneath which the chin curved outward to a point. There was no nose to speak of; indeed, the whole countenance might have been taken for that of a sun-dried corpse had it not been for a pair of large black eyes, still full of fire and intelligence, which gleamed and played . . . like jewels in a charnel-house. (320-321)

Whereas the African male is black and often admirable by virtue of his maleness, Gagoola is yellow, a degenerate shade of black that codes her body within Orientalism. Her gender and age disappear in the paradox of the ancient fetus. Like the ugly women in Carroll's narrative, her body provides a space within which the difference between male and female disintegrates, along with the difference between adult and child. As women do in *Alice's Adventures,* she enjoys exercising a form of power over her subjects that is murderously antithetical to the maternal role. Men who share her power take on "cruel and sensuous" feminine features, indicating that they share her degeneracy as well (317).

To arrive at the point where they actually confront and overcome this woman, three English adventurers have to travel across a landscape mapped out in much the same sexual terms as Gagoola's body. "I am rendered impotent even before its memory," the narrator confesses. "There straight before us, were two enormous mountains . . . shaped exactly like a woman's breasts" (286). According to the map left to them by a Portuguese adventurer who perished centuries before in search of the mines, the Englishmen must cross a scorching desert and then scale pinnacles that resemble "a woman's breasts" but are in fact a pair of "extinct volcanoes" (287). Those who manage to surmount these treacherous peaks descend into territory dominated by homicidal witches before reaching the cave that guards the entrance to the fabled diamond mines.

Lest his readers fail to grasp the heavy-handed symbolism, Haggard provides a map to help them visualize the terrain across which his heroes were traveling—his version of the unconquered territory to the north of the Transvaal in South Africa (Figure 5.11). The map represents this territory as a female figure. According to the logic of this figure, the incredible wealth within the belly of Africa draws men across a supine female body, enticing them into an opening which could be either the mouth or the genitals and being either is implicitly both at once. One cannot help noting the resemblance between the map and the body of Gagoola, whose eyes "gleamed and played . . . like jewels in a charnel-house." Both point to the enticing secrets contained within the female body of Africa, knowledge of which is likely to prove lethal for the Europeans. Given the fact that he saw fit to give Africa itself the same body that Europe had given to mad-

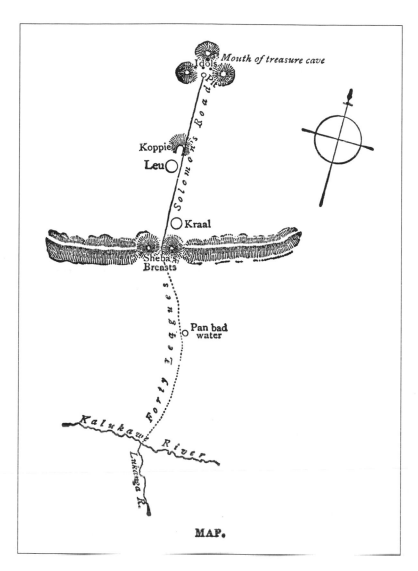

FIGURE 5.11   Map of Route to King Solomon's Mines
(1885). H. Rider Haggard.

women and whores, we can well imagine why Haggard brought his story to a close by killing off most of its women as well as the men who had fallen under their spell. In so doing, the story asks its readers to imagine bringing order to another people by containing the source of conflict within a female body and bringing that body under masculine control.

Occidentalism

In describing the poetics of this body of cultural material, I am arguing for the power of visual representation, a power that only certain images acquire, those of the most banal sort. Modern historiography makes it much easier to understand how Europeans represented Africans and Asians than how bits and pieces of those representations circulated back and forth between fact and fiction to redefine the white middle-class person. Nevertheless, from what we have seen of the exchange between England and its others, it seems altogether possible that an entire class of people—not only authors and intellectuals, but all manner of readers as well as writers—eventually understood who they were as Europeans in relation to an imaginary woman. And in thinking of other cultures in terms of her dark and powerful body, these people deemed themselves peculiarly fit to govern Asia and Africa. A paper published in the *Proceedings of the Royal Colonial Institute* for 1869 attributes the unrivaled success of English colonies to the fact that British men were so capable of self-regulation. The report allows that in the "French love of family kind, their cherishing of home ties, their somewhat patriarchal simplicity of life, there is much to admire, much for Englishmen to imitate." But, the author continues, "in the utter absence amongst the French of the vital self governing principle, there is, I apprehend, the fatal source of national stagnation."[50] If the French lack of self-regulation made them inferior to the English, still their reverence for the family placed the French well above the peoples whom they colonized. While the logic contained in popular images of the female body exalted the national character of each imperial nation, it actually extended beyond nationalism, as the quotation implies, to produce a similar form of male bonding throughout middle-class Europe, bonding that was necessary for empire.

King Solomon's Mines locates England's superiority over Africa not only in the Englishman's capacity for self-regulation but also in the bond between men. There is never any question in the novel that the homosocial bond is a more important and exalted one than heterosexual love.[51] Cultures where women mix into politics are primitive cultures whose women are markedly unfeminine. The domesticity of European women in turn testifies to the advanced state of its culture. Such a basis for national superiority certainly was used to justify the political subordination of women.[52] In making them politically dependent on men, however, the same logic made masculinity symbolically and psychologically dependent on women. Thus each of Haggard's heroes must have a woman in his past. By telling us that marriageable women existed long ago and far away, he assures the reader that no "petticoat" will deflect the emotion fusing the three highly individuated men into a single heroic character. At every turn, the perpetuity of the state and the health of the culture depend entirely on maintaining homosocial devotion. But as the ubiquity of bad and ugly women in the tale suggests, such devotion in turn requires their presence along with the absence of English women. Eve Kosofsky Sedgwick has been helpful in describing this triangulated configuration as one in which the woman is absolutely necessary.[53] The degraded double of the ideal English woman ensures that the bond among family-minded men remains strong even when they are far away from home. Women of dusky flesh at once embody erotic desire and reduce it to the sordid thrill of gazing. The tales of imperial conquest resemble the photography of whores, madwomen, and natives in that their characteristic maps, pictorial landscapes, and richly detailed description of other peoples inscribed another culture with messages that made it intelligible to Europeans. With seeing, furthermore, came knowing, and with knowing, a sense of themselves as subjects over and above the objects of such a gaze. The eroticism adhering to the disfigured surface of other bodies produced the desire to look at and know those bodies, a desire that only reinforced the homosocial bond. This desire materialized in a figure that bonded fantasy to realism, a popular image of what could not be realized within British culture without challenging the autonomy of that culture as well as its continuity in time.

By reminding us that objects are neither inert nor speechless, *Alice's Adventures in Wonderland* seems to offer readers a very different moral to its story. If we feel that objects have gained unprecedented power over subjects in this story, it is perhaps because they do, as Carroll suggests, have the power to classify us as fit for certain social spaces. And if in fact the messages those objects convey offer, in the form of a desirable object, a self that we desire to be, then we have to question the difference between the subjects we believe we are and the image-objects that make it possible for us to see ourselves that way. *Alice* will not allow the reader to imagine middle-class culture either without a dazzling array of unrelated objects or without men and women convinced that their status as subjects has something to do with their ability to classify and control that world of objects. Indeed, the survival of boy as well as girl protagonists depends on their ability to manage images. Not only must they decode the bewildering array of visual information that comes with the foreign messages accompanying commodities, on the one hand, and the cultural inscription on a foreign landscape, on the other; they must also be seen in certain ways by other observers. Thus Alice frequently verges on homicide, and the band of brothers display signs of a physical strength they do not in fact possess.

These resemblances to their brutally degenerate counterparts, led, in both cases, by a vicious woman, are performed in the service of difference. If Alice demonstrates that an enlarged or distorted body is, like her appetite, not really her own, then Haggard's little tribe of Englishmen confirm the fact that brains, honor, and commitment to one another are more powerful than any use of force. The manipulation of images in defiance of the laws of realism serves in both cases to bring those images under the control of words—in the form of the stories themselves—that are contained within and domi-nated by the very categories of realism against which children's litera-ture only seems to be rebelling. By playing with images, the modern individual acquires mastery over things, not the least of which is his or her own body.

CHAPTER SIX

Authenticity after Photography

LITERARY HISTORY WOULD HAVE US THINK OF MODERNISM AS "the great divide," a body of literary, visual, and plastic arts that mounted a successful assault on realism and took command of the cultural field.[1] And so say modernists themselves. In her manifesto essay, "Mr. Bennett and Mrs. Brown," Virginia Woolf famously argued that in rehearsing all the material facts about a character, fiction completely missed the point and failed to tell us who they were, what made them tick, and by what external factors their lives would therefore be most affected. What was most real was not something we could understand simply by looking at it. Truth, as Woolf understood it, lay on the other side of images, and she maintained that most of her Victorian predecessors failed to understand the difference and reproduced compellingly reductive stereotypes that kept one from contemplating the unfathomable complexities of each and every individual life. To mount this argument on behalf of modernist aesthetics, Woolf reduced realism to a mere caricature of itself by choosing Arnold Bennett to personify it. The whole complex game of determining the category to which an object or image rightly belonged, the fragility of the visual order, the awareness it could never conceal its own limits, its elasticity, its ability to render visible desire and fears that were fundamentally invisible—all this vanished as Woolf settled on the work of her Edwardian predecessor to exemplify realism. This same reductive gesture would be repeated by several novelists many times over and in many ingenious forms. The end result was a redefinition of realism, the very problematic in terms of which the modernists themselves formulated aesthetic theories, wrote poetry and fiction, and produced art-quality photographs. Rather than acknowledge that fact, they represented realism as an obsolete literary genre that nevertheless continued to display an arrogant desire to know and even possess chunks of the world by looking no further than its surface.

Yet to represent those elements of human nature that she was convinced would always elude Bennett's powers of visual description, Woolf and her cohort had to rely on stereotypical images every bit as much as he did. To what does Woolf introduce us if not to a visual type, when she describes Mrs. Brown as "one of those clean, threadbare old ladies whose extreme tidiness—everything buttoned, fastened, tied together, mended and brushed up—suggests more extreme poverty than rags and dirt"?[2] To recall Mrs. Brown's male companion on the train, moreover, Woolf puts him in "good blue serge with a pocket knife and a silk handkerchief, and a stout leather bag."[3] Having thus described a couple with whom she once shared a coach from Richmond to Waterloo, she can exercise a kind of power over that subject matter which is in fact quite reminiscent of Dickensian narration. "Obviously," she says of the man in the good blue serge suit, "he had an unpleasant business to settle with Mrs. Brown; a secret, perhaps sinister business, which they did not intend to discuss in my presence."[4] As in Dickens, we receive a surplus of visual information. As in Dickens, that information refuses to yield a definitive reading of the situation and so generates a gap between visual and verbal information. As in Dickens, moreover, this gap in turn creates an appetite for more such information. Even if the real Mrs.

Brown cannot be adequately represented in conventional images, it is nevertheless from such images that we must infer what has been left out.

Dickens defers to an image as a truth to be read in the same terms as one reads the generic protocols of photography. He insists that we understand a visual description, not in relation to its object, but by virtue of its difference from every other kind of visual information. Woolf, in contrast, offers that image as a substitute for and barrier to the truth of individual identity, much as Mrs. Brown's neat appearance "suggests more extreme poverty than dirt and rags." She, in other words, would have us read conventional images in terms of what they conceal and thus what they do not allow us to know. On this basis she asks us to assume that her Mrs. Brown represents what humanity had been before nineteenth-century realism reduced it to a predictable set of conventional images. If this truth was one that could only be represented by exposing the limits, distortions, and deceptions of visual stereotypes, however, that truth could not possibly have the same originary status that modernism would persuade us it does. The modernist concept of an authentic subject that existed prior to and independent of the photograph was surely a subject that modernism constructed retrospectively. To put it simply, the modernist concept of authenticity was a post-photographic way of imagining one's relation to the real. In this chapter I describe modernism accordingly, as a set of techniques that relocated identity on the other side of the image and sought to reveal what was there before realism misrepresented that more primary reality of self and object. In this respect, modernism confirmed the very principle it characterized as both naive and arrogant, namely, the primacy of certain images.

Modernism's hostility toward both mass culture and women is all too well known.[5] Indeed, literary and cultural criticism has shown that, however strange and various, the formal innovations associated with modernism worked toward the single end of distinguishing authentic artistic expression from those art forms which made themselves accessible to ordinary consumers.[6] In doing so, these same formal moves strived to remasculinize art.[7] My own investigation of what modernism did to the world that realism had made both legible and reproducible must begin where most such inquiries end. Why modernists—or anyone else for that matter—should have felt compelled to disavow mass culture is no more obvious to me than why they should exhibit such intense ambivalence toward women. I seriously doubt that fear of feminization could have motivated all those unconventionally gendered and uniquely talented individuals to produce the brilliant array of novels, poems, paintings, photographs, sculptures, and performances that they did. Nor do I believe that such a socially acceptable phobia was what brought their various forms of creative energy together under one rather tight conceptual umbrella. Even if it could be shown that so many artists actually shared an aversion to women and mass culture, furthermore, we would still have no way of explaining why their specific expressions of contempt for the popular and conventional were able to redefine art for all of modern culture.[8] Thus the modernist endeavor to remasculinize art should be seen as a means to another end, I believe, rather than the prime mover and final cause of modernism's rejection of the mission and methods of literary realism. Only by redefining modernism's distrust of the legibility of visual representation of the body as an aesthetic strategy rather than its cultural objective, can we begin to consider the more interesting question of what modernism accomplished by its extraordinarily various and yet single-minded assault on both mass culture and femininity.

In pursuit of an answer, I will look closely at the change that English fiction and photography underwent during the last decade of the nineteenth and early decades of the twentieth century, as these particular media acquired the status of high-culture art forms. I have indicated all along that my choice of media is a strategic one. By the 1860s, I have argued, fiction and photography had taken up a mutually authorizing relationship that had extraordinary influence over how modern people saw the world and situated themselves in relation to it. Modernism's quarrel with Victorian aesthetics sought to undo the collaboration between words and images that I have identified with realism. Modernists working in a range of media declared that henceforth images should display objects that could not be verbally described and, by the same token, words should refer to a reality that could not be pictured in conventional images.[9] Given that the first novels to make this move from a popular to an elite art form did so within a few short years of the first fine-art photographs, we might expect these media to have pursued parallel trajectories in developing the formal techniques we identify with modernism in fiction and photography, respectively. We would be wrong.

To break off the relationship on which they both rose to hegemony, these two popular media worked in apparent opposition to each other. Victorian fiction achieved the authority to represent the world as one saw it by making reference to rather ordinary kinds of information, especially photographs. These were the stock and trade of literary realism.[10] These were also the materials that modernism found most misleading and obstructive. And if fiction could no longer claim to tell the truth by referring to such images, then how much more problematic was the task for photography? To the degree that a photograph's very existence as an image seemed to depend on objects and people outside the photographic frame, the medium itself argued for a one-to-one relationship between an image and its subject matter.[11] Given that modernism's aversion to mass culture and femininity expressed itself in an assault upon the visual order established by nineteenth-century realism, modernist photography is the place to go for cultural insight into both aversions.

The Art Which Is Not One

In promoting the notably abortive set of experiments in art photography known as pictorialism, Alfred Stieglitz, the protégé of P. H. Emerson, worked with the image in ways that resembled the techniques of Julia Margaret Cameron and Oscar Rejlander more than those of his mentor.[12] To turn photographic images into art, Stieglitz assumed that the art image had to reveal properties of the subject concealed beneath its visible surface. Thus he sought to make photography counter its own object-dependency and so renounce the very realism that had fostered its development as a popular medium. Initially, Stieglitz and his colleagues borrowed painterly techniques to sever the bond between image and object on the theory that doing so would allow them to picture the unseen interiorities which they, along with such novelists as Woolf, Joyce, and Lawrence, considered the definitive subject of art.[13] An example or two of pictorialist techniques are sufficient to demonstrate what went wrong. In a photograph of 1904 entitled *Struggle,* Robert Demachy introduced brushstrokes by applying a gummy substance to the negative, hoping to remove the figure of a naked woman from its photographic context and link it to the title of his image (Figure 6.1). In the 1903 version of a well-known sequence of portraits of Rodin, Edward Steichen superimposed a second negative on the first so that the space outside the sculptor's head would represent the enormous genius fomenting within it (Figure 6.2).

The whole point of borrowing painterly techniques was to distinguish the work of the pictorialists from the kind of photography that had dominated the epoch of realism, but this particular way of marking differences within photography was also destined to mark photography as decidedly inferior to painting. In 1904, Stieglitz was not alone in declaring pictorialism a failure. His experiment prompted a rash of manifestos urging photography to divorce itself from painting. One such attack compares pictorialism to an elusive woman, who manages "to suppress all outlines and details and lose them in delicate shadows so that meaning and intention become hard to discover."[14] In using hard objects to represent the murky territory of the subject, pictorialism may have turned its back on the popular demand for photographic realism. But in emulating painting, these same photographers inadvertently set their images upon the slippery slope to a familiar form of sentimentalism that used an imperiled body as the outward and visible sign of an inward state of suffering. What I want to emphasize here is the capacity of certain images to cancel out aesthetic value, not because those images happened to stick to certain objects, but because they happened to stick to other images already charged with meaning. The very repetition that lends

FIGURE 6.1   *VI. Struggle* (1904). Robert Demachy.

a pose its reassuring predictability produced the sedimentation of meaning and elicited the canned response associated with both mass culture and bourgeois femininity.

Thus, by 1904, a new aesthetic doctrine calling itself "Straight Photography" sought to purify images of the semiotic baggage they brought with them from their life in popular tradition. All talk of

FIGURE 6.2   *I. Rodin* (1903). Edward J. Steichen.

self-expression vanished from the critical discourse surrounding photography.[15] Proponents of the new photographic aesthetic sought to
eliminate not only the inner eye of imagination but also the crafts-
manship associated with the human hand. Despite these antiseptic
measures, the new aesthetic doctrine was anything but gender-free.
In pitting art against popularity, it pitted art against femininity as
well. Photographers used a sexually charged language to conceptualize the project of turning their subject matter into art images, and
they invariably registered success and failure as a loss or gain in
masculinity. Photographers were urged to control the negative by

Authenticity after Photography

mastering the objects that supplied the raw material for their images. Along with exhortations not to manipulate the negative were instructions endowing the art photographer with the qualities of an optical predator who watches and waits with a preternatural sensitivity to objects' visual qualities until they assume exactly the position he desires. "I consider every fluctuation of color, light and shade, study line values and space divisions," explains a spokesman for this method, "patiently waiting until the scene or object of my *pictured vision* reveals itself in its supremest moment of beauty" (my italics).[16] This subtly gendered redefinition of the relationship between object and observer yielded images we now identify with photographic modernism.

To demonstrate how these photographers purged the image of what they found both derivative and feminizing in earlier photography, I have chosen a few examples of domestic scenes, nudes, and celebrity portraiture, all common subject matter for Victorian photographers, all used in the failed experiments of the pictorial school as well. One cannot help noticing the transformation of domestic objects as they become raw material for the new kind of art image (Figure 6.3). We are completely missing the point, in my estimation, when we attribute such an experiment with shape, light, and angle to modernism's investment in form for its own sake. Paul Strand is doing much more than displaying his formal ingenuity when he strips ordinary household objects of the very cultural associations essential to their popular appeal. Strand quite literally detaches such images from the domestic economy in which their subject matter acquired sentimental value from the individuals who sat in that chair or hung those sheets along a clothesline. He frames the images of ordinary household objects so as to emphasize the visible qualities that place them in relation to images of similar geometric form. Within this new symbolic economy, the nature or kind of subject matter testifies to its own material transformation.

As with domestic objects, so too with the woman who was the center of the modern household. No doubt it was particularly impor-

FIGURE 6.3   *Geometric Backyards, New York 1917.* Paul Strand.

tant for these photographers to defeminize the embodiment of femininity, the female body. Stieglitz's famous photographs of Georgia
O'Keeffe's torso (Figure 6 4) have little in common with the conspicuous painterliness of the work of Robert Demachy. Stieglitz
forces the viewer to confront the fact that the body in the photograph is an image, since only an image could be cropped and positioned at such an angle. As an image, the female body represents
neither itself nor what it formerly represented within sentimental,
pornographic, or realistic frames of reference. All these and more
possibilities for meaning are of course there in Stieglitz's photographs of O'Keeffe, but they are there to be canceled out in a way
that simultaneously identifies the photograph as "a Stieglitz" and

Authenticity after Photography

FIGURE 6.4   *Georgia O'Keeffe* (1919). Alfred Stieglitz.

renders its conventional subject matter absolutely mute—indeed, anatomically mouthless. From here, it is not much of a leap to the nudes of Edward Weston, always shot from a surprising angle, thus always a partial object even when the whole body is obviously contained within the frame (Figure 6.5).

To arrive at a fully articulated modernism, Stieglitz had to work with and within the tradition of realism precisely because his chosen medium came into being as the most exact fulfillment of that tradi-

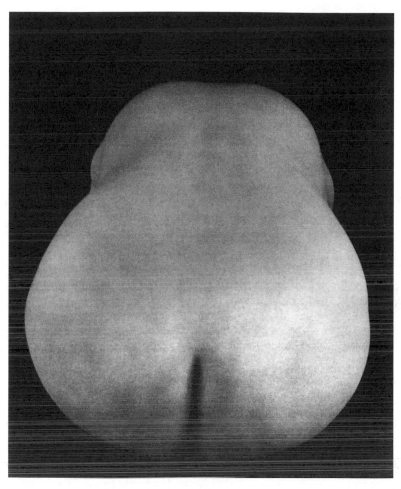

FIGURE 6.5   Untitled (1927). Edward Weston.

tion. His portraits of O'Keeffe severed the bond between the photographic image and anything like a natural body, redefining their raw
material, or O'Keeffe herself undressed, as images pure and simple.
In this way, Stieglitz forced photography to renounce the rhetoric of
the perfect copy that points back to its traditional subject matter. In
her discussion of surrealist photography, Rosalind Krauss describes a
similar strategy of displacement. By making us conscious of the photograph as image, as Krauss explains, surrealism calls attention to the

Authenticity after Photography

255

process of doubling "that elicits the notion that to an original has been added its copy. The double is the simulacrum, the second, the representative of the original. It comes after the first, and in this following, it can only exist as figure, or image. But in being seen in conjunction with the original, the double destroys the pure singularity of the first."[17] Doubling, she continues, not only turns the presence of someone or something into a succession of copies, it also "transmutes raw matter into the conventionalized form of the signifier."[18] Where popular photography sticks to its object so as to make the doubling process seem a natural one, the Stieglitz nude takes the doubling process itself as its subject matter. It testifies to the originality of the copy—an originality that comes from Stieglitz himself, as the producer of that copy.

What the paradox of the original copy did to the gender of its human subject matter becomes particularly clear in celebrity portraits by modernist photographers. The early masters of photography were as interested in capturing the image of exceptional individuals as in reproducing traditional class and racial stereotypes, and they established the formal conventions indicating that the individual portrayed was exceptional. The ordinary individual tends to be subsumed in the pose. "That," we tell ourselves with hardly a second thought, "is the way a woman, or a professional person, or a pleasant shopkeeper looks and consequently asks to be observed." The celebrity, however, because he or she provides both the original for and the copy of that image, has more of a two-way relationship with a photograph, and this relationship deserves our further attention. The celebrity portrait depends for its existence on the willingness of famous people to pose. By the same token, it was not long after the invention of photography when such individuals were virtually obliged to have their photographs taken, since celebrity portraiture could bestow on them a uniqueness that no individual face and figure possessed in and of themselves.

More important for my purposes is the question of how modernist portraiture differentiates itself from other celebrity portraits. In some respects, the images of O'Keeffe, Henry James, Ezra Pound,

FIGURE 6.6   *Henry James* (1906). Alvin Langdon Coburn.

James Joyce, Gertrude Stein, and others produced by art photographers after 1910 did in fact usurp the position of the object as the
thing that contained the truth of the celebrity subject (Figure 6.6).
At the same time, however, the celebrity image began to differentiate
itself sharply from the conventional image of a man or woman belonging to the respectable classes. In his portraits of O'Keeffe, for

Authenticity after Photography

FIGURE 6.7　*Georgia O'Keeffe* (1918). Alfred Stieglitz.

example, Stieglitz displaces the infinitely reproducible stereotypical image by cropping and positioning her head together with her hands so as to destroy the natural autonomy of face and hands, body parts his earlier photographs had already identified as hers (Figure 6.7). What the modernist photograph cut away from the celebrity, however, it invariably restored by way of the image. Stieglitz used camera angle, lighting, and focus to lend O'Keeffe's image—each and every image of her that he exhibited—its own formal autonomy, an autonomy only he could give it.

I am keenly aware of using terms that invite us to consider further the gendered dynamic of such objectification: Are these not displacements of "her body" with "his gaze"? Before I address the well-known argument that seeing is masculine and being seen therefore a feminine condition, however, I want to lay the ground for qualifying an application of the male-female binary to this kind of photography.[19] I remain unconvinced that the relationship between a photograph and the subject it objectifies is entirely a one-way street, especially when that subject happens to be a full-fledged image-consuming member of modern culture. To transform his perception of such an individual into art photography, to be sure, the modernist photographer manhandled the portrait of a female face or body. By cropping, tilting, and casting a face or body in a radically unsentimental light, he did violence to what we generally regard as the "normal" or "public" image of that individual. This dispute with earlier portraiture is built into modernist photography and becomes part and parcel of its art. In violating the natural autonomy of his subject matter, however, Stieglitz never repeated the error of pictorialism. He refused to let the body stand in for some emotion it appears to be experiencing and thereby conveys to the viewer, and he did so by playing the game of realism in reverse. The photographs that resulted may very well suggest that his subject matter inspired the photographer to distort the conventional portrait in a particular way, but those formal innovations empower the individual subject only to overturn that power relationship and privilege instead a secret contained within the imagination of the art photographer. In contrast to those, say, of Julia Margaret Cameron, such portraits insist that *they* have conferred uniqueness on the celebrity rather than the other way around.[20]

I have held the obvious feminist criticism of modernist photography at bay by staying within the genre of celebrity portraiture. In fact, however, few examples of modernist photography respected the generic distinctions between images of the domestic interior, the nude, and the celebrity portrait. So, too, when we consider how many of the modernists—photographers, painters, poets, and novelists alike—turned for material to their often scandalous relationships with other artists and intellectuals, it is tempting to conclude that crossing the generic lines between the family portrait, pornography, and celebrity photography was somehow necessary both to their self-definition as artists and to their work. A photograph of Paul Strand's wife, entitled simply *Rebecca*, illustrates one of the means by which modernists eroticized their artistic experiments and so made their portraits more enticing to the respectable public they appeared to scorn (Figure 6.8). Such portraiture created a body peculiar to modernism.[21]

This body simultaneously reproduced and displaced the body as displayed in pornographic photography with an art image that set modernism's sexuality apart from mainstream heterosexual monogamy. Like the celebrity's portrait, these visual representations of what were known to be intimate relationships confined the secret bred of that intimacy to a closed coterie. While it is certainly true that such representations of the body gave the masculine photographer mastery over the implicit femininity of his medium, it can be argued that even when the model was male, his portrait appears before us as a replacement and disfiguration of the woman, as in the case of Weston's nudes (Figure 6.9). More important, however, is the photographer's remove from the observer. Because it indicates the photographer's ability to see that body directly and manipulate its visual information, the celebrity photograph sets him apart from other (implicitly masculine) observers; those viewers see only what the photographer wants them to see, and they will never have the knowledge of his photographic subject matter that he shares with members of his coterie.[22]

The woman in this scenario may well be the object of the gaze and, in this respect, subordinated to the photographer. She, however, does share the secret of modernism's openly bohemian sexuality and, in taking on this knowledge, assumes a position of epistemological superiority to the convention-bound observer. As the embodiment of such knowledge, she may have gained as much from the notoriety as he.[23] In addition to the sexual relationship between the photographer and his model, Stieglitz's photographs of O'Keeffe make us keenly aware of his choice of angles and use of lighting, as well as the repertoire of images available to him, and they do so

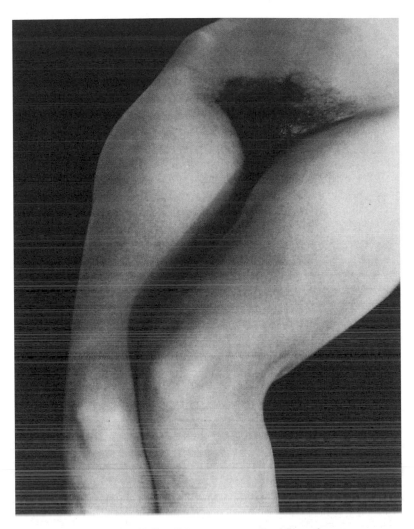

FIGURE 6.8 *Rebecca, c. 1922.* Paul Strand.

without indicating why he has made the precise selection he has; the fact that his object choice was both sexual and aesthetic automatically puts it beyond the viewer's ken. This parting of the photographer's way of seeing from that of the observer produced a division between seeing and knowing that defies reduction to any binary difference between male and female.

Authenticity after Photography

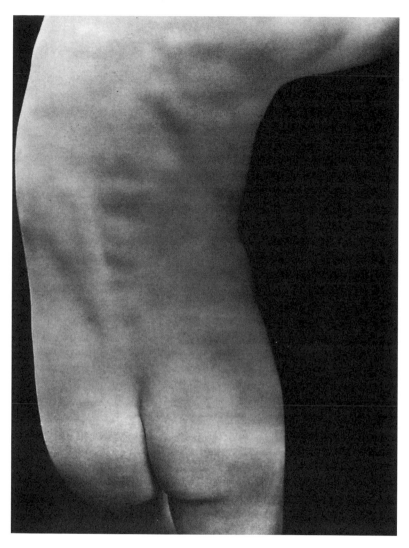

FIGURE 6.9   Untitled (1925). Edward Weston.

Fiction after Photography

Novelists had to make different moves than photographers in order
to transform a popular medium into a work of art. The difference
between the two sets of formal maneuvers was determined as much
by their common objective as by the difference between the media in

which they worked. Both novelists and photographers identified art with formal techniques that opposed the conventions identified with popular realism and neutralized mass culture's capacity to elicit canned responses from the consumer. Both brought this aesthetic to bear on the conventions for representing the human body. Of all the objects that mass culture had taken up and rendered in reproducible stereotypes, "the body" was the centerpiece and object *par excellence*. The body so packaged provided and still provides modern individuals with the means of locating themselves within a differential system of poses.[24] Indeed, when positioned as the object of the gaze, even the male body is feminized, as demonstrated by Weston's nudes, because we see it as a distortion of another body image—a strictly middle-class production.

At some point in the nineteenth century, it is fair to say, many women were born with such a class body by virtue of the fact that they grew up middle-class in one of the modern Western nations. It soon became impossible, as John Tagg has observed, for this body to enter the streets of the modern metropolis without losing its value as such, for one was supposed to display that body only within the domestic sanctuary and even there, only according to rather elaborate rules.[25] These rules were manifest not only in the fashions of the times, in the privacy of the tea table and feminine amusements, but also in the distinction that popular photography scrupulously maintained between family portraits and pornography. When an image of the respectable woman was destined for public distribution, as, for example, in a pleasing scene from domestic life, a model would often supply the figure of that woman with eyes diverted from the camera, much as Esther's face appears in the Hablot Browne illustration for *Bleak House* (see Figure 3.2). It was as if these indications of invisibility ensured the privacy of the private sphere. A photograph or illustration could consequently identify itself as pornographic simply by undressing the middle-class body and displaying what no photographer was supposed to see, much less make available for public consumption.

Photograph by photograph, in collusion with fiction and the

developing human sciences, Victorian photographers produced a stereotypical image that came to represent "the female." Against this standard, any variation could be measured: consumptive women, madwomen, promiscuous women, working-class women, and African women, as well as children and men. Mary Ann Doane has argued that in classical cinema the female body became "the body," and a woman's relationship, as subject, consequently grew much closer to her body as a visual object than a man's.[26] She had to be feminine; ideally she would become maternal; but she could not be exposed as female in the sense implied by the popular body. The allurements of the fully exposed body necessarily canceled out both its maternity and its femininity, since these were private functions of the woman and manifested themselves accordingly—through her behavior toward others, but never as the source of erotic gratification. While the respectable woman could be said "to have" a female body, her relation to that body resembles what D. A. Miller calls "the open secret."[27] Her identity as a feminine and maternal woman indicated that she had an erotic life which she had scrupulously withheld from public view. To grasp the extent to which this open secret shaped Victorian fiction, one need only recall how any one of Charlotte Brontë's heroines shrinks into corners and niches or fades into the background behind her more flamboyant rivals and companions. Jane Eyre, Lucy Snowe, and Carolyn Hellstone will do anything to avoid the limelight, and Brontë consequently allows us to see them only as they watch men watching other women make spectacles of themselves.[28]

The two halves of the popular body—the feminine and the female—were indeed two halves of a single cultural formation. That construct was organized by a contradiction between the body which contained and concealed a woman's sexuality, on the one hand, and the body as manifestation of that sexuality, on the other. The feminine and the female could not coexist within a single photograph, since they ostensibly addressed entirely different audiences who looked at the body in entirely different ways. Around the end of the nineteenth century, about the same time when Stieglitz first tried to detach the photographic image from its object, the drive to see that object began to command the technological resources that would gratify its lust with pornographic movies. The result, as Linda Williams explains, was a body that appears simply to extend the logic of visibility, as the camera appears to follow an imagined penis—which has acquired not only a mind but eyes of its own as well—on the way to its objective inside the female body.[29] For the obvious reason that the pornographic camera promises to reveal something fundamentally unseeable—namely, the source of pleasure concealed within the woman's body—cinematic narrative resorts to substitution in order to represent such gratification in visual terms. The pornographic movie uses the body's surface to visualize the pleasure occurring somewhere underneath. Rather than showing the viewer what a woman's desire ordinarily looks like, however, this metaphoric use of the body's surface produces a historically new body, one that objectifies the desire of male consumers.

I believe that Victorian photography created the binary opposition in terms of which this cinematic logic unfolded. Fifty years of pornographic photography had reduced the female body to its visible traces, broken it up into various parts, shot those parts from unusual angles, and reconstituted them in albums and stereoscopic sequences, as well as through sheer repetition, to produce a master stereotype—the erotic object itself.[30] Victorian consumers may well have conceptualized that object as the body of a middle-class woman divested of its privacy, stripped, and visually probed, but pornographic photography produced a body that was in fact brand new and ontologically hostile to its respectable other half. Such a body did not simply expose the secret contained within the elite cultural body, it also redefined sexuality itself as something that was materially inscribed and therefore visible on the body's surface. What one discovered in viewing the pornographic body was not the sexuality of respectable women, then, but the surface of another body, the body of a class or an ethnic group who "allowed" their women to be seen.

The formal techniques that set the modernist novel apart from earlier fiction had to work against both halves of this body, as did the techniques that managed to distinguish the new art photography from the genres of photography that had dominated until that moment. To a man, novelists who wanted to produce works of literature went after the contradiction that organized the popular body by keeping its two halves apart—the feminine body (which exposed nothing but the socially acceptable signs of gender) from the female body (which displayed the truth of its sexuality). In his essay "Pornography and Obscenity," D. H. Lawrence makes this point explicitly, as he applies the term "pornographic" to fiction that equates sexual gratification with seeing. When it withholds the visual elements of sexual experience from readers, he contends, such fiction simply displaces erotic desire with the desire to see. "I'm sure poor Charlotte Brontë . . . did not have any deliberate intention to stimulate sexual feelings in the reader," he admits, "yet I find *Jane Eyre* verging towards pornography and Boccaccio seems to me always fresh and wholesome."[31] More surprising than his unusual application of the term "pornography" is Lawrence's habit of using graphic sexual description in an effort to distinguish his own fiction from the kind of novels Charlotte Brontë wrote. More curious still, as I will demonstrate, is the fact that the sexually explicit component of his work, rather than any technical innovation, is what allows us to put him in the same camp with Joyce and Woolf.

I have selected a lovemaking scene from *Lady Chatterley's Lover* to suggest how literary modernism transformed the popular body into a work of art. Of particular interest is what Lawrence does with the body of a respectable woman in the following passage:

> It was not really love. It was not voluptuousness. It was sensuality sharp and searing as fire, burning the soul to tinder.
>
> Burning out the shames, the deepest, oldest shames, in the most secret places. It cost her an effort to let him have his *thing*, like a slave, a physical slave. Yet the passion licked round her, consuming, and when the sensual flame of it pressed through her bowels and breast, she really thought she was dying: yet a poignant, marvelous death.
>
> She had often wondered what Abélard meant, when he

said that in their year of love he and Helöise had passed through all the stages and refinements of passion. The same thing, a thousand years ago: ten thousand years ago! The same on Greek vases, everywhere! The refinements of passion, the extravagances of sensuality!

In the short summer night she learnt so much. She would have thought a woman would have died of shame. Instead of which, the shame . . . was at last roused up and routed by the phallic hunt of the man, and she became to the very heart of the jungle of herself.[32]

The author in this scenario has clearly usurped the position of a novelist like Charlotte Brontë, who was in her own time credited with pushing domestic fiction to the very brink of respectability. Even she could not refer to actual "breasts" and "bowels" without crossing over the carefully drawn line separating domestic fiction from pornography, a generic difference that was invariably reestablished during periods of canonization and therefore essential to the novel's identity as such. The author of *Lady Chatterley's Lover* takes up a position in the traditional seat of novelistic power, by which I mean the position of the female sensibility as it wrestles with desire. He does so, however, in order to force his chosen genre across the line distinguishing those elements of private life that could be exposed without compromising their privacy from those elements that become obscene the moment they see the light of public day.

Like the pornographic film, the passage produces an object that could not be visualized by any other means. And like the pornographer, Lawrence uses female orgasm to represent the boldest expression of human desire: something registering on the mind, because it happens within the body, but something that eludes visibility, because what happens on the surface of the body stands in for an entirely different order of events. Once stripped of social stereotypes, the female body becomes language in the artist's hands, and his lovemaking remakes her. To indicate that such a transformation is successfully under way, Lawrence's prose abandons conventional sentence structure and grows paratactic, repetitious, and descriptive. What was thus amplified, extended in time, and made palpable, he insists, was *not* in fact something that could be displayed on the body's surface. Where the popular body would display its sexual pleasure for a masculine consumer, the Lawrentian body presumes to offer us something still more basic to a woman's nature.

To explain what modernism defined as more authentic than a woman in the throes of passion, let me begin by noting that the literary language of lovemaking mobilizes formal procedures quite distinct from those enabling photography to transform the popular body into art-quality images. In reading Lawrence, we do not encounter a surface that simultaneously indicates and withholds the sexual secrets shared by the photographer and his coterie. On the contrary, Lawrence used the female body to objectify another order of events taking place beneath its surface. He may have promised the reader the visual gratification of pornography, but he delivered something on the order of an out-of-body experience instead. Sexuality was not something that the female body could contain, as pornography assumed it did, so much as something that pulsed through the body, connecting it to universal humanity and ultimately to nature herself. This metaphoric use of what would otherwise be just another pornographic body defines the most fundamental element of human nature as fundamentally invisible. We have to discover the secret of sexual identity by other than visual means.

James Joyce's *Ulysses* tends to use the popular body in another way—more as a microscope that compresses the world into a single scene than as a telescope that expands outward from a center of visibility by inflating physical details into literary universals.[33] Where women are concerned, Lawrence can easily be accused of dramatizing their sexual lives in order to objectify his own theory of love, while on at least one truly memorable occasion Joyce allows the woman to narrate her own transformation from mere body into a metaphor for all of humanity.[34] As a result, the Joycean narrative does not strive to unearth a secret buried within a woman's body so much as to show us how the world would look from a position within that body. *Ulysses* reorganizes a vast array of British cultural materials so that we encounter them through the reverie of a common Irish woman. Such use of the body is clearly what prompts Franco Moretti to describe Joyce's Dublin as "a more striking miniature of the world system than anything produced in the previous century."[35]

For the duration of Molly Bloom's soliloquy, a female body provides the imaginary boundaries of a text that incorporates Dublin and, within Dublin, presumably the rest of the world. Her reverie portrays all social relationships as sexual engagements with or disengagements from her body. Take this excerpt, for example:

> Ill put on my best shift and drawers let him have a good eyeful let his micky stand for him Ill let him know if thats what he wanted that his wife is fucked yes and damn well fucked too up to my neck nearly not by him 5 or 6 times . . . and Ive a mind to tell him every scrap and make him do it in front of me serve him right its all his fault if I am an adultress as the thing in the gallery said O much about it if thats all the harm ever we did in this vale of tears God knows its not much doesnt everybody only they hid it I suppose thats what a woman is supposed to be there for or He wouldnt have made us the way He did so attractive to men then if he wants to kiss my bottom Ill drag open my drawers and bulge it right out in his face as large as life he can stick his tongue 7 miles up my hole [36]

Here indeed the narrative seems to belong to Molly. Elsewhere in the novel, furthermore, she or some other version of the popular body serves as the imaginary center from which the narrative appears to come and to which it must return. But does this mean that Joyce sifted through all of British cultural history, only to settle on a common woman's sexual parts, their base sensations, and her coarsest terms for them as the source of meaning for an epic statement about his culture?

To answer this question, we must put formal differences aside and understand Joyce in much the same terms as we did Lawrence.

Joyce comes to Molly's body with language borrowed from pornography, albeit pornography of a less sanctimonious and more Rabelaisian variety than Lawrence played with. It is only when men thus approach and stir her to life that Molly or any of her avatars exist for readers, and her reverie creates a body that swirls around the points of masculine display, contact, entry, and separation. Like Lawrence, Joyce sets up this limited repertoire of references to the popular body in order to transform that body into one that cannot be seen, because it is a purely textual phenomenon, the highly artificial nexus of various strands of cultural history. Here, once again, we seem to gain entry to the female body as the author pares away prosaic convention and, in so doing, presumably puts us in touch with something more basic to human existence than all the psychological peaks and valleys that Charlotte Brontë had been willing to muster. Once again, the male sex organ appears to provide the only instrument capable of rousing the female in the woman to a state of visibility. Although permeable at every opening, foul of mouth, anathema to hierarchy, and mixed with a host of others—indeed, serving as the host to many others—Molly does not constitute the kind of opposition that might seriously challenge a patriarchal culture. As a working Irish woman, she is no less metaphorical, her meaning no less metaphysical, than Constance Chatterley's. Indeed, it is modernism's brilliance to make such different literary figures play precisely the same role in distinguishing true from false masculinity.

E. M. Forster's *Maurice* neither desires to undress the respectable woman of novelistic tradition nor feels compelled to transform the pornographic spectacle of her fully sexualized body into the language of literature. Yet this novel accomplishes the modernist objectives of remasculinizing fiction and elevating it to an art form all the same. Moreover, in that Forster does so with the same clarity of purpose that we saw in Lawrence and Joyce, his novel serves as a striking instance of the exception proving the rule. *Maurice* deals with an old Cambridge romance that refuses to die. Whereas his boyhood lover has thrown over his homosexual infatuation for the adult responsibilities of marriage, Maurice cannot do so. "Natural" desire returns, as it does for Constance Chatterley, as a full-blown romance with his lover's gamekeeper. In the following description of their first passionate encounter, we can, once again, observe the novel at work incorporating and displacing a version of the popular body:

> "Oh let's give over talking. Here—" and [Alec, the game-keeper] held out his hand. Maurice took it, and they knew at that moment the greatest triumph ordinary man can win. Physical love means reaction, being panic in essence, and Maurice saw now how natural it was that their primitive aban-donment . . . should have led to peril. . . . And he rejoiced because he had understood Alec's infamy through his own— glimpsing, not for the first time, the genius who hides in man's tormented soul. Not as a hero, but as a comrade, had he stood up to the bluster, and found childishness behind it, and behind that something else.[37]

Conventional language breaks off. Whereupon a fleeting reference to erotic contact between physical bodies initiates a swerve inward away from anything resembling the popular body, a "glimps[e of] . . . the genius who hides in man's tormented soul," a descent into primi-tivism, and the lyrical elevation of prose to indicate that we have left the domain of respectable fiction and ventured into the unknown, because invisible, territory of high art.

It is true that when he included sexually explicit material in his novel, Forster preserved the polite prose style that both Lawrence and Joyce rejected. By using the conventional language of romance to describe sex acts that put man quite literally in touch with man, however, Forster in fact flew more directly in the face of polite con-vention than either Joyce or Lawrence did. He was all too aware of what could happen if he replaced the woman of conventional fiction with a man and described that man's sexual attraction to another man in the same terms his readership considered appropriate for heterosexual love.[38] In his "Terminal Note," Forster explains what was at stake in making these substitutions: "A happy ending was imperative . . . I was determined that in fiction anyway two men should fall in love and remain in it for the ever and ever that fiction allows, and in this sense Maurice and Alec still roam the greenwood" (33).

The implications of his substitutions extend well beyond For-ster's agenda. He replaced Lawrence's Lady Chatterley with a man, Maurice. Instead of her emasculated husband Clifford, Forster's hero yearns for a boyhood lover and finds the sexual satisfaction he needs with that lover's gamekeeper, much as Constance Chatterley did with Mellors. By means of this one substitution, Forster turned the con-ventions of the adultery plot against themselves, so that they asserted the primary and compelling nature of homosexual desire. Joyce and even Lawrence may be said to offer more exemplary versions of modernist style, as they portray what may strike us as a far more conventional brand of adultery, but in neither case does conven-tional wisdom hold up. The desire by means of which Lawrence and Joyce put their own distinctive spins on the adultery plot invariably culminates in images of onanism, bestiality, orality, and anal penetra-tion. Men in their novels seem more attracted to the breast and anus than to the female genitals. Thus we would not be wrong in using Forster's revision of the heterosexual love story to exemplify the endeavor to position masculinity outside and in opposition to the domestic conventions that modernism viewed as feminine and feminizing.

Despite their obvious differences in style and preferred assault on normative sexuality, the passages I have used to illustrate the procedures of modernism require us to bring remarkably similar assumptions to the act of reading. Each self-consciously uses porno-graphic subject matter to dramatize the limitations of the visible world and lay claim to a truth beyond it. To find a language for the primitive impulses on which it based such claims to authenticity, modernism went to marginal people and practices that nineteenth-century authors and intellectuals from Thomas Malthus through Max Nordau had represented as essential to human identity and yet hostile to reason, taste, social authority, familial relations, and endur-ing love. What had been peripheral—the working class, the Irish, the homosexual—resurfaced at the core, as a new subject, a lost childhood, a buried erotic life that lay closer to the very center of consciousness than any of the desires that literate people were apparently willing to acknowledge in themselves or allow into publication. In place of the feminine woman, writers as different as Lawrence, Joyce, and Forster each turned to her degraded counterpart, the popular body as depicted in pornographic literature. So much the worse, it would seem, for fiction that was striving to be art. But as this figure emerged from what Lawrence described as the underworld of mass culture, the fiction in which she did so gained new authority over the novel-reading public. That fiction identified whatever the reader saw by conventional means as an obstruction and denial of the truth. Indeed, according to literary modernism, the conventional means of seeing prevented one from grasping intuitively not only the basis for the most conventional relationships, but what one shared with children, savages, whores, and homosexuals as well.

It was one thing for a group of disgruntled expatriates to challenge the conventional relationship between seeing and knowing. It was quite another matter for educated readers to receive these novels in the spirit in which they were written. In 1933, District Judge John M. Woolsey legitimated the claim of a relatively small number of artists and intellectuals when he made it illegal to ban the sale of *Ulysses* in the United States. For it to be officially declared pornography, written material had "to stir the sex impulses or to lead to sexually impure and lustful thoughts."[39] Woolsey and two of his friends apparently stayed up all night and read the entire novel, only to find that it not only failed to arouse them sexually, it also offered "very powerful commentary on the inner lives of men and women."[40] The court concluded that "when such a real artist . . . *seeks to draw a picture* of the lower middle class in a European city," it should not "be impossible for the American public legally *to see that picture*" (the italics are mine, the circumlocution Woolsey's).[41] To determine that *Ulysses* was art rather than pornography, then, Woolsey had to believe that if the sexually explicit language composing Molly Bloom's soliloquy did not arouse him, it was not pornographic: Joyce had succeeded in making a degraded version of the popular body represent something other than that body, a truth that could not otherwise be seen. Thus Woolsey conceded modernism's first premise that the inner lives of men and women were composed of pornographic scenarios and could be so pictured, even though the preponderance of literature written since the late eighteenth century had not depicted human consciousness in pornographic terms. The judge could pronounce Joyce's novel literature, because he felt that its graphic sexual descriptions referred not to sexual experience per se but to the "inner lives" of Irish people. Nor, there is reason to suspect, did he believe the Irish represented only the Irish in *Ulysses*. Never questioning the stereotype of the Irish as a people lacking sexual constraint, Woolsey was all too willing to believe they enacted human urges too primitive to be seen elsewhere in Europe or America.[42] On both counts, he decided that Joyce's graphic descriptions were not supposed to be read transparently.

Modernism's Symptom

My point in using photography to rethink literary modernism has been to suggest that all forms of modernism offer ways of dealing with the fact of mass visuality: the production of a field of vision that not only possessed the tangibility and wholeness of a world, but that also provided the common ground for readers of fiction, a world to which any novel could refer with considerable confidence. The production of such a world necessarily transformed the reader-observer brought up on omniscient fiction and popular photography into a reader-viewer who was arguably more passive in the face of visual information than at any previous moment in modern history. While our accounts of this period in cultural history acknowledge many different changes in the constitution of the reading subject (from membership in a class of producers to membership in a class of consumers, for example, or from a culture defined by political economy to a culture defined by sexology), the increasingly visual basis of cultural experience remains largely invisible and yet omnipresent as a metaphor in these accounts.[43] What tends to register instead is a changing relation to woman.

At a certain point in time, this body appeared to yield nothing by divulging itself fully, and identity came to be understood more by what the subject had to excorporate and set in opposition to itself, than by the figures which it incorporated and sought to reproduce. It stands to reason that, at such a point in time, the female body would begin to serve as the symptom of masculinity. Rather than threatening the subject's integrity and durability, as I explained in the Introduction, the symptom lends the subject those very qualities, according to the later writings of Lacan and those who turn his model of identity formation to cultural analysis. If the symptom were to dissolve, according to this view, then the subject itself disintegrates. Thus to say that woman is the symptom of man means that man himself exists only through woman; his very ontological consistency depends on her.[44] Rey Chow borrows this formulation to reverse the usual approach to Western representations of racial difference as something that limits, denigrates, and thereby oppresses an actual "native." What she argues instead is that "as the white man's symptom, as that which is externalized in relation to the white-man-as-subject, the space occupied by the native is essentially object-ive, the space of the object" in the traditional Cartesian formula.[45] She compares various attempts on the part of postcolonial critics to restore these objects to their subject status with the concerted attempt on the part of second-wave feminism to restore the truth to women's distorted and partial identities by theorizing subjectivity. By assuming that a particular object of knowledge is there to be liberated from misrepresentation, according to Chow, both projects deny that native and woman are entirely fabricated embodiments of material excluded from Western masculinity, and thus projections on which white men depend for their identity as such.

Whenever they assume that images per se are bad, both feminism and postcolonial theory observe the logic of modernism as well.[46] If "woman" is, as Lacan suggests, simply the external anchor for male identity, and if, as Chow reformulates the model, the "native" serves

Authenticity after Photography

275

in a similar capacity for the imperial West, then we can on the same basis consider the reproducible transparent image as the symptom of modern culture itself: that which constitutes oppositionally the twin categories of art and the modern subject, lending to its most cherished products both continuity over time and a point of origin in the vision of exceptional men. Chow suggests as much, when she points out that by attempting to recover the subjectivity of oppressed groups, most critiques of imperialism attempt "to combat the politics of the image, a politics that is conducted on surfaces, by a politics of depths, hidden truths, and inner voices." Thus does such criticism fail to consider "the most important aspect of the image—its power precisely as image and nothing else."[47] Modernism's consistent attempt to detach the object from its image can be read according to the logic of the symptom as at once an acknowledgment and a denial of modernism's dependency on the very kind of images that can take the place of objects. What is at stake in continuing to disavow the degree to which we as subjects and the world of objects are already images?

It is as anachronistic, I believe, to regard one's place in the visual order as less than real and to yearn for fullness of being beyond the image that identifies that place, as it was, in the age of Stieglitz and Lawrence, to mistake images for the things and people they represent. To yearn for such fullness of being is to embrace a post-photographic notion of authenticity that modernism conjured up retrospectively. By considering the modernist turn in fiction and photography as the moment when the primacy of popular images was both acknowledged and effectively suppressed, I have tried to demonstrate why there can be no escaping such images. The body on which we stake our sense of futurity, individuation, rights, and community is neither a pornographic construct nor a medley of modernist body parts. That body is not only an image but arguably the most real thing about us as well.[48] On the other hand, to embrace the visual order as exuberantly as some versions of postmodernism do is simply to take up the other side of the opposition and set the body as image against what we imagine to be the real body, but which is in fact another body image. Between modernism's twin options there lies a conceptual abyss that can only be negotiated by a politics of the signifier, a theory capable of evaluating images, intervening in their reproduction, and holding them responsible for identifying needs and instigating desires.

❧ NOTES ❧

INTRODUCTION: WHAT IS REAL IN REALISM?

1. See Martin Jay, *Downcast Eyes: The Denigration of Vision in Twentieth-Century French Thought* (Berkeley: University of California Press, 1994) for a thorough description of this trajectory. In *Picture Theory* (Chicago: University of Chicago Press, 1994), W. J. T. Mitchell contends that poststructuralism's concern with "grammatology," "discourse," and the like echoes "Wittgenstein's iconophobia and the general anxiety of linguistic philosophy about visual representation" (11–13).

2. In "Welcome to the Cultural Revolution," for example, Rosalind Krauss argues that "a certain type of visual sign is now ascendant in that part of the academy that likes to think of itself as avant-garde. Identified as *image,* its material structure has collapsed and, disembodied, it now rises as Imaginary, hallucinatory, seductive: the shared property of Psychoanalytic Studies, Cultural Studies, and the incipient field of Visual Studies." *October* 77 (1996): 92.

3. Nancy Armstrong, *Desire and Domestic Fiction: A Political History of the Novel* (New York: Oxford University Press, 1987).

4. Georg Lukács, *Studies in European Realism,* trans Edith Bone (New York: Grosset & Dunlap, 1964), 8.

5. Georg Lukács, "The Crisis of Bourgeois Realism," *The Historical Novel,* trans. Hannah and Stanley Mitchell (Lincoln: University of Nebraska Press, 1983), 171–250.

6. Ian Watt, *The Rise of the Novel: Studies in Defoe, Richardson and Fielding* (Berkeley: University of California Press, 1957); Harry Levin, *The Gates of Horn: A Study of Five French Realists* (New York: Oxford University Press, 1963); George Levine, *The Realistic Imagination: English Fiction From Frankenstein to Lady Chatterley* (Chicago: University of Chicago Press, 1981); Elizabeth Deeds Ermarth, *Realism and Consensus in the English Novel* (Princeton: Princeton University Press, 1983); D. A. Miller, *The Novel and the Police*

(Berkeley: University of California Press, 1988); Naomi Schor, *Breaking the Chain: Women, Theory, and French Realist Fiction* (New York: Columbia University Press, 1985); Michael Fried, *Realism, Writing, Disfiguration: On Thomas Eakins and Stephen Crane* (Chicago: University of Chicago Press, 1987).

7. Fredric Jameson, "Reification and Utopia in Mass Culture," *Signatures of the Visible* (New York: Routledge, 1990), 11–12.

8. Ibid., 12.

9. In *The Cult of Images: Baudelaire and the 19th-Century Media Explosion* (Santa Barbara: UCSB Art Museum, 1977), Beatrice Farwell describes an explosion of mass-produced lithographic images that rapidly displaced "the folkloric aspect" of "popular imagery" with "urbanity" and "sophistication" during the period between 1820 and 1860 in France. Although the English were neither so careful nor so consistent in preserving the record of this media event, it is likely that lithography had a similar impact on England as well. "It is clear," Farwell contends, "that in its early years, much photographic work made for commercial sale dealt in the same kind of imagery as lithography." Also see Patricia Anderson, *The Printed Image and the Transformation of Popular Culture 1790–1860* (Oxford: Clarendon Press, 1991), for a compelling description of the pictorial literacy of the working classes up through the decade when photography assumed the role occupied by lithography in this regard.

10. Geoffrey Batchen, *Burning with Desire: The Conception of Photography* (Cambridge: MIT Press, 1997), 53.

11. "Photography: Its History and Applications," *Living Age* 92 (1867): 195.

12. Ibid.

13. "A Suppressed Art," *Once A Week* 19 (1864): 368.

14. Lady Elizabeth Eastlake, "Photography," *The Quarterly Review* 101 (1857): 443.

15. Indeed, as Larry J. Schaaf demonstrates, William Henry Fox Talbot was acutely aware of his predecessors while working on calotype technology. He was narrowly beaten out as the inventor of photography by Louis Daguerre, and during the decade when he held a patent on the process, other intellectuals were developing similar methods on their own. *Out of the Shadows: Herschel, Talbot, and the Invention of Photography* (New Haven: Yale University Press, 1992).

16. Ibid., 159.

17. William Henry Fox Talbot, "A Brief Historical Sketch of the Invention of the Art," *Classic Essays in Photography*, ed. Alan Trachtenberg (New Haven, Conn.: Leete's Island Books, 1980), 29.

18. Abigail Solomon-Godeau, *Photography at the Dock: Essays on Photographic History, Institutions, and Practices* (Minneapolis: University of Minnesota Press, 1991), 14.

19. Jacques Derrida, *Archive Fever: A Freudian Impression*, trans. Eric Prenowitz (Chicago: University of Chicago Press, 1996), 1–3.

20. Thomas Richards, *The Imperial Archive: Knowledge and the Fantasy of Empire* (London: Verso, 1993), 11. As Richards points out, "At mid-century [an archive] meant ordering information in taxonomies; by century's end 'classified' had come to mean knowledge placed under the special jurisdiction of the state," 6.

21. In the words of Roland Barthes, "A specific photograph . . . is never distinguished from its referent (from what it represents), or at least is not *immediately* or *generally* distinguished from its referent." Such a distinction "requires a secondary knowledge or act of reflection. By nature, the Photograph . . . has something tautological about it: a pipe, here, is a pipe." *Camera Lucida: Reflections on Photography*, trans. Richard Howard (New York: Hill and Wang, 1981), 5.

22. Derrida, *Archive Fever*, 4–5. If the self-effacement of the archivist allows the archive to appear "in the nude, without archive," the question arises: "does one need a first archive in order to conceive of originary archivability? Or vice versa?" 80.

23. Allan Sekula, "The Body and the Archive," *October* 39 (1986): 3–64.

24. In *A. A. E. Disdéri and the Carte de Visite Portrait Photograph* (New Haven: Yale University Press, 1985), Elizabeth Ann McCauley provides a good sense of the quantity, range of subjects, and impact on the tradition of painting characterizing the boom in *cartes de visite* in France begun by A. A. E. Disdéri in the late 1850s and picked up by a number of his peers during the 1860s. These images included figures from the worlds of art and entertainment, as well as family portraits and prominent political figures.

25. William C. Darrah, *Cartes de Visite in Nineteenth Century Photography* (Gettysburg, Pa.: W. C. Darrah, 1981), 4.

26. Sekula draws on a contemporary of Bertillon and Galton, Charles Sanders Peirce, to make the distinction between the methods of the two criminologists. Assuming "the photograph was nothing more than the physical *trace* of its contingent instance," he contends, Bertillon exploited the indexical properties of the image. Galton saw the symbolic properties of the medium and, "in seeking the apotheosis of the optical, attempted to elevate the indexical photographic composite to the level of the *symbolic*, thus expressing a general law through the accretion of contingent instances." "The Body and the Archive," 55.

27. Francis Galton, *Inquiries into Human Faculty and Its Development* (London: Macmillan, 1883), 5–6.

28. Barthes's well-known distinction between the *studium* and *punctum* can explain the partial success and ultimate defeat of both endeavors. What he calls the *studium* resides in the pictorial qualities of a photograph that tell us how to read it. To enact this "contract between creator and consumers,"

an image must ensure that we have, in a sense, already seen it before we see it (28). In this familiar space, all too rarely, Barthes confesses, "a 'detail' attracts me. I feel that its mere presence changes my reading, that I am looking at a new photograph" (42). "By the mark of *something*," he continues, "it is no longer 'anything whatever'" (49). It is important to note that a photograph can be neither all *studium* nor all *punctum*, since the somewhat disappointing sense of having seen such an image depends on the absence of an obtrusive detail that would break its surface tension and transport us to the other side. At the same time, a photograph's ability "to annihilate itself as a *medium*, to be no longer a sign but the thing itself," occurs momentarily and strictly within a familiar frame of reference. If Bertillon's individuated images had no ability to identify the appropriate criminal except as those images diverged from totally fabricated norms or abstract types, then Galton's types had no authority as categories unless they could suppress the details that endowed individual photographs with an ability to point to some referent outside themselves.

29. In "A Short History of Photography," *Classic Essays on Photography*, ed. Alan Trachtenberg, Walter Benjamin attributes "the removal of the object from its shell, the fragmentation of the aura" to an increasing need "to take possession of the object . . . in an image and the reproductions of an image" (209). In the early regional photography of David Octavious Hill, Benjamin sees "something that is not to be silenced, something demanding the name of the person who lived then, who even now is still real and will never entirely perish into art" (202). "At that early stage, object and technique corresponded to each other as decisively as they diverged from one another in the immediately subsequent period of decline. Soon improved optics commanded instruments which completely conquered darkness and distinguished appearances as sharply as a mirror" (27). Photographs produced during the last two or three decades of the nineteenth century part ways decisively from their objects and simply reproduce other images.

30. This is, after all, the lesson of *Camera Lucida*, that the element of repetition, or *studium*, cannot exist without the estranging detail, or *punctum*, that reconnects the signified of the photograph to its referent, as if they were one and the same.

31. Louis Althusser, "Ideology and Ideological State Apparatuses (Notes towards an Investigation)," *Lenin and Philosophy and Other Essays*, trans. Ben Brewster (New York: Monthly Review Press, 1971), 174.

32. Jacques Lacan, "The mirror stage as formative of the function of the I as revealed in psychoanalytic experience," *Écrits: A Selection*, trans. Alan Sheridan (New York: W. W. Norton, 1977), 1–2.

33. Kaja Silverman, *The Threshold of the Visible World* (New York: Routledge, 1996), 18.

34. In *Gender Trouble* (New York: Routledge, 1989), Judith Butler pro-

vides the clearest description of the process, whereby the other becomes a secret (invisible) component of the subject, generating a lifetime of self-performances (57–72).

35. Rey Chow, *Writing Diaspora: Tactics of Intervention in Contemporary Cultural Studies* (Bloomington: University of Indiana Press, 1993), 30.

36. As Barthes explains, the photographic subject is to some degree already an image before he or she steps before the camera: "I constitute myself in the process of 'posing,' I instantaneously make another body for myself, I transform myself in advance into an image. This transformation is an active one." *Camera Lucida*, 10–11. Considering photography from a sociological rather than a personal perspective, John Tagg nevertheless insists on the same element of performance, or self-production: "The portrait is . . . a sign whose purpose is both the description of an individual and the inscription of social identity. But at the same time, it is also a commodity, a luxury, an adornment, ownership of which confers status. The aura of the precious miniature [is not lost, as Benjamin would have it, but] passes over into the early daguerreotype. The same sense of possession also pervades the elaborately mounted collections of *cartes de visite* of public figures." *The Burden of Representation: Essays on Photographies and Histories* (Amherst: University of Massachusetts Press, 1988), 37.

37. In "The fetishism of the commodity and its secret," *Capital*, vol. 1 (New York: Vintage Books, 1977), 163-177, Karl Marx uses this figure to represent the commodity as an object whose abstract social value has displaced its material properties as an object. Once the table emerges as a commodity, the table both remains a table and "it changes into a thing that transcends sensuousness. It not only stands with its feet on the ground, but, in relation to all other commodities, it stands on its head, and evolves out of its wooden brain grotesque ideas, far more wonderful than if it were to begin dancing of its own free will" (164), as does, for example, the séance table.

38. Though dealing with literary representation, rather than objects in the marketplace, Lukács represents the encroachment of description occurring during the second half of the nineteenth century in no less apocalyptic terms: When "writers attempt a vain competition with the visual arts . . . they become mere still lives. Only painting has the capacity for making a man's physical qualities the direct expression of his most profound character qualities. And it is no accident that at the time descriptive naturalism in literature was degrading human beings to components of still lives, painting was losing its capacity for intensified perceptual expression." "Narrate or Describe?" *Writer and Critic and Other Essays*, ed. and trans. Arthur D. Kahn (New York: Grosset & Dunlap, 1970), 138.

39. In the well-known opening to his *Simulacra and Simulation*, trans. Sheila Faria Glaser (Ann Arbor: University of Michigan Press, 1994), Jean Baudrillard describes modernity in terms of the Borges fable of a map that

had been made so accurately and well that it became, for all intents and purposes, the thing it represented. I am, again, interested in the hyperbolic terms in which Baudrillard represents this substitution: "This imaginary of representation, which simultaneously culminates in and is engulfed by the cartographer's mad project of the ideal coextensivity of map and territory, disappears in the simulation whose operation is nuclear and genetic, no longer at all specular and discursive. It is all of metaphysics that is lost," 2.

40. Marx, "The fetishism of the commodity and its secret," 165; Lukács, *The Historical Novel*, 250; Baudrillard, *Simulacra and Simulation*, 6.

41. As Slavoj Žižek emphasizes, the kind of misrecognition on the part of a culture that necessitates such extravagant misreadings of history is performative and possesses "a positive ontological dimension," or truth in its own right. *The Sublime Object of Ideology* (New York: Verso, 1989), 66.

42. For an example of this debate, see *Identities*, ed. Henry Louis Gates, Jr., and Anthony Appiah (Chicago: University of Chicago Press, 1995), especially Avery Gordon and Christopher Newfield, "White Philosophy," 380–400, and Walter Benn Michaels, "The No-Drop Rule," 401–412.

I   THE PREHISTORY OF REALISM

1. See, for example, Martin Price's discussion of Austen's frequent reference to this debate in her novels, "The Picturesque Moment," *From Sensibility to Romanticism: Essays Presented to Frederick H. Pottle*, ed. Frederick W. Hilles and Harold Bloom (New York: Oxford University Press, 1965), 256–268.

2. Addressing precisely this question of the relation between England and what she aptly calls "the aesthetic nation," Elizabeth Helsinger points out that the members of the aesthetic nation, "like those of the political nation after 1832, are still men of property, though that need not mean private ownership of the land itself. Books like [J. M. W. Turner's] *Picturesque Views in England and Wales* offered middle-class consumers a way of possessing England (the land) and hence claiming membership in it (the nation) some years before political reforms redefined the concept of property to admit them to the franchise. But in the 1820's and 1830's, neither the defenders of English landscapes as national property nor the majority of middle-class political reformers meant to stretch the meaning of possession to include the working classes." "Turner and the Representation of England," *Landscape and Power*, ed. W. J. T. Mitchell (Chicago: University of Chicago Press, 1994), 106.

3. According to Ann Bermingham, "The fetish of rusticity in the early Victorian suburb represented the survival of the popular picturesque sensibility and the incorporation precepts into a program of social planning. . . . In its purest form," she continues, "the suburb was an abstraction of the rustic tradition, a utopian ideological construction that provided a refuge

from the disappointing realities of both urban and rural life." *Landscape and Ideology: The English Rustic Tradition, 1740–1860* (Berkeley: University of California Press, 1986), 167–168.

4. John Taylor describes the increase in the number of photographers in England: "The first entry for photographers is in the census of 1851, when there were just fifty-one professionals. By 1861 this number had grown to 2,534, which would have served a small community of patrons. The business expanded gradually till 1881 when there were 6,661 employees, with a large increase by 1901 when the number stood at 14,999." *Reading Landscape: Country-City-Capital,* ed. Simon Pugh (Manchester: Manchester University Press, 1990), 181.

5. William Gilpin, *Three Essays: On Picturesque Beauty; On Picturesque Travel; and On Sketching Landscape: To Which is Added a Poem, On Landscape Painting,* second edition (London, 1794), iii. All references to Gilpin's *Three Essays* are to this edition and are identified by page numbers in the text.

6. Edmund Burke, *A Philosophical Enquiry into the Origin of our Ideas of the Sublime and Beautiful* (New York: Oxford University Press, 1990), 13. All citations to Burke's *A Philosophical Enquiry* are to this edition and are identified by page numbers in the text.

7. By way of explaining how man can take the highest form of pleasure in the very things that threaten to annihilate him, Burke has this to say: "what generally makes pain itself . . . more painful, is, that it is considered as an emissary of this king of terrors [death]. When danger or pain press too nearly, they are incapable of giving any delight, and are simply terrible; but at certain distances, and with certain modifications, they may be, and they are delightful." *A Philosophical Enquiry,* 36–37. Art, he contended, was required to create that distance and so contains the threat of annihilation.

8. Here, too, we find Gilpin sticking close to Burke, who identified curiosity as "the first and simplest emotion which we discover in the human mind" and, on this basis, claimed that "some degree of novelty must be one of the materials in every instrument which works upon the mind." *Three Essays,* 29. Burke looks for novelty in the objects we observe, in other words, while Gilpin is concerned with how they look.

9. By showing that the thrill of sexual conquest and the quest for knowledge are linked metaphorically in eighteenth-century poetry and epistemology, as well as his writing on the picturesque, Simon Pugh places Gilpin's theory squarely within Enlightenment thought: "Just as the poet takes control of the woman's body, a passive commodity, through division into parts, through inventory and itemisation, likewise the landscape should be 'composed,' says Gilpin, 'as the artist composed his celebrated venus, but selecting accordant beauties from different originals.' The rhetorical tradition of 'division' and 'partition' both divides up matter to 'increase and multiply' but also opens it up and opens it up to view, to 'enlightenment,' by uncover-

ing something hidden." "Loitering with intent: from Arcadia to the Arcades," *Reading Landscape*, 152.

10. Lest such attacks on Romantic enthusiasm swing readers to the other side of Burke's opposition between pleasure and judgment, where they might come to understand the pleasure of the picturesque as no pleasure at all, Gilpin builds in such safeguards as the following statement throughout his argument: "The province of the picturesque eye is to *survey nature;* not to *anatomize matter.* It throws it's glances around in the broad-cast stile. It comprehends an extensive tract at each sweep. It examines *parts,* but never descends to *particles." Three Essays,* 26.

11. According to Gilpin's instructions, the observer should select the point of view offering the most interesting set of visual features ("A few paces to the right, or left, make a great difference. The ground which folds awkwardly here, appears to fold more easily there.") and then fix that point of view "with two or three principal points, which may just mark on your paper. This will enable you the more easily to ascertain the relative situation of the several objects." *Three Essays,* 63. The next priority is to represent "the *characteristic features* of a scene" in terms of the gradations of light and dark best captured with a lead pencil and wash of india ink. Only then is distance introduced by tinting the foreground, middleground, and background with different colors. *Three Essays,* 64–84. After the outlines are drawn and the ink wash has been made and tinted, details, which may include "figures," are added with this caution: "But in figures thus designed for the ornament of a sketch, a few light touches are sufficient. Attempts at finishing offend." *Three Essays,* 77–78.

12. Indeed, Gilpin insists, in the case of "an unpicturesque assemblage of objects; and, in general, all untractable subjects, if it be necessary to represent them, [they] may be given as plans, rather than as pictures." *Three Essays,* 66.

13. William Gilpin, *Observations on the River Wye, and several parts of South Wales, &c. relative chiefly to Picturesque Beauty, made in the Summer of the Year 1770* (Oxford: Woodstock Books, 1991), 32. All references to Gilpin's *Observations* are to this edition and are identified by page numbers in the text.

14. By the time Wordsworth wrote the poem immortalizing the Abbey, Gilpin's journey was rather well known, so much so that in 1789 Horace Walpole reported in a letter to Hannah More that he had been "amusing myself by sailing down the Wye, looking at the abbeys and castles, with Mr. Gilpin in my hand to teach me to criticise, and talk of foregrounds, and distances, and perspective and prominences, and all the cant of connoisseurship." Quoted in Ann Bermingham, "English Landscape Drawing around 1795," *Landscape and Power,* ed. W. J. T. Mitchell (Chicago: University of Chicago Press, 1994), 87.

15. For the men who dominated aesthetic discourse and the ideology choreographing their various definitions of taste, see Daniel Cottom, "Of Taste," *The Cultural Imagination: A Study of Ann Radcliffe, Jane Austen, and Sir Walter Scott* (New York: Cambridge University Press, 1985).

16. In "English Landscape Drawing around 1795," Ann Bermingham links the argument for nature and against abstraction directly to anti-Jacobin polemics. Because of this relationship, instructions on how to draw certain objects in a landscape were ideologically charged. For this reason, she explains, Uvedale Price could fault Gilpin for paying too much attention to the disposition of details, while at the same time, William Marshall Craig, himself the author of a book of drawing instructions, attacked Gilpin because he did allow natural objects to serve as his model. "Unlike Gilpin's arbitrary signs, which were open to interpretation and rhetorical applications," Bermingham explains, "Craig's literal, natural sign would be impervious to manipulation, change, and misunderstanding, because it would be locked in a mirrorlike relation to the thing it represented." We could say the same thing of Price's criticism of Gilpin's abstract style, once we acknowledge that Price's reference is not nature but the tradition of landscape painting. *Landscape and Power*, 92.

17. These rules were perhaps first articulated in *A Treatise on the Coins of the Realm in a Letter to the King* by Charles Jenkinson, the first Earl of Liverpool, soon after becoming President of the Board of Trade in 1786. According to A. E. Faeveryear, *A Treatise* offered both a summary of "the best opinion upon the subject at the time" and the first code of regulations "for managing a gold-standard currency with token coins." Faeveryear notes that Liverpool's argument endorsed "two quite distinct principles: 1) that the coins would pass at their nominal value so long as their total intrinsic value in metal and workmanship equaled their nominal value, and 2) that they would take their value according to the rate at which they could be exchanged for gold coins, in other words, their value would be maintain by their convertibility." A. E. Faeveryear, *The Pound Sterling: A History of English Money* (London: Clarendon, 1931), 175-177.

18. See, for example, Burke, *A Philosophical Enquiry*, 17, 25.

19. The argument of Henry Thornton, who appeared before secret committees of the two Houses of Parliament on the Bank of England, reveals the economic logic that won the day in 1797: "It may . . . be safely assumed, that when the main sources of a country's wealth are unimpaired; when its population, its industry, its manufacturing and trading capital, its general commerce, its credit, its colonial possessions, its political strength and independence, its laws and constitution remain; and when, moreover, its paper is confined within its accustomed bounds; the absence of its gold . . . is an evil which is likely neither to be durable, nor in any respect very important."

Henry Thornton, *An Enquiry into the Nature and Effects of the Paper Credit of Great Britain 1802*, ed. F. A. Hayek (London: George Allen and Unwin, 1939), 158–159.

20. *A Letter to the Right Honorable William Pitt on the Influence of the Stoppage of Issues*, quoted in Faeveryear, *The Pound Sterling*, 189.

21. Writing to Hannah More during the crisis of 1825, Marianna Thornton describes the chaos in her father's banking firm of Pole, Thornton & Co. On a "dreadful Saturday I shall never forget," she recounts, "the run increased to a frightful degree, everybody came in to take out their balance, no one brought any in . . . [and] the House was left literally empty." The "moment of peril" made one partner "insist on declaring themselves Bankrupts at once." Another partner "cried like a child of five year old." The burden fell upon her father, who proceeded to rid himself of the ineffective partners and take on another new, young man like himself. "Can you believe it?," expostulates his daughter, "I really hardly can . . . It still appears to me magic that when we only looked forward to his rising in years to come, he is at once placed at the head of one of the first, in some respects the very first, Banking House in Town. He was off again in the dark on Monday morning to the Bank of England," who apparently loaned him 400,000 pounds in Bank of England notes. "So ends this fearful tale," Marianna's letter of December 7, 1825, concludes, "and from the deepest sorrow, we are all at once the happiest of the happy. To me a special Providence seems to watch over these walls." On December 12 that same year, she writes again to Hannah More, a letter that begins with these words: "I little thought when I closed my last happy letter to you how soon it would all be reversed—and that a few hours would realize our worst anticipations." The bank had gone under in that brief span of time. The sequence of letters continues to show these extraordinary reversals of fortune recurring on a weekly basis and to describe them in appropriately melodramatic terms. "The Crisis of 1825: Letters from a Young Lady," *Papers in English Monetary History*, ed. T. S. Ashton and R. S. Sayers (Oxford: Clarendon, 1932), 98–108. See also Richard Brown, *Society and Economy in Modern Britain 1700–1850* (London: Routledge, 1991), 200.

22. In his study of Gide's *The Counterfeiters*, Jean-Joseph Goux usefully describes "the reciprocal metaphor linking money and language in close parallels. . . . The type of language that could be compared to *gold money* would be a full, adequate language. In it and through it, the real would be conveyed without mediation." But, he continues, "if we now consider a system in which language is compared to *representative paper currency*, . . . the relationship between language and being begins to be problematic. Just as in the economic sphere there arises the question of *convertibility*, that is, the existence or not of a deposit serving to back the tokens in circulation, likewise in the domain of signification the truth value of language will be-

come a crucial concern. Language will no longer be conceived as fully expressing . . . reality or being; it will necessarily be conceived as a means, a relatively autonomous instrument, by which it is possible to represent reality to varying degrees of exactitude." *The Coiners of Language*, trans. Jennifer Curtiss Gage (Norman: University of Oklahoma Press, 1994), 14, 17. See also Patrick Brantlinger's account of debt during the period between 1750 and 1832 in *Fictions of State: Culture and Credit in Britain, 1694–1994* (Ithaca: Cornell University Press, 1996), 88–135.

23. "The Bill of Exchange and Private Banks in Lancashire, 1790–1830," *Papers in English Monetary History*, 49.

24. Thus we find that in urging Parliament to lift the restriction on gold, David Ricardo thinks about restriction in quite different terms from those of the argument which held off restriction until 1797. Paper having proved incapable of providing a standard for itself, he looks to gold as the one commodity capable of regulating paper, since it is outside the system of exchange: "The issuers of paper money should regulate their issues solely by the price of bullion, and never by the quantity of paper in circulation. The quantity can never be too little while it preserves the same value as the standard." Despite this pro-gold position, Ricardo acknowledged certain advantages to the self-regulating system of currency that had been in place since 1797: "If the plan now proposed, of paying bank notes in bullion, be adopted, it would be necessary either to extend the same privilege to country banks, or to make bank notes a legal tender, in which latter case there would be no alteration in the law respecting country banks, as they would be required, as they now are, to pay their notes when demanded in Bank of England notes." "Proposals for an Economical and Secure Currency, with Observations on the Profits of the Bank of England," second edition (1816), *The Works of David Ricardo*, ed. J. R. McCulloch (London: John Murray, 1881), 407.

25. Price's argument on behalf of a "natural" landscape that maintained the traditional relationship between landowner and those who worked the land and Knight's counterargument to the effect that since only those of refined sensibility could enjoy the landscape, it should be arranged to appeal to that sensibility, can be found, respectively, in Price's *Essays on the Picturesque* (1794) and Knight's *An Analytical Inquiry into the Principles of Taste* (1805).

26. Knight's anti-Burke position has been described thus: "It was upon Burke's theories that Price had established his discussion of the picturesque, so Knight, in attacking Price, also sets about demolishing Burke's system. . . . Burke had, he felt, placed too much emphasis on the role of 'sensual impressions' neglecting the influence of our mental faculty on our aesthetic responses. . . . External objects merely prompt complex trains of associations which are themselves established from previous experience." Michael Clarke

and Nicholas Penny, "Visible Appearances," *The Arrogant Connoisseur: Richard Payne Knight, 1751–1824,* ed. Michael Clarke and Nicholas Penny (Manchester: Manchester University Press, 1982), 82. See also Nigel Everett, *The Tory View of Landscape* (New Haven: Yale University Press, 1994), 103–122.

27. Richard Payne Knight, *An Analytical Inquiry into the Principles of Taste* (London, 1805), 245. All references to Knight's *Analytical Inquiry* are to this edition and are identified by page numbers in the text.

28. In *The Tory View of Landscape,* 98, Nigel Everett claims that, despite their disagreements as to whether art or nature should shape the landscape, both Knight and Price accepted Burke's position that what the French Revolution had done to the European countryside would threaten the English social order, were England's landscape allowed to be similarly transformed. In Europe, as Everett explains, "this common patrimony had been thrown aside by a revolution that was an urban conspiracy of men whose occupations encouraged narrowness of mind and a spirit of envy—tradesmen, lawyers, literary hacks, minor priests, and academics. Among their first acts was to create a market in paper credits based on the confiscated estates of the Church and the landed interest, with the twin ideas of financing the public debt and destroying the traditional influence of the country." Where Burke sought to counteract a danger spilling over from Europe into England, Knight and Price saw the possibility of transformation coming from within. Price, in particular, was convinced that many of the habits of improvement were little different from those of the despots Burke condemned, and he sought to restrict the picturesque accordingly.

29. In their Introduction, Stephen Copley and Peter Garside note that Kent's reputation as an agrarian "reformer" is now overshadowed by that of Arthur Young and William Marshall, even though Kent was more highly esteemed during the late eighteenth century. Kent specialized in designing the layout of estates, according to principles described in his *Hints to Gentlemen of Landed Property* (1775), and in drawing up leases, both of which made him a likely target for Knight's attack on those who were transforming the English landscape. "Introduction," *The Politics of the Picturesque,* ed. Stephen Copley and Peter Garside (Cambridge: Cambridge University Press, 1994), 14–17.

30. In "Nine Revisionist Theses on the Picturesque," *Representations* 38 (1992): 76–100, Kim Ian Michasiw reads Gilpin—correctly, I believe—as proposing an Enlightenment game—"a sequence of decomposings and recomposings that amuse according to an arbitrary set of rules" (94). One element of a game that transforms objects into images and gives them value within their own differential system, an element essential to the pleasure of the game, is that it leaves the landscape untouched; the thrill of the picturesque depends entirely on the inviolable otherness of nature, which allows the person without the means to own large tracts of land to possess the

landscape in images. By following picturesque procedures, such individuals simulated the kind of territorial marking that only a great landowner could actually perform upon the land. But what started out as a rational amusement tailored specifically for powerless tourists soon turned into something else, as a second generation transformed the rules of Gilpin's game into "a way of seeing" (94). As such, Michasiw contends, the picturesque aesthetic began to "function as a class marker and may have a determining force in the working relations between those class fragments embracing it and the land. This last possibility is particularly pronounced in the case of two sorts of picturesque adepts: those owning large tracts of land and those going off to claim or to rule larger tracts of other peoples' lands in the role of imperial agents" (94). Much as I agree with Michasiw's rethinking of the picturesque aesthetic, especially the importance he grants to the anti-elitist thrust of Gilpin's argument, I have to question his assumption that Gilpin was writing for the "lesser gentry, whose way of life was passing away in the last decades of the eighteenth century as surely as was that of the small freehold farmer." Indeed, I have tried to make clear that Gilpin's definition of the picturesque exists in ideological tension with the theories that preceded (e.g., Burke) and followed his (e.g., Knight and Price).

31. Bermingham, *Landscape and Ideology*, 72.

32. Jane Austen, *Northanger Abbey* (Harmondsworth: Penguin, 1986), 126.

33. We should keep in mind that this genre of painting was not available to the general public at the end of the eighteenth century and well into the nineteenth. Access to this iconography was therefore highly restricted until Victorian culture would make both these paintings available to a much larger slice of the population.

34. An American example might demonstrate how common it would become during the nineteenth century to think about language in economic terms and vice versa. Although we tend to remember Ralph Waldo Emerson for his organic metaphors for linguistic expression, his use of money is especially revealing: "When simplicity of character and the sovereignty of ideas is broken up by the prevalence of secondary desires . . . new imagery ceases to be created, and old words are perverted to stand for things which are not; a paper currency is employed when there is no bullion in the vaults." Under these circumstances, Emerson thought it was the poet's obligation to "pierce this rotten diction and fasten words again to visible things; so that picturesque language is . . . a commanding certificate, or fully underwritten currency." *The Selected Writing of Ralph Waldo Emerson*, ed. Brooks Atkinson (New York: Random House, 1992), 15–16.

35. Knight's solution to the problem created when the landscape as image had been detached from hereditary land corresponds semiotically to the shift from a gold to a paper standard, as Goux explains it: "Substituting a

paper banknote for hard gold implies that nominal value is isolated to the point of being autonomized as a sufficient quality for circulation. The token replaces the metallic medal only when the latter is reduced to the token function alone, when it is used solely with a view to exchange, for exchange, and in exchange, to the expulsion of all other possible functions; thus the token can credibly be assigned the role previously played by a medal." *The Coiners of Language,* 139.

36. J. C. Loudon, "Introduction," *The Landscape Gardening and Landscape Architecture of the Late Humphry Repton, Esq.* (London: Longman, 1840), v. All references to Loudon's "Introduction" are to this edition and are identified by page numbers in the text.

37. Humphry Repton, *Observations on the Theory and Practice of Landscape Gardening* (1803), ed. J. C. Loudon (London: Longman, 1840), 176–177. All references to Repton's *Observations on the Theory and Practice* are to this edition and are identifed by page numbers in the text.

38. Humphry Repton, *Sketches and Hints on Landscape Gardening* (1795), ed. J. C. Loudon (London: Longman, 1840), 108. Repton's *Enquiry into the Changes of Taste in Landscape Gardening* (London: J. Taylor, 1806) concludes with a letter he had written twelve years earlier to Uvedale Price, whose undisguised attack on the art of landscape gardening obliged Repton to "take up its defence" (140). In doing so, Repton sets his own taste apart from that shared by Price and Knight in a way that has obvious class connotations: "both Mr. Knight and you [Price] are in the habits of admiring fine pictures, and both live amidst bold and picturesque scenery: this may have rendered you insensitive to the milder scenes that have charms for common observers" (155).

39. Repton, *Sketches and Hints on Landscape Gardening,* 114.

40. David Worrall explains how the picturesque merged with a policy of turning useful land to "waste," fencing off large tracts of property that had traditionally been available to travelers, and appropriating common land, and he turns to Humphry Repton to sum up the political contradictions inscribed in the logic of the picturesque aesthetic by the second decade of the nineteenth century. "Agrarians against the Picturesque: ultra-radicalism and the revolutionary politics of land," *The Politics of the Picturesque: Literature, Landscape and Aesthetics since 1770,* ed. Stephen Copley and Peter Garside (Cambridge: Cambridge University Press, 1994), 249–250.

41. Repton's concern with interiors seems to increase with his age. In his last work, *Fragments on the Theory and Practice of Landscape Gardening,* ed. J. C. Loudon (London: Longman, 1840), originally published in 1816, we find chapters devoted to "Windows" and how they might enhance interior living and to "Interiors" which compare the "Ancient Cedar Parlour and Modern Living Room." All citations to Repton's *Fragments* are to this edition and are identified by page numbers in the text.

42. As described by Repton, this perspective on the landscaping bears clear affinities with what Mary Louise Pratt has termed "anti-conquest" strategies of colonialism, strategies of representation, in her words, "whereby European bourgeois subjects seek to secure their innocence in the same moment as they assert European hegemony . . . The main protagonist of the anti-conquest is a figure I sometimes call the 'seeing-man,' an admittedly unfriendly label for the European male subject of European landscape discourse—he whose imperial eyes passively look out and possess." *Imperial Eyes: Travel Writing and Transculturation* (New York: Routledge, 1992), 7.

43. W. J. T. Mitchell argues that landscape "doesn't merely signify or symbolize power relations; it is an instrument of cultural power, perhaps even an agent of power that is (or frequently represents itself as) independent of human intentions. Landscape as a cultural medium thus has a double role with respect to something like ideology: it naturalizes a cultural and social construction, representing an artificial world as if it were simply given and inevitable, and it also makes that representation operational by interpellating its beholder in some more or less determinate relation to its givenness as sight and site." "Introduction," *Landscape and Power*, 2–3. I would argue that the traditional country house lost its iconographic significance at this moment and began to operate as a specifically modern apparatus, one that insisted on the exemplary, reproducible quality of the image and the standard of taste it implied.

44. Leonore Davidoff and Catherine Hall argue convincingly that the Loudons' publications helped to shape the way a newly wealthy urban middle class lived their private lives. More important for my purposes is their claim that during the period when England was on the paper standard, owning a home and fathering a family that displayed economic success and fiscal responsibility was as good as money in the bank. Possession of the iconography described by the Loudons ensured these people credit, with the result that they emerged from three decades of economic turbulence in a position of unprecedented power. *Family Fortunes: Men and Women of the English Middle Class 1780–1850* (Chicago: University of Chicago Press, 1987). Ann Bermingham describes this transformation in art-historical terms in *Landscape and Ideology*, 147–174. See also F. M. L. Thompson, ed., *The Rise of Suburbia* (New York: St. Martin's, 1982).

45. According to Pierre Bourdieu, "symbolic capital" should "be understood as economic or political capital that is disavowed, mis-recognized and thereby recognized, hence legitimate, a 'credit' which, under certain conditions, and always in the long run, guarantees 'economic profits.' . . . In short, when the only usable capital is (mis)recognized, legitimate capital called 'prestige' or 'authority,' the economic capital that cultural undertakings generally require cannot secure the specific products produced by the field—nor the 'economic' profits they always imply—unless it is reconverted

into symbolic capital." "The Production of Belief: Contribution to an Economy of Symbolic Goods," trans. Richard Nice, *Media, Culture and Society* 2 (1980): 132. By "cultural capital," I mean much the same thing Bourdieu does by "symbolic capital." Given that I consider all forms of capital "symbolic," however, I prefer the term "cultural capital" for those sign systems into which money must be converted before it can create class distinctions.

46. Quoted in Davidoff and Hall, *Family Fortunes*, 189.

47. In "The Affirmative Character of Culture," Herbert Marcuse identifies a turning point in the history of capitalism when culture begins to offer a symbolic resolution to problems that cannot be resolved in material terms. For culture to be effective in this way, it must provide tangible, compensatory gratification: "If the individual is ever to come under the power of the ideal to the extent of believing that his concrete longings and needs are to be found in it—found moreover in a state of fulfillment and gratification, then the ideal must give the illusion of granting present satisfaction. It is this illusory reality that neither philosophy nor religion can attain. Only art achieves it—in the medium of beauty." *Negations* (Boston: Beacon Press, 1968), 119.

48. As Martin Price notes, disdain for the picturesque on precisely these grounds makes its way into the novel, especially those of George Eliot, where it was found to lack both accuracy in description and genuine emotion. "The Picturesque Moment," 282–286.

49. John Ruskin, "On the Turnerian Picturesque," *Modern Painters*, vol. IV (London: J. M. Dent, 1907), 1–14. All references to Ruskin's "Turnerian Picturesque" are to this edition and are identified by page numbers in the text.

50. Ruskin found England uniquely willing to embrace this presentism. Elsewhere in Europe, he claimed, "all is continuous; and the words, 'from generation to generation,' understandable there. Whereas here we have a living present, consisting merely of what is 'fashionable' and 'old-fashioned;' and a past, of which there are no vestiges; a past which peasant or citizen can no more conceive; all equally far away" (4). For a discussion of Ruskin on the picturesque, see George Landow, *Aesthetic and Critical Theories of John Ruskin* (Princeton: Princeton University Press, 1971).

51. Sir Arthur Conan Doyle, *Sherlock Homes: The Complete Novels and Stories, Vol. II* (New York: Bantam Books, 1986), 417–418.

52. Charles Dickens, *Hard Times* (New York: W. W. Norton, 1990), 9.

53. William Henry Fox Talbot, "A Brief Historical Sketch of the Invention of the Art," *Classic Essays on Photography*, ed. Alan Trachtenberg (New Haven: Leete's Island Books, 1980), 28.

54. Lady Elizabeth Eastlake, "Photography," *The Quarterly Review* 101 (1857): 459.

55. Ibid., 465.

1. Jonathan Crary, *Techniques of the Observer: Vision and Modernity in the Nineteenth Century* (Cambridge: MIT Press, 1990), 129.

2. Ibid., 67–96.

3. In "Unbinding Vision: Manet and the Attentive Observer in the Late Nineteenth Century," *Cinema and the Invention of Modern Life*, ed. Leo Charney and Vanessa R. Schwartz (Berkeley: University of California Press, 1995), Crary pursues the implications of his earlier study of "technologics of the observer": "Since Kant, of course, part of the epistemological dilemma of modernity has been about the human capacity for synthesis amid the fragmentation and atomization of a cognitive field. That dilemma became especially acute in the second half of the nineteenth century, along with the development of various techniques for imposing specific kinds of perceptual synthesis, from the mass diffusion of the stereoscope in the 1850s to early forms of cinema in the 1890s. Once the philosophical guarantees of any a priori cognitive unity collapsed, the problem of 'reality maintenance' became a function of a contingent and merely psychological faculty of synthesis, whose failure or malfunction was linked in the late nineteenth century with psychosis and other mental pathologies" (47–48).

4. In "The Age of the World Picture," Martin Heidegger contends that not every epoch in human history understands itself as a picture: "The world picture does not change from an earlier medieval one into a modern one, but rather the fact that the world becomes picture at all is what distinguishes the essence of the modern age" (130). He contends, further, that the fact that "the world becomes picture is one and the same event of man's becoming *subiectum* in the midst of that which is" (132). *The Question Concerning Technology and Other Essays*, trans. William Lovitt (New York: Harper Torchbacks, 1977).

5. M. Christine Boyer links a new interest in seeing both to a new interest in traveling and to the development and spread of lithographic technology: "Invented by Alois Senefelder in 1796, lithography was a quick and inexpensive method of printing, and by the 1820s its popularity had spread from Munich to England and France." *The City of Collective Memory: Its Historical and Architectural Entertainments* (Cambridge: MIT Press, 1994), 284. Patricia Anderson describes the pictorial world that *Penny Magazine* attempted to open up for working-class readers in 1832 as one that photography would substantiate during the period from the late 1850s to the end of the century: "elaborate diagrams of scientific and mechanical devices; artistically rendered pictures of foreign lands, plants, and animals; accurate representations of religious monuments and noteworthy ruins; detailed scenes of contemporary life and architecture; individualized portraits of famous peo-

ple; and well-executed illustrations of works of art." *The Printed Image and the Transformation of Popular Culture 1790–1860* (Oxford: Clarendon Press, 1991), 54. Beatrice Farwell reiterates this principle in her account of the explosion of popular imagery during the same period in France: "It was not only lithography whose subject matter found easy translation into photographs. Wood-engraved pictures in the news magazine were as likely to have been cut from photographs as from original drawings." *The Cult of Images: Baudelaire and the 19th-Century Media Explosion* (Santa Barbara: UCSB Art Museum, 1997), 12.

6. *Blackwood's Edinburgh Magazine* 51 (1842): 518.

7. *Living Age* 28, 352 (15 February 1851): 299.

8. Herbert Story-Moskelyne, "The Present State of Photography," *The National Review* 8 (April 1859): 379, 381–382.

9. Roy Flukinger, *The Formative Decades: Photography in Great Britain, 1839–1920* (Austin: University of Texas Press, 1985), 11.

10. Norman Bryson is among those to distinguish what he calls "the Glance" from "the Gaze," a term borrowed from Lacan and popularized by feminist film criticism: "Theoretical interest in the image, over the past few decades, has been largely preoccupied with the new order of the image represented by Photographs," he notes, "leaving the spectator of painting conspicuously untheorized." *Vision and Painting: The Logic of the Gaze* (New Haven: Yale University Press, 1983), 87. Bryson implies that this new work in film and especially photography allows him to refigure Western painting as a dialectic of the Glance, the production and consumption of visual information bound by the limits of embodiment in space and time, as opposed to the Gaze, which arrests and displaces the motion and productivity of the Glance. Because photography appears to be the principle of motion-productivity incarnate, we might be tempted to equate our relation to such images with the Glance. But if the Glance is what photography catches and freezes without any traces of the displacement of human eye by camera lens, then it is more accurate to say that the photograph collapses Glance and Gaze in a way that transforms the nature and social effect of both. In saying this, I am suggesting why I do not find "the Gaze" an especially useful theoretical category to engage where photography is concerned: the concept demands too rigidly binary an understanding of visual phenomena—as either masculine or feminine, either active or passive, either powerful or subjected, either subject or object—precisely where photography often collapses these differences. To this, let me add a second disclaimer. This book occasionally draws comparisons between painting and photography, but my remarks come exclusively from the perspective of a literary scholar interested in photography and attempt to show how the photograph transformed the traditional concept of portraiture to make it more compatible with literary realism.

11. Pierre Bourdieu uses the habit of taking photos on the most inti-

mate of all experiences, the honeymoon, to make this point: "The truly complete honeymoon is revealed by the couple [known as J.B. and his wife] photographed in front of the Eiffel Tower, because Paris is the Eiffel Tower, and because the true honeymoon is the honeymoon in Paris. One of the pictures in J.B.'s collection is bisected by the Eiffel Tower; at the bottom is J.B.'s wife. What seems to us an act of barbarism or barbarity is actually the perfect fulfillment of an intention: the two objects designed to solemnize one another are placed right in the centre of the photograph, as centring and frontality are the most decisive ways of stressing the value of the object captured in this way. As a result, the photograph becomes a sort of ideogram or allegory, as individual and circumstantial traits take second place." *Photography: A Middle-brow Art*, trans. Shaun Whiteside (Stanford: Stanford University Press, 1990), 36.

12. John Tagg, for example, argues that "the meaning and value of photographic practice could not be adjudicated outside specific, historical language games. Photography is neither a unique technology nor an autonomous semiotic system." "The Discontinuous City: Picturing and the Discursive Field," *Strategies* 3 (1990): 147. Indeed, on the assumption that photography's enormous popularity was a symptom of the will to dominate, most scholarship neglects to ask why certain images had so much appeal, why indeed those in domination took more pictures of themselves than of anybody else.

13. Bourdieu, *Photography*, 15.

14. Timothy Mitchell, "Orientalism and the Exhibitionary Order," *Colonialism and Culture*, ed. Nicholas B. Dirks (Ann Arbor: University of Michigan Press, 1992), 289–317. Quotations from this work are identified by page numbers in the text.

15. Of a later development, the "World's Fair," Boyer observes that "these exhibitions actually became simulated travelogues, guidebooks to the world of exotic places and encyclopedias of appropriated treasures. Every site became the focal point of other places, every location was the start of a series of possible routes passing through other nations. Traveling across the fairgrounds was literally a panoramic shot of goods and places, constantly provoking a dilemma of how to link one fragmented scene to the next." *The City of Collective Memory*, 259.

16. Gérard de Nerval, *Oeuvres*, 1: 883, quoted in Mitchell, "Orientalism and the Exhibitionary Order," 311.

17. Bourdieu explains the relationship between the hegemony of middle-class family life and the sheer amount of domestic photography, almost from the beginning of its public availability, but especially after successive inventions brought technology for making faster, simpler, and cheaper images: "As the need to take photographs is usually only a need for photographs, it is understandable that all the factors which determine an inten-

sification of domestic life and a reinforcement of family ties should encourage the appearance and intensification of photographic practice: the practice decreases with age because of a decline in involvement in social life and particularly in the life of the scattered family, which does away with the reasons for taking photographs." *Photography*, 25.

18. As Bourdieu observes, "just as the peasant is expressing his relationship with urban life when he rejects the practice of photography, . . . the meaning which *petits bourgeois* confer on photographic practice conveys or betrays the relationship of the *petite bourgeoisie* to culture, that is, to the upper classes (bourgeoisie) . . . and to the working classes from whom they wish to distinguish themselves." *Photography*, 9.

19. Lennard Davis argues that novelistic descriptions of place had a similar impact on readers. People did not consider the slums an integral part of their reality, much less find them interesting, prior to the detailed description of such places in the fiction of Balzac and Dickens, which subsequently, according to Davis, "took on a relative life of its own." *Resisting Novels: Ideology and Fiction* (New York: Methuen, 1987), 89–91.

20. Henri Lefebvre, *The Production of Space*, trans. Donald Smith (Cambridge: Blackwell, 1991), 73.

21. David Harvey, *The Urban Experience* (Baltimore: Johns Hopkins University Press, 1989), 33.

22. Charles Dickens, "Busy with the Photograph," *Household Words* (22 June 1854): 243. A statement from *The National Review* (April 1859) goes more directly to the point: "It is no rare phrase that characterises the exciting age on which our lives are thrown as the age of the electric telegraph and of photography . . . Each of these great practical triumphs of a scientific age has sprung into existence and fructified and covered the world with its results during a period so short, that the hair of the very men who introduced them is not yet gray." "The Present State of Photography," 365.

23. Boyer, *The City of Collective Memory*, 253.

24. Eve Blau, "Patterns of Fact: Photography and the Transformation of the Early Industrial City," *Architecture and Its Image: Four Centuries of Architectural Representation*, ed. Eve Blau and Edward Kaufman (Montreal: Centre Canadien d'Architecture, 1989), 44.

25. Malcolm Andrews, "The Metropolitan Picturesque," *The Politics of the Picturesque: Literature, Landscape and Aesthetics since 1770*, ed. Stephen Copley and Peter Garside (Cambridge: Cambridge University Press, 1994), 285.

26. Quoted in Andrews, "The Metropolitan Picturesque," 284.

27. In her analysis of Manila's new metropolitan form, Neferti Xina M. Tadier argues that in undergoing modernization, "the state understands traffic as it understands the economy—as a system of practices upon the efficiency of which the nation's development depends." It is true that "the

liberalized flow or 'drive' [of traffic] allows one who is afforded the privilege of overseeing the city to occupy a self removed from face-to-face confrontations with its social contradictions, which are heightened in congested moments." But, Tadier observes, the "desire articulated by this new metropolitan form . . . does not emanate from a subject outside that articulation; rather, the articulation itself helps to produce the effect of subjectivity," which she describes as "a self that can transcend the human mass." "Manila's New Metropolitan Form," *differences* 3 (1993): 162–164.

28. See Mitchell, "Orientalism and the Exhibitionary Order," 305.

29. Tom Gunning, "Tracing the Individual Body: Photography, Detectives, and Early Cinema," *Cinema and the Invention of Modern Life*, 16.

30. In contrast with the photography of such early reformers as John Thomson and Paul Martin, as well as the later work of Jacob Riis, Blau observes that "Annan's shows no direct engagement with the inhabitants he is documenting. The reformers and photographers of street life went into the slums in search of their inhabitants—to discover and record how and where they lived. For Annan the subject was the *place* itself, not its denizens, except insofar as they were a visible part of the reality of that place." "Patterns of Fact," 49.

31. Griselda Pollock has argued convincingly that these illustrations collaborated with photography to turn the misery and squalor of the East End into suitable objects of touristic pleasure: "While the Parisian bourgeoisie took up residence in the new apartment blocks of Haussmanized Paris and hung pictures of rural and semi-rural France on their walls, the English middle classes fashioned an ideological 'country' in which to live. *London: A Pilgrimage* proffered a particular kind of urbanism for their consumption, a picturesque text with a romantic, Gothic visualization." "Vicarious Excitements: *London: A Pilgrimage* by Gustave Doré and Blanchard Jerrold, 1872," *New Formations* 4 (1988): 47.

32. To show how photography differed from fiction and illustration by emptying some of the most populated sections of Glasgow, Ellen Handy compares Annan's images with Dickens's descriptions of the slums in *Our Mutual Friend*, noting not only the techniques by which the photographer depopulated the old city, but also his method of sanitizing the same sites that Dickens heaped with refuse and covered with unwholesome moisture. "Dust Piles and Damp Pavements: Excrement, Repression, and the Victorian City in Photography and Literature," *Victorian Literature and the Pictorial Imagination*, ed. Carol T. Christ and John O. Jordan (Berkeley: University of California Press, 1996), 122.

33. Given the bluntly documentary purpose of his 1868 volume of thirteen images titled simply *Photographs of Glasgow*, it is rather ironic that Annan's photographs were recast in a nostalgic format in 1878, when public demand following an exhibition led the Glasgow City Improvement Trust to

publish forty carbon prints under the title of *Photographs of Old Closes, Streets, etc. of Glasgow taken 1868–1877*. In the photogravure edition of Annan's Glasgow photos, published in 1900, thirteen years after his death, Blau tells us, "the subversion of the sense of the original set was carried further . . . Only twenty-eight of these had been in the original set, and some of them had been retouched to remove blurs and other imperfections, so that it had little left of the original survey" by the time certain images were excerpted from the collection and valued for their intrinsic aesthetic qualities. "Patterns of Fact," 49–50.

34. See Gerhard Joseph's discussion of blurring and transparency in "The Sharp and the Blurred," *Tennyson and the Text: The Weaver's Shuttle* (Cambridge: Cambridge University Press, 1992).

35. Tom Gunning, "Phantom Images and Modern Manifestations: Spirit Photography, Magic Theater, Trick Films and Photography's Uncanny," *Fugitive Images: From Photography to Video,* ed. Patrice Petro (Bloomington: Indiana University Press, 1995), 42–71. For a full scholarly account of nineteenth-century spiritualism and the authority women acquired as mediums, see Alex Owen, *The Darkened Room: Women, Power and Spiritualism in Late Nineteenth-Century England* (London: Virago, 1989).

36. William Gilpin, *Three Essays: On Picturesque Beauty; on Picturesque Travel; on Sketching Landscape,* second edition (London, 1794), 20.

37. Ibid., 28.

38. *Westminster Review* 6 (October 1854): 604–608.

39. Andrews, "The Metropolitan Picturesque," 285.

40. At the bottom of the social ladder, beneath "nomads," as Boyer explains, quoting Mayhew, "were the 'crawlers': mostly old women 'reduced by vice and poverty to that degree of wretchedness which destroys even the energy to beg,' becoming in the end so lethargic that death would be a better condition." *The City of Collective Memory,* 288.

41. There are inevitably two positions on the question of reform, and Thomson's oeuvre is no exception. Arguing against the position established by Stephen White's biography of Thomson, Richard Stein recasts Thomson's concern for the individuality of street people in terms compatible with my own view: "In Thomson's London all the figures become 'examples' of something, 'true types' as in Mayhew: the very formality of the photographic iconography suggests that to respond to them requires some larger set of generalizations . . . In this sense, our apparent proximity to the poor in early documentary photography simultaneously involves a new technique of distance—and a new technique of distancing related to, but not wholly derived from, the technological possibilities of the medium itself." "Street Figures: Victorian Urban Iconography," 249–250.

42. Boyer observes that while "London itself blended in an excessive manner realistic and fantastic imagery," the city "was especially susceptible to

Gothic representation." It "had an utterly confused town plan, more like a collection of small town and desperate slums rather than a unified whole. Even Regent Street, the only London passage of any architectural pretension, was pieced together in sections more reminiscent of a crooked stovepipe than a magnificent boulevard of pleasure. The English Gothic Revival, however, turned this shady obscure London with its grotesque shadows and indefinite forms into an advantage, finding its ugliness a moment of the sublime." *The City of Collective Memory*, 279–280.

43. Andrews, "The Metropolitan Picturesque," 287.

44. A public who felt its own worth could be represented in its surroundings, clothes, and possessions was understandably suspicious about this capacity for recontextualization. The anonymous author of an essay entitled "Photographic Portraiture" complains about the ability of photographs to let Mrs. Jones "stand in that park-like pleasure-ground, when we know that her belongings and surroundings don't warrant more than a little back-garden big enough to grow a few crocuses," while "Her majesty [is] to be seen in the shop windows, in which she is so posed that a tuft of verdure in the background appears to form a head-dress such as the Red Indians wear." "Photographic Portraiture," *Once a Week* 8 (31 January 1863): 149.

45. Dickens, "Busy with the Photograph," 243.

46. John Thomson, *China and Its People in Early Photographs: An Unabridged Reprint of the Classic 1873/4 Work* (New York: Dover, 1985), vol. I, Plate IX.

47. Investigating Hannah Cullwick's contribution as a model to the images that made A. J. Munby, her friend and eventually husband, notorious, Carol Mavor describes Hannah's sensitivity to the racial implications of the soot that coated her body as a charwoman: "When she was a lady, she painted herself white: whitening her dark, reddened hands with smart white gloves and, most certainly, dusting her face not with soot, but with the 'Ophelia powders' so popular then." *Pleasures Taken: Performances of Sexuality and Loss in Victorian Photographs* (Durham, N.C.: Duke University Press, 1995), 95.

48. Tagg, "The Discontinuous City," 140.

49. Eastlake, "Photography," 459–460.

50. "Photography: Its History and Application," 210.

51. Mavor argues persuasively that if, by manipulating Hannah's image, Munby took pleasure in transforming her body and the spaces she could therefore occupy, then Hannah found gratification in their curious collaboration too. According to Mavor, "She made invisibility into an art. She wore her thirteen-and-one-half-inch biceps as proudly as she wore her dirt. Her dirt, her masculine stride, her lack of womanly manners enabled her to go through the streets of the city freely, without the usual constraints placed upon the Victorian lady." *Pleasures Taken*, 73.

52. Joseph, *Tennyson*, 78.

53. It could be argued that Cameron's portraits, in striving to be art-quality images, were to their subjects what Gainsborough's portraits had been to the ruling elite during the previous century. For a description of the extraordinary recognition Cameron received as a portrait artist, despite consistent criticism of her technical mastery of photography, see Pam Roberts, "Julia Margaret Cameron: A Triumph over Criticism," *The Portrait in Photography*, ed. Graham Clarke (London: Reaktion Books, 1992), 47–70.

54. In 1860, Victoria became the first British sovereign to permit photographs of herself to go on sale to the general public. Margaret Homans offers the most complete and sophisticated discussion of how photographs of the Royal family, despite the superiority of the Queen's position to that of her Consort, struggled to observe the same conventions on which Cameron based her aesthetics. See both "To the Queen's Private Apartments: Royal Family Portraiture and the Construction of Victoria's Sovereign Obedience," *Victorian Studies* 37 (1993): 1–41, and "Victoria's Sovereign Obedience: Portraits of the Queen as Wife and Mother," *Victorian Literature and the Pictorial Imagination*, ed. Carol T. Christ and John O. Jourdan (Berkeley: University of California Press, 1995). For a discussion of how Victoria reversed Cameron's aesthetics in posthumous representations of Albert and herself as his widow, see my "Monarchy in the Age of Mechanical Reproduction," forthcoming in a special issue of *Nineteenth-Century Contexts* devoted to Victorian photography and edited by Richard Stein.

55. *Living Age* 92 (1867): 208.

56. Bryan Lukacher, "Powers of Sight: Robinson, Emerson, and the Polemics of Pictorial Photography," *Pictorial Effect/Naturalistic Vision*, 39.

57. "Photography," *The Quarterly Review* 443.

58. "Photography: Its History and Applications," *Living Age* 92 (1867): 217.

59. See, for example, *Metropolis London: Histories and Representations since 1800*, ed. David Feldman and Gareth Stedman Jones (London: Routledge, 1989); Gavin Weightman and Steve Humphries, *The Making of Modern London 1815–1914* (London: Sidgwick & Jackson, 1983); *The Victorian City: Images and Realities*, Volumes I, II, ed. H. J. Dyos and Michael Wolff (London: Routledge and Kegan Paul, 1978); Anthony S. Wohl, *The Eternal Slum: Housing and Social Policy in Victorian London* (Montreal: McGill-Queen's University Press, 1977).

60. Pierre Bourdieu argues that domestic photography does not preserve a structure of feeling so much as provide a basis for that feeling; as the only group that would prove capable of preserving its identity in modern urban society, the bourgeois family could be said to exist by virtue of verbal and visual images that produce the feelings necessary for the unit's survival. *Photography*, 28.

61. It is worth noting, in this regard, how Henry Peach Robinson's instructions to would-be portrait photographers aestheticize the individual body: "A single figure should be complete in itself; it should not appear as though it had been cut out of a group, and it should be incapable of having another figure added to it without injury. The head being the chief object, every line should be composed in relation to it, and the student will find the rules of pyramidal composition invaluable to him here. He must consider contrast of lines and balance, variety, repose, and, above all, unity and simplicity." *Pictorial Effect in Photography* (London: Pip & Carter, 1869; rpt. Pawlet, Vt.: Helios, 1969), 90.

62. "Photography: Its History and Applications," 218.

63. Dickens, "Busy with the Photograph," 245.

64. Karl Marx, *Capital*, vol. I, trans. Ben Fowkes (New York: Random House, 1977), 165, 167. All citations to Marx's *Capital* are to this edition and are identified by page numbers in the text. Dickens, like Marx, uses the language of necromancy to talk about photography and devices associated with it. He begins an essay on the stereoscope by claiming "there is a good deal of romance to be found even in the details of pure science," and by asserting that some of these devices produce effects belonging "wholly to the days of sorcery." "The Stereoscope," *Household Words* (3 September 1853): 37, 42.

65. Elizabeth Deeds Ermarth, *Realism and Consensus in the English Novel* (Princeton: Princeton University Press, 1983), 34.

3 FOUNDATIONAL PHOTOGRAPHS

1. Lady Elizabeth Eastlake, "Physiognomy," *Quarterly Review* 90 (December 1851): 62.

2. Nicholas Dames has convincingly argued the case that what appears so abnormal about Lucy Snowe is her appropriation of phrenology for the language of love. Insofar as phrenology is founded on experiment and convinces by induction, it is an unlikely vehicle for the most intimate and nuanced feelings. Yet, as Dames explains, "phrenological exchanges . . . create what they find, and what they preeminently create in this novel is desire." "The Clinical Novel: Phrenology and *Villette*," *Novel* 29 (1996): 385.

3. Mary Cowling, *The Artist as Anthropologist: The Representation of Type and Character in Victorian Art* (Cambridge: Cambridge University Press, 1989), 34.

4. To make photographic images yield a type, Francis Galton, for example, had to superimpose many photographic images on a single negative. The result, he argued, was not a fabrication but the same kind of proof that resulted from statistical computations: "Composite pictures, are . . . much more than averages; they are rather the equivalents of those large statistical

tables whose totals, divided by the number of cases, and entered in the bottom line, are the averages. They are real generalizations, because they include the whole of the material under consideration. The blur of their outlines, which is never great in truly generic composites, except in unimportant details, measure the tendency of individuals to deviate from the central type." "On Generic Images," *Proceedings of the Royal Institution*, vol. 9 (1879), 166.

5. In *The Imaginary Puritan* (Berkeley: University of California Press, 1992), 114–117, Leonard Tennenhouse and I make much the same argument about the so-called print revolution in England. If print exploded after 1796, we contend, the cause was not parliament's failure to renew the Licensing Act of 1692. On the contrary, in order for so many English men and women to put their words in print after 1796, they had to think of themselves as sources of language and desire that could be put into writing and then broadly distributed. Indeed, England had enjoyed a cultural climate where literate people could think in these terms during the 1640s and 1650s, when abolishment of the star chamber made it impossible to enforce censorship regulations.

6. Elizabeth Anne McCauley, *A. A. E. Disdéri and the Carte de Visite Portrait Photograph* (New Haven: Yale University Press, 1985), 42–45.

7. Ibid., 35.

8. William C. Darrah, *Cartes de Visite in Nineteenth Century Photography* (Gettysburg, Pa.: W. C. Darrah, 1981), 4.

9. Frances Dimond, "Preface," *Crown and Camera: The Royal Family and Photography 1842–1910*, ed. Frances Dimond and Roger Taylor (Harmondsworth: Penguin, 1987), 8.

10. Margaret Homans provides a helpful summary of Victoria's manipulation of family photography: "Paradoxically, she holds her sovereignty because of the popularity she accrues by appearing as an ordinary wife . . . If she wanted to promote a worldview in which the middle-class wife's subordination underwrites middle-class supremacy, she became both the agent and the product of her own ideological designs." "Victoria's Sovereign Obedience: Portraits of the Queen as Wife and Mother," *Victorian Literature and the Victorian Pictorial Imagination*, ed. Carol T. Christ and John O. Jordan (Berkeley: University of California Press, 1995), 182. Thomas Richards characterizes the relationship between the image and the commercial culture of the high Victorian period in these terms: "The image of Victoria incarnated relations among things by imposing on them a sentimental typology that simultaneously summoned up two complementary consumer worlds, the material world of the Victorian court and the ethereal world of the beyond (in sentimental culture, a luxurious and well-stocked afterlife had already become a model for the easy-street daydreams of commodity culture)." *The*

Commodity Culture of Victorian England: Advertising and Spectacle 1851–1914
(Stanford: Stanford University Press, 1990), 104.

11. "Photographic Portraiture," *Once a Week* 8 (13 January 1863): 148.

12. A. Wyntar, *"Cartes de Visite," Living Age* 72 (January-March 1862): 673.

13. The Victorian habit of photographing the dead is now well known. Compelling this practice was the historically unprecedented belief, on the part of a group capable of taking and preserving an image directly from the body, that the image was part of that individual, a remnant of its uniqueness, and testimony that the person had been there, thus a kind of place-saver. A statement from 1868 suggests as much: "It happens too often that death leaves no remembrance of parent or child, friend or lover, except a portrait that, in so many cases, becomes of priceless worth, and the reflection must give pain to many that even this will pass away." "The Future of Photography," *Living Age* 99 (October-December 1868): 821. For another instance of photographs standing in for the thing itself, see Allan Sekula on the early use of photographs to identify criminals, "The Body and the Archive," *October* 39 (1986): 3–64.

14. In her informative study of the visual culture available to members of the working classes, Patricia Anderson pinpoints 1832 as an important turning point: "A new illustrated publication, the *Penny Magazine*, would enter the market and offer people the choice of an unprecedented variety of printed imagery." Anderson credits this publication with beginning to diminish the "vast difference between the pictorial world of the English worker and the crowded walls of an Academy exhibition." It can hardly be coincidental that the categories of the world that *cartes de visite* would visualize for the middle-class readership would resemble those that *Penny Magazine* had opened up for a whole new class of observers: "elaborate diagrams of scientific and mechanical devices; artistically rendered pictures of foreign lands, plants, and animals; accurate representations of religious monuments and noteworthy ruins; detailed scenes of contemporary life and architecture; individualized portraits of famous people; and well-executed illustrations of works of art." *The Printed Image and the Transformation of Popular Culture 1790–1860* (Oxford: Clarendon Press, 1991), 49, 54.

15. Stephen Bann identifies a moment in the history of painting where photography intrudes: "in each case, it is the excess of unknowable physiognomy over the signs of status, the self-manifestation of a body refusing to be read, that constitutes the special effect of authenticity." "Erased Physiognomy: Théodore Géricault, Paul Strand and Gary Winogrand," *The Portrait in Photography*, ed. Graham Clarke (London: Reaktion Books, 1992), 45. Authenticity is something we tend to locate either in the early photography of Adams and Hill or in such modernists as Strand and Winogrand. I would

suggest, however, that we see some of this excess even in the most conventional studio photography, that an implicit argument between specific subject matter and the generic protocols of popular photography never fails to make that subject matter present, if only momentarily.

16. See Joan Scott, "Experience," *Feminists Theorize the Political,* ed. Judith Butler and Joan W. Scott (New York: Routledge, 1992). Scott points out that an experience tends to be described as something an individual sees. There is, she argues, a problem with accounts that offer such visual evidence: "The project of making experience visible precludes analysis of the workings of the [ideological] system and of its historicity; instead it reproduces" the terms of that system (25).

17. Ronald R. Thomas points out that 1851, the year before *Bleak House* went into publication, opened a new era in the technology of photography, with the invention of the collodion, or wet-plate process, that "moved photography solidly into the commercial world, as innumerable high-quality prints could now be made from a single negative." This innovation, Thomas contends, allowed "mass-produced portraiture [to become] popular among the middle classes, widely distributed to friends, avidly collected, and proudly displayed in family albums as substitutes for the more costly oil portrait, commissioned only by the wealthiest and most fashionable families." "Making Darkness Visible: Capturing the Criminal and Observing the Law in Victorian Photography and Detective Fiction," *Victorian Literature and the Victorian Imagination,* ed. Carol T. Christ and John O. Jourdan (Berkeley: University of California Press, 1995), 138.

18. Charles Dickens, *Oliver Twist* (Oxford: Clarendon Press, 1966), 70. All citations are to this edition and are identified by page numbers in the text.

19. Despite his insistence on Monks's acuity as a physiognomist, Michael Hollington observes that the stepbrother's recognition of Oliver is not based on the visible features of his face at all. It is "no doubt through some innate affinity of blood but also perhaps because of his inverted religiosity" that Monks is so good at spotting Oliver: "'If a crowd of devils were to put themselves into his exact shape, and he stood amongst them, there is something that would tell me how to point him out'" is Monks's response to Fagin when "he asks him whether he's sure it's Oliver." "Dickens and Cruikshank as Physiognomers in *Oliver Twist,*" *Dickens Quarterly* 8 (1990): 250.

20. Or, as Garrett Stewart argues, "before the advent of photography, a 'person' may have felt her 'essence' to be indistinguishable from her living image without being separable from it. Photography widened this difference to a rift." "Reading Figures: The Legible Image of Victorian Textuality," *Victorian Literature and the Victorian Visual Imagination,* 349.

21. Lindsay Smith demonstrates that this change did not occur within

fiction alone but across the literature of the period. The poetry and theory of Ruskin, Morris, and the Pre-Raphaelites work within the same problematic as "photographic realism": "the camera came to intrude, in diverse ways, into a variety of nineteenth-century discourses. Not only does its novel presence transform acts of looking, most obviously calling into question the concept of a faithful transcription by the artist of the external world, but its transformation of methods of reproduction affects major social, aesthetic, philosophical, and metaphysical categories and interrelationships." *Victorian Photography, Painting, and Poetry* (Cambridge: Cambridge University Press, 1995), 3.

22. J. Hillis Miller and David Borowitz, *Charles Dickens and George Cruikshank* (Los Angeles: William Andrews Clark Memorial Library, 1971), 45.

23. Ibid.

24. Michael Steig, *Dickens and Phiz* (Bloomington: Indiana University Press, 1978), 10. All citations to Steig are to this edition and are identified by page numbers in the text.

25. Q. D. Leavis, "The Dickens Illustrations: Their Function," F. R. and Q. D. Leavis, *Dickens the Novelist* (London: Chatto and Windus, 1970), 344.

26. Charles Dickens, *Bleak House,* ed. George Ford and Sylvère Monod (New York: W. W. Norton, 1977), 5. All citations to *Bleak House* are to this edition and are identified by page numbers in the text.

27. As D. A. Miller explains, "The hermeneutic problem put to characters by the discrepancy between outside and inside (such that the former can never be counted on to represent the latter, which it is rather constituted to disguise) is never a problem for us, for whom the outside, riven with expressive vents, quite adequately designates the nature of the subject it thus fails to conceal." *The Novel and the Police* (Berkeley: University of California Press, 1988), 206.

28. Henry Peach Robinson, *The Pictorial Effect in Photography* (London, 1869; rpt. Pawlet, Vt.: Helios, 1971), 192.

29. Ibid., 198. Robinson is emphatic about maintaining the traditional mimetic relationship between photographic image and natural object. In ruling out trick photography, we should note, he does not insist on a one-to-one relationship between image and object, only that the image be true to nature: "The photographer must not let his invention tempt him to represent, by any trick, any scene that does not occur in nature; if he does, he does violence to his art, because it is known that his finished result represents some object or thing that has existed for a space of time before his camera" (78).

30. Quoted in Thomas, "Making Darkness Visible," 155.

31. "By mid-century," according to Anthony Wohl, "Victorian England was in danger of becoming submerged in a huge dung heap of its own

making." *Endangered Lives: Public Health in Victorian Britain* (London: J.M. Dent, 1983), 86. Reinforcing the spatial division of London according to class, the poor were far more likely to be submerged in this way than the well-do-do.

32. To understand the cultural logic of this final transformation, we might think of the exposure of Lady Dedlock's dead face as a middlebrow equivalent of the high-culture transformation undergone by the Lady of Shalott. According to Kathy Alexis Psomiades' insightful reading of that moment in Tennyson's poetry, "by moving from private to public, the Lady changes her nature. Leaving the ruined castle to sail down to Camelot, she no longer produces but *is* art . . . Lancelot's comment refers only to her body: 'She has a lovely face.' . . . Once disembodied, she is now all body; once all subject, she is now all object; and with her last moments of subjectivity, she stages herself as art." *Beauty's Body: Femininity and Representation in British Aestheticism* (Stanford: Stanford University Press, 1997), 26.

33. Jacques Lacan, "Seminar on 'The Purloined Letter,'" *Yale French Studies* 48 (1972): 55.

34. Ibid., 60.

35. See D. A. Miller, *The Novel and the Police*, 60–63.

36. Ronald Thomas, "Making Darkness Visible," 140.

37. Robinson is especially sensitive to the double imperative involved in taking a good portrait. Sitters, he contends, should not be allowed to select the poses they want their own to emulate. "Besides being of very little use, there is also actual harm in a 'set' of poses the structure of which is not understood, as will be seen if a sitter is allowed to select the position in which he will be taken." At the same time, he insists, each person is best captured photographically when "arranged with great taste and judgment," by which he means according to their type: "Sailors, coastguards, children, or the more prim-looking visitors, all look what they are." *Pictorial Effect in Photography*, 52, 84.

38. According to the editors of the Norton Critical Edition, the manuscript of *Bleak House* "shares the usual characteristics of most of Dickens's manuscripts, though it is in some respects worse—i.e., harder to read than many of them. Its pages are often crowded, and there are numerous deletions, corrections, and insertions throughout." "Textual History," *Bleak House*, 803.

39. In contending that Esther takes over for Lady Dedlock as the heroine of *Bleak House*, I in no way mean to imply that Esther is actually more of "a person" with any more of a stable identity than her predecessor. Except for the importance of the image, Cynthia Northcutt Malone makes much the same argument concerning Esther's identity that I have made concerning her mother's, suggesting that the shift from Lady Dedlock to Esther is

simply one more in the succession of displacements that constitute the former's identity. "'Flight' and 'Pursuit': Fugitive Identity in *Bleak House*," *Dickens Studies Annual* 19 (1990): 107–124.

40. Oscar Wilde, *The Picture of Dorian Gray* (London: Penguin, 1949), 39. All references to *The Picture of Dorian Gray* are to this edition and are identified by page numbers in the text.

41. Chris Jenks argues that the *flâneur* offers an alternative and inherently critical view of modernity that "uncovers compulsive currents within the city along with unprescribed boundaries of exclusion and unconstructed gateways of opportunity." "Watching Your Step: The History and Practice of the *Flâneur*," *Visual Culture*, ed. Chris Jenks (New York: Routledge, 1995), 154. The remapping of the city that results from this wandering viewpoint necessarily contradicts a system that locates visually identifiable types in specific social spaces.

42. Pondering the relationship between Dorian's portrait and the photographic image, Garrett Stewart concludes that "what is left behind by this objectification of the body by the camera's *objectif* (lens) is precisely *subjectivity*. This seems to be . . . Wilde's point. The visible rot of Dorian's picture, as instantaneous in its increments as if it were itself photographically recorded stage by stage, is in fact based on no visible origin or model. What it (re)presents exists only somewhere invisibly, in him who reads it." "Reading Figures," 350. The idea that ugliness exists in the eye of the beholder fudges the question of where these images come from, I believe, and why the beholder, in this case Basil Hallward, sees the portrait both before and after its degeneration in the same terms that Dorian and presumably the reader do as well. Having made this observation, in other words, Stewart still needs to explain why subjectivity takes the form of certain body images.

43. Max Nordau, *Degeneration* (Lincoln: University of Nebraska Press, 1968), 9.

44. Ibid. Given his insistence that individuals should conform to their types, or at least not play around with the integrity thereof, it makes perfect sense that Nordau should have dedicated his massive study of the degeneration of types "to Caesar Lombroso, Professor of Psychiatry and Forensic Medicine at the Royal University of Turin." Lombroso is known today for having used photographs to demonstrate that prostitutes and other criminal groups conformed to certain physical types, which of course they didn't.

45. Ed Cohen describes Wilde's trial in terms that confirm my position. Despite Wilde's efforts to distinguish himself from the type of "the sodomite" by insisting on his status both as an artist and as his own work of art, early on popular journalism apparently won the struggle to determine who Wilde was: "The images of the two men [i.e., the Marquis of Queensberry and Oscar Wilde] provide a studied contrast, almost as if they represented

the 'do' and 'don't' panels in a Victorian etiquette book. This tableau, in turn, became a set piece in the descriptions of the trials so that, for example, when the *Star* reported the opening of the second day of the trial, it reiterated these postures exactly." *Talk on the Wilde Side: Toward a Genealogy of a Discourse on Male Sexualities* (London: Routledge, 1993), 141.

46. Regina Gagnier describes Wilde's awareness of advertising and the market in images and how he used the type of the dandy to challenge the prevailing type of the middle-class man. Her account also explains why the public reacted with such hostility to Dorian Gray: "Like Baudelaire's 'Woman,' the British dandy wears the mask . . . as self-advertisement," using "artifice to 'produce' something more uncommon than the debased productions of industrial labor and inherited wealth. Although Balzac, Barbey, and Baudelaire explicitly pose the dandy as liberator, as the new source of human superiority, implicit in their essays is a more chilling framework for the dandy: having discerned the commercialism of his society, he offers himself as a product, he sells his aura." *Idylls of the Marketplace: Oscar Wilde and the Victorian Public* (Stanford: Stanford University Press, 1986), 82. As a novelist, Wilde demonstrates a full understanding of the dual potential of the dandy type and the likelihood that the negative image would dominate public opinion. This could be why he saw himself, as he claimed, neither as Dorian nor as Lord Henry, but as the painter Basil Hallward, done in by his own image-making.

4 RACE IN THE AGE OF REALISM

1. In *The Industrial Reformation of English Fiction: Social Discourse and Narrative Form, 1832–1867* (Chicago: University of Chicago Press, 1985), 149, for example, Catherine Gallagher contends that the industrial novels of the 1850s "focus attention on one of the genre's most problematic *données*. In *Hard Times* and *North and South* . . . Dickens and Gaskell explore the very foundations of their art, exposing its structural inconsistencies. In fact, both of these realistic novels become, as we will see, reflections on their narrative methods."

2. In an essay entitled "Reportage or Portrayal," Georg Lukács distinguishes between "genuine reportage," which "permits a lively, effective and penetrating depiction of a section of reality, even without any insight into the overall process and its interconnections," and a fetishistic concern with details, which "conceives a social product as ready-made and final." *Essays on Realism*, ed. Rodney Livingstone, trans. David Fernbach (Cambridge: MIT Press, 1980), 54–55. While Lukács would reserve the term *realism* for the kind of fiction that relies on the first kind of description, it is more usual to find both reportage and portrayal included under the rubric of realism.

3. In *Framing the Victorians: Photography and the Culture of Realism* (Ithaca: Cornell University Press, 1996), 20, Jennifer Green-Lewis contends what I also hold to be true: "The most urgent philosophical and literary debates of the nineteenth century have traditionally been polarized by the dichotomies of logical positivism and metaphysical idealism, realism and antirealism (or romance). Despite their differences, proponents on either side were drawn to photography as symbol of insufficiency of empiricism's account of reality or, conversely, as proof of the totality of its vision."

4. Michel Foucault, *Discipline and Punish: The Birth of the Prison,* trans. Alan Sheridan (New York: Vintage, 1979).

5. Michel Foucault, *The History of Sexuality: An Introduction,* trans. Robert Hurley (New York: Pantheon, 1978).

6. See the Introduction, pp. 24–26.

7. Patrick Brantlinger attributes the number of gothic novels to something like this sense of anxiety: "Although the connections between imperialism and other aspects of late Victorian and Edwardian culture are innumerable, the link with occultism is especially symptomatic of the anxieties that attended the climax of the British Empire." *Rule of Darkness: British Literature and Imperialism, 1830–1914* (Ithaca: Cornell University Press, 1988), 227–228.

8. In discussing the difficulty of distinguishing "magic realism" from "fantastic literature," Fredric Jameson makes a point that I have pursued in this chapter with exclusively English materials. What "is at issue in both cases," he insists, "is a certain type of narrative or representation to be distinguished from 'realism.'" Those who see magic realism as the authentically Latin American counterpart of European surrealism emphasize "not so much a fantastic narrative . . . as a metamorphosis in perception and in things perceived." "On Magic Realism in Film," *Signatures of the Visible* (New York: Routledge, 1990), 128.

9. Terry Eagleton, for example, reads the Brontës' fiction as "the opaque but decipherable signs" of the pressures of an industrializing world outside the text. Underlying such criticism is the assumption that while, as he puts it, "the sisters would certainly have seen a good deal of destitution" just beyond the parsonage, the material world stopped at their doorstep. *Myths of Power: A Marxist Study of the Brontës* (New York: Barnes and Noble, 1975), 13.

10. In using only *Wuthering Heights* to show how fiction peripheralized certain groups of British subjects, I may leave the impression that the ethnic periphery had a homogeneity it certainly did not have. Eric Hobsbawm and Terence Ranger, for example, describe how the English deliberately created a tradition for the Scots and the Welsh, as they did for the various territories of India, that gave each of these cultures within the empire its own exotic

past, each as distinct from the others as it was distinct from the English past. *Invention of Tradition,* ed. Eric Hobsbawm and Terence Ranger (Cambridge: Cambridge University Press, 1983), 1–14.

11. It was only in the 1880s, for example, that John Beddoe developed his famous Index of Negrescence to establish racial difference among the various races of Great Britain, one pole of which was marked by an "Africanoid" type of Celt. *The Races of Britain* (London: Trubner, 1885), 9–11.

12. See, for example, E. P. Thompson, *The Making of the English Working Class* (New York: Vintage, 1966); Edward Said, *Orientalism* (New York: Random House, 1979); Gayatri Chakravorty Spivak, "Subaltern Studies: Deconstructing Historiography," *In Other Worlds: Essays in Cultural Politics* (New York: Methuen, 1987); George W. Stocking, *Victorian Anthropology* (New York: Macmillan, 1987); Anita Levy, *Other Women: The Writing of Race, Class, and Gender, 1832–1898* (Princeton: Princeton University Press, 1991).

13. Michael Hechter argues that along with Scotland, Wales, and Ireland, certain areas within England were reconceptualized as an ethnic periphery. The English counties and regions that came to be considered ethnic were those that had traditionally been organized for grazing and open wasteland rather than for raising crops in enclosed fields. The former use of land followed the "Celtic field system." Although this system had all but disappeared by the period I am discussing, Hechter observes that the areas where it had dominated were precisely the peripheral areas that tended to resist the more common English practice of cereal and grass growing and the more typically English distribution of land through private ownership and primogeniture. Yorkshire, where Emily Brontë lived and wrote, was one of those areas. *Internal Colonialism: The Celtic Fringe in British National Development, 1536–1966* (Berkeley: University of California Press, 1975), 58–59.

14. Katie Trumpener's definitive study, *Bardic Nationalism: The Romantic Novel and the British Empire* (Princeton: Princeton University Press, 1997), demonstrates that the novels of Walter Scott, Maria Edgeworth, and the Brontës were only the tip of the iceberg, so immense was the body of literature that aided and abetted internal colonialism. See also Mary Ellis Gibson's fine review essay covering three recent books (including Trumpener's) on this topic: "Representing the Nation: Poetics, Landscape, and Empire in Nineteenth-Century Culture," *Victorian Literature and Culture* 27 (1999): 337–352.

15. "Most typically, such terror translates into the ostensible unreadibility of the colonized subcontinent: from the early travelogues in the seventeenth century to the proliferation of Anglo-Indian fiction in the nineteenth, the dominant Western metaphor for India suggests a spatial intransigence, or a geography so figural that—like the Marabar Caves—it can be read by Western eyes only after its transmutation into a threadbare

and dangerous literalism. This unreadability is of course simply one instance of a discursive transfer of power, which fetishizes a colonial fear of its own cultural ignorance into the potential threats posed by an Indian alterity." Sara Suleri, *The Rhetoric of English India* (Chicago: University of Chicago Press, 1992), 6.

16. In discussing the significance of the various parts of the head, as Mary Cowling points out, R. R. Noel "provide[s] a remarkably clear instance of the identification of the lower orders of advanced societies with primitive races: if we compare the heads of modern savages of the lowest type, and of the brutal and ruffianly natures, still to be met with in highly civilised communities, with the heads of men distinguished for intellectual and moral qualities . . . [we find] they are in the relatively greater development in the heads of the average European, and still more palpably in those of eminently moral and intellectual men, of the frontal and coronal regions . . . In the skulls of the 'primitive Spelaean people,' [now extinct] of modern savages, and of the lowest and most rural class of European populations . . . the parts just mentioned are low and imperfectly developed." *The Artist as Anthropologist: The Representation of Type and Character in Victorian Art* (Cambridge: Cambridge University Press, 1989), 124–125. In *Little Citizens: The Child Victim, the State, and the Victorian Novel* (Charlottesville: University of Virginia Press, 1999), Laura C. Berry offers an insightful analysis of the figuration of the laboring poor as a ravenous man, a Malthusian nightmare come to life. This figure suggested that indigent populations would not only eat us out of house and home but would also eat up the differences between us and them (see especially chap. 1).

17. Barthes concludes his description of the *punctum* as the partial feature, the intrusive accident, the "prick" of time that nails an image to the world outside the frame, by noting that this dimension of a photograph is always a reminder of death. In looking at a photograph, he explains, "I observe with horror an anterior future of which death is the stake. By giving me the absolute past of the pose, . . . the photograph tells me death in the future. What *pricks* me is the discovery of this equivalence." *Camera Lucida: Reflections on Photography*, trans. Richard Howard (New York: Hill and Wang, 1981), 96.

18. Quoted in John Taylor, "The Alphabetic Universe: Photography and the Picturesque Landscape," *Reading Landscape: Country-City-Capital* (Manchester: University of Manchester Press, 1990), 181.

19. Renato Rosaldo, "Imperialist Nostalgia," *Culture and Truth: The Remaking of Social Analysis* (Boston: Beacon Press, 1989), 69.

20. Ibid., 70.

21. Ibid.

22. In "The Alphabetic Universe," Taylor describes the changes that

tourism wrought upon the landscape as pervasive and swift. See also E. P. Thompson's account of the dismantling of local artisan cultures in *The Making of the English Working Class*, 543–552.

23. Arjun Appadurai points out that while the new technologies of visuality gave the consumer a sense of mastery over an expanding visible universe, the same technologies also shifted and nuanced the middle-brow standard of taste and sold that consumer a notion of what he or she should know, should desire, indeed should be. "Introduction: Commodities and the Politics of Value," *The Social Life of Things*, ed. Arjun Appadurai (Cambridge: Cambridge University Press, 1986), 3–63.

24. I have taken this term, as well as the cultural logic it stands for, from Hechter's title, *Internal Colonialism: The Celtic Fringe in British National Development, 1536–1966*.

25. Charles Percy Sanger concludes his detailed historical analysis of the laws governing marriage and inheritance in *Wuthering Heights* with this remark: "There is, so far as I know, no other novel in the world which it is possible to subject to an analysis of the kind I have tried to make." "The Structure of *Wuthering Heights*," in Emily Brontë, *Wuthering Heights*, ed. William Sale, Jr. (New York: Norton, 1972), 25. All citations to *Wuthering Heights* are from this edition and are identified by page numbers in the text. How does one reconcile Brontë's scrupulous attention to the legal restrictions on marriage and inheritance with her strong suggestions that many of the marriages and patterns of inheritance taking place in the novel are perverse if not criminal acts? We have to assume that while she had a detailed knowledge of the legal literature on these matters, Brontë was also aware of competing cultural rules for kinship and rights of land use.

26. Quoted in Richard Dorson, *The British Folklorists: A History* (Chicago: University of Chicago Press, 1968), 83.

27. Richard Dorson, ed., *Peasant Customs and Savage Myths: Selections from the British Folklorists* (Chicago: University of Chicago Press, 1968), I, 1.

28. Ibid., I, 11.

29. Quoted in David Vincent, *Literacy and Popular Culture, England 1750–1914* (Cambridge: Cambridge University Press, 1989), 156.

30. Dorson, *Peasant Customs and Savage Myths*, I, 38.

31. In his "Preface to the Second Edition of the Lyrical Ballads," poems that claim to be based on those collected by folklorists, William Wordsworth as much as makes this point, when he contends: "it will be the wish of the Poet to bring his feelings near to those of the persons whose feelings he describes, nay, for short spaces of time, perhaps, to let himself slip into an entire delusion, and even confound and identify his own feelings with theirs." *Criticism: The Major Texts*, ed. Walter Jackson Bates (New York: Harcourt, Brace, and World, 1952), 340.

32. Thoms began his career as a folklorist by apologizing for his subject

matter and lamenting the recalcitrance of local beliefs and customs. By 1846, however, when he launched his column in *The Atheneum*, he offered as a rationale for that column these two observations: "—the first, how much that is curious and interesting in these matters is now entirely lost—the second, how much may still be rescued by timely exertion. What Hone endeavored to do by his 'Every-Day Book' &c., *The Atheneum*, by its wider circulation, may accomplish ten times more effectually—gather together the thousands of readers, and preserve them in its pages." Dorson, *Peasant Customs and Savage Myths*, I, 53. Dorson prefaces this declaration by Thoms as "the stock grievance echoed by all folklorists" from the inauguration of Thoms's column in 1846 to the present day, Dorson, *Peasant Customs and Savage Myths*, I, 52.

33. George Borrow, *Lavengro: The Scholar—The Gypsy—The Priest* (New York: Dover, 1991), vii. It is worth noting that Borrow's extended account of his travels through Wales, entitled *Wild Wales* (1862), participated directly in the project that Hobsbawm and Ranger call "the invention of tradition." It is helpful to regard men such as Borrow as intellectual tourists. By seeing, they presumed to know, and by writing down what they had seen, such men sought to establish their superiority as sensitive and sophisticated observers. I quote at some length a biographer's impressions of Borrow in order to suggest that these impressions could just as easily apply to Brontë's Lockwood: "Borrow's work is never documentary: everything he wrote is a function of his remarkable character. He is always singularly urbane but his is a brand of urbanity that alerts the reader to an unsettling ambivalence of tone, something that hints, suggests, or even makes blatantly obvious, that not everything is being said that might be said. The intrepid Victorian traveller so frequently writes like an extrovert that his reader can be quite chagrined to realize he is not . . . That Borrow, in telling us so much, refuses to tell us all makes us inquisitive about his private life." Michael Collie, *George Borrow, Eccentric* (Cambridge: Cambridge University Press, 1982), 1–2.

34. In *The Politics and Poetics of Transgression* (London: Methuen, 1986), 125–203, Peter Stallybrass and Allon White identify some of the ways in which local customs, especially those maintaining a pre-individualistic understanding of social identity, survived on into the modern age at local sites, in the practices associated with leisure time and the peculiar organization of bourgeois neuroses.

35. In "Images of Decay: Photography in the Picturesque Tradition," *October* 54 (1990), Wolfgang Kemp identifies two sources of the appeal of such images of decay. First, "the admirer of the picturesque sets himself apart from the standards of taste of the average consumer of art. He adopts a distanced relation to the object of his look by consciously disregarding the object's utilitarian value" (107). The second source of pleasure is related to the first but turns away from aesthetics in the direction of practicalities: "The

picturesque offers no ready symmetries, no easily identifiable compositional schemes. Recognizing and appreciating these qualities is an important achievement for the adept of the picturesque, perhaps even the decisive achievement in the process of learning to see. In short, the picturesque is also a didactic principle" (108).

36. Asa Briggs, *A Victorian Portrait* (New York: Harper and Row, 1989), 139.

37. Jacques Derrida begins his analysis of the issue of "truth" in Van Gogh's "shoe painting" with this remark: "we've got a ghost story on our hands here all right." *The Truth in Painting*, trans. Geoff Bennington and Ian McLeod (Chicago: University of Chicago Press, 1987), 257. Derrida describes Meyer Shapiro's critique of Heidegger's reading of the shoes as a conflict between two different ways of returning the pair of shoes to an absent owner. To say "the shoes of" is much the same as saying "the ghost of" in this analysis. Another clearly related question arises from the fact that the shoes both do and do not appear in the photographs I have been discussing. The Scottish fisher girl is marked as a fake, for example, because she is obviously in someone else's shoes, which automatically shifts our attention away from the owner of those shoes and onto the flesh that has no right to fill them; the truth of the model would become visible only in a pornographic image that removed all the clothing that is not hers, clothing that appears to have no rightful owner. Her "truth" exists in opposition to that of respectable women, which becomes visible only in portraits that display their economic status and quality of taste in the clothing that belongs to them—that indeed *is* their body—or, alternatively, in spirit photographs where the body indicates the absence of any flesh at all.

38. My discussion of miniaturization is indebted to Susan Stewart's *On Longing: Narratives of the Miniature, the Gigantic, the Souvenir, the Collection* (Baltimore: Johns Hopkins University Press, 1984).

39. The problem with naming the people who were not doing the classifying is that I must to some degree reproduce the very classification system I am describing. I refer to these people alternately as "natives," "indigenous peoples," "local" or "regional" populations, and occasionally "ethnics," when they were in fact British people.

40. Charlotte Brontë, "Editor's preface to the New Edition of *Wuthering Heights*," *Wuthering Heights*, 9.

41. Ibid., 10.

5 SEXUALITY IN THE AGE OF REALISM

1. Of particular importance in this regard was the rise of physical anthropology championed in England by the Anthropological Society of London. In *Victorian Anthropology* (New York: Macmillan, 1987), George W.

Stocking, Jr., explains how the publication of Darwin's *The Origin of Species* in 1859 changed what had been the prevailing theory of racial difference first elaborated by J. C. Prichard in 1808. Prichard rejected polygenesis, or the theory of multiple origins for man, in order to maintain the absolute difference between man and animal. He used the concept of degeneration to account for the variety of bodies that human beings inhabited and the very different cultural traditions they practiced. Challenging this monogenesist position were those who saw, as Robert Knox wrote in *The races of men: A philosophical enquiry into the influences of race over the destinies of Nations* (1850), that "no good reason exists for regarding man as a distinct creation from the living world" (quoted in Stocking, 69). On the basis of physical evidence, polygenesists argued that different races had originated from different centers of creation and remained unchanged through most of human history. Different races assimilated to each other's climates only with difficulty, according to this view, and interbred infrequently. From these inferences, they concluded that mankind was not one but several species. Darwin's theory of evolution challenged the twin assumptions that man began as many species that had subsequently remained much the same, but post-Darwinian anthropology nonetheless retained many aspects of polygenesis: "the emphasis on classification in biological terms; the correlation of physical type and cultural achievement; the incorporation of a static racial hierarchy into a dynamic evolutionary sequence; the rejection of [the] biblical assumption [that man differed from the rest of nature]; and the insistence that man be studied as part of the natural world" (183). Stocking summarizes Darwin's impact on Victorian anthropology in these terms: "In the beginning, black savages and white savages had been psychologically one. But while white savages were busily acquiring superior brains in the course of cultural progress, dark-skinned savages had remained back near the beginning. Although united in origin with the rest of mankind, their assumed inferiority of culture and capacity now reduced them to the status of missing links in the evolutionary chain. Their cultural forms, although at the center of anthropological attention, . . . [were studied] in order to cast light on the processes by which the ape had developed into the British gentleman" (185). For an account of this attempt to formulate an all-encompassing paradigm linking biological superiority to European features, see Ronald Rainger, "Race, Politics, and Science: The Anthropological Society in the 1860s," *Victorian Studies* 22 (1978): 51–70.

2. Edward Said's *Orientalism* (New York: Vintage, 1979) is still the exemplary study of this imaginary relationship. Orientalism, according to Said, was a project that "kept intact the separateness of the Orient, its eccentricity, its backwardness, its silent indifference, its feminine penetrability, its supine malleability." Though mainly a product of scholarship, he maintains, Orientalism nevertheless saw to it that "the Orient existed as a place isolated from

the mainstream of European progress in the sciences, arts, and commerce" (206).

3. Étienne Balibar, "Racism and Nationalism," in Étienne Balibar and Immanuel Wallerstein, *Race, Nation, Class: Ambiguous Identities,* trans. Chris Turner (New York: Verso, 1991), 42.

4. Ibid., 43.

5. Mary Louise Pratt uses the term "contact zone" to refer "to the space of colonial encounters, the space in which peoples geographically and historically separated come into contact with each other and establish ongoing relations, usually involving conditions of coercion, radical inequality, and intractable conflict. I borrow the term 'contact' here from its use in linguistics, where the term contact language refers to improved languages that develop among speakers of different native languages who need to communicate with each other consistently, usually in context of trade. . . . Like the societies of the contact zone, such languages are commonly regarded as chaotic, barbarous, lacking in structure." *Imperial Eyes: Travel Writing and Transculturation* (New York: Routledge, 1992), 6.

6. V. Y. Mudimbe, *The Invention of Africa: Gnosis, Philosophy, and the Order of Knowledge* (Bloomington: Indiana University Press, 1988), 6–7.

7. Katie Trumpener argues that "during the late eighteenth and early nineteenth century, Britain conquered, colonized, and consolidated a vast new empire in North America, Asia, Australia, and Africa. Its formation was anticipated by, then meshed with, the formation of Britain as the 'United Empire of Great Britain and Ireland.' The modern British state, as Michael Hechter has influentially argued, resulted from the internal colonization of Wales, Ireland, and Scotland, building its economic strength on the systematic underdevelopment and impoverishment of these domestic colonies. One British imperialism produces another. The conquest and administration of domestic colonies served as a trial run for the colonization of the overseas empire." *Bardic Nationalism: The Romantic Novel and the British Empire* (Princeton: Princeton University Press, 1997), 249. Although I agree with this formulation up to a point, I believe the stress should be placed on the difference between the two arenas of colonization and the forms of racism they required.

8. One notable instance of such a reaction occurs in the closing pages of *Descent of Man, and Natural Selection in Relation to Sex,* vol. II, ed. John Tyler Bonner and Robert M. May (Princeton: Princeton University Press, 1871; rpt. 1981), as Charles Darwin turns against his own theory of evolution and renounces his relation to primitive man in these phobic terms: "As for my own part I would rather be descended from that heroic little monkey, who braved his dreaded enemy in order to save the life of his keeper; or from that old baboon, who, descending from the mountains, carried away in triumph his younger comrade from a crowd of astonished dogs—as from a savage

who delights to torture his enemies, offers up bloody sacrifices, practises infanticide without remorse, treats his wives like slaves, knows no decency, and is haunted by the grossest superstitions" (404–405). Here, in concluding *Descent,* Darwin shifts briefly and hysterically from the monogenesist view of man he held throughout his work to something like a polygenesist view whereby European man might descend from the ape independently of his African and Oceanic counterparts.

9. For a description of the reflux of Asianness, see Nicholas Daly, "That Obscure Object of Desire: Victorian Commodity Culture and Fictions of the Mummy," *Novel* 28 (1994): 24–51.

10. In *The Rhetoric of British India* (Chicago: University of Chicago Press, 1992), 19, Sara Suleri explains how what began as an ethnographic master plan—*The People of India: A Series of Photographic Illustrations with Descriptive Letter Press of the Races and the Tribes of India* (published serially between 1868 and 1875)—turned out to be "a model of alterity so explosively multifarious that the invading race itself is threatened to be subsumed into [the] powerlessness [of those it has subordinated]. Rather than supply the invader with a key to a system of cultural control, caste represents the symbolic invisibility of the peoples of India, and the disempowering fear that the colonizer cannot function as the other to a colonized civilization that had long since learned to accommodate a multiplicity of alterities into the fabric of its cultures."

11. Judith Walkowitz, *Prostitution and Victorian Society: Women, Class, and the State* (Cambridge: Cambridge University Press, 1980).

12. William Acton, *Prostitution Considered in Its Moral, Social, and Sanitary Aspects* (London: Cass, 1972), 85.

13. Henry Mayhew's *London Labour and the London Poor,* vol. IV (New York: Dover, 1968) provides an excellent demonstration of how criminology interlocked conceptually with the anthropological study of primitive cultures. Less than ten pages into his study of the criminal types comprising the category of "those who will not work," Mayhew felt curiously compelled to define prostitution and provide an encyclopedic description of all its varieties from ancient times to the present day in all the countries of the world: "The general design of this inquiry will be to draw a view of the position occupied by the female sex in different ages and countries, to measure the estimation in which it is held, to fix the accepted standard of morality, to ascertain the recognised significance of the marriage contract, the laws relating to polygamy and concubinage, the value at which feminine virtue and modesty were held, and thus to consider the prostitute in relation to the system of which she formed a part" (37). In this way, Mayhew's research extended the use of a particular brand of heterosexual monogamy from criminalizing the English underclasses to primitivizing other cultures. Simply put, he converted the particular way in which his culture classified women into a universal system for evaluating human beings.

14. Great Britain, *Reports from the Select Committees on the Contagious Diseases Bill and Act* (1866), *British Parliamentary Papers: Health, Infectious Disease,* vol. 4 (Shannon: Irish University Press, 1970), 727.

15. Ibid., 120.

16. Ibid., 730.

17. Ibid., 119.

18. Ibid., 44.

19. Ibid.

20. Ibid., 729.

21. Ibid., 733.

22. This act allowed a grace period of 42 days before the baby had to be registered, and it did not require stillbirths to be registered. Thus there was still considerable opportunity to conceal a baby's existence. For a discussion of this problem, see Lionel Rose, *Massacre of the Innocents: Infanticide in Great Britain, 1800–1939* (London: Routledge, 1986), 121.

23. Ibid., 182–186.

24. Elaine Showalter, *The Female Malady: Women, Madness, and English Culture 1830–1880* (New York: Pantheon, 1985), 106.

25. Ibid., 107.

26. It should be noted that the procedures for examining prostitutes under the Contagious Diseases Acts were already working, however unconsciously, within a model that detected symmetrical disfigurations at both ends of the female body. William Acton proposes the following list of symptoms gathered from twenty-four female patients admitted to St. Bartholemew's Hospital (26 November 1840): "1. Bubo, sore at the entrance to vagina. 2. Sores. 3. Condylomata, excoriation. 4. Itch, gonorrhoea, excoriation. 5. Suppurating bubo, gonorrhea. 6. Warts, gonorrhea. 7. Very large sores on thighs. 8. Two large sores on vulva, two buboes. 9. Gonorrhoea, excoriated tongue. 10. Excoriations around the anus. 11. Condylomata of the vulva (very red), two buboes. 12. Very large condylomata, excoriation of the throat. 13. Condylomata, itch, and a curious eruption. 14. A small sore on vulva, eruption on body, sore throat. 15. Discharge from vagina, raised condylomata. 16. Sores on the labium, perhaps primary. 17. Condylomata. 18. Eczema, itch, phagedaenic sores. 19. Condylomata, excoriation very extensive. 20. Very large condylomata, white excoriation between toes, and on throat. 21. Condylomata, very extensive affectation of the tongue. 22. Condylomata. 23. Discharge from vagina, superficial ulceration. 24. Two buboes, condylomata." It is noteworthy that when Acton names an afflicted body part, it is either in the mouth or the genital area. He not only zones and links these two areas in examining infected prostitutes but also turns this list into a system for gathering future data. "As each patient is inspected," he suggests, "make a cross upon the proper line, and when the consultation is

over, you will have a tabulated view of the forms of disease it has presented to your notice." *Prostitution Considered,* 52.

27. This practice is closely related to the claims of a reverse Darwinism. See, for example, Daniel Pick, *Faces of Degeneration: A European Disorder, c. 1848–1918* (Cambridge: Cambridge University Press, 1989); Sandor L. Gilman, *Difference and Pathology: Stereotypes of Sexuality, Race, and Madness* (Ithaca: Cornell University Press, 1985), 191–216; and David G. Horn, "The Norm Which Is Not One: Reading the Female Body in Lombroso's Anthropology," *Deviant Bodies,* ed. Jennifer Terry and Jacqueline Urla (Bloomington: Indiana University Press, 1995), 109–128. It is not surprising to discover that attacks on the women's movement of the nineteenth century might represent feminist activists as physiologically different from the "normal" European woman. Cynthia Eagle Russett quotes a Victorian anthropologist who "denounced the 'superficial, flat-chested, thin-voiced Amazons, who are pouring forth sickening prate about the tryanny of men and the slavery of women.'" *Sexual Science: The Victorian Construction of Womanhood* (Cambridge, Mass.: Harvard University Press, 1989), 27.

28. In "Gender, Race, and Nation," *Deviant Bodies,* ed. Jennifer Terry and Jacqueline Urla, Anne Fausto-Sterling asks why nineteenth-century scientists were so preoccupied with the physical features distinguishing Hottentot women, since "the peoples whom the early Dutch explorers named Hottentot had been extinct as a coherent cultural group since the late 1600s." Fausto-Sterling investigates the process by which an African woman named Sarah Bartmann was during her life and after her death in 1815 classified as alternately Hottentot and Bushwoman by Georges Cuvier's relatively conscientious dissection and comparison of her body to those of other racially marked women. "Human racial difference," Fausto-Sterling concludes, "while in some sense obvious and therefore 'real,' is in another sense pure fabrication, a story written about the social relations of a particular historical time and then mapped onto available bodies" (21).

29. See Darwin Marable, "Photography and Human Behavior in the Nineteenth Century," *History of Photography* 9 (1985): 141–147, and Allan Sekula, "The Body and the Archive," *October* 59 (1986): 3–64.

30. Keith F. Davis, *Désiré Charnay, Expeditionary Photographer* (Albuquerque: University of New Mexico Press, 1981).

31. In the colonies, the European prostitute created a special kind of categorical confusion. Margaret Macmillan writes: "Although a speaker at a meeting on 'Social Evil' in Bombay in 1891 congratulated himself that there was not a single English girl among them, it was feared that Indians might not be able to see the distinction. Not surprisingly, there was also concern in official and unofficial circles over pornography that involved European women." *Women of the Raj* (London: Thames and Hudson, 1988), 53.

32. From early on, the nascent art of advertising used the colonial body to ply its wares. See, for example, Thomas Richards, *The Commodity Culture of Victorian England: Advertising and Spectacle, 1851–1914* (Stanford: Stanford University Press, 1990), 119–167.

33. Lewis Carroll, *Alice's Adventures in Wonderland and Through the Looking Glass* (New York: New American, 1960). All citations are to this edition and are identified by page numbers in the text.

34. In "Falling Alice, Fallen Women, and Victorian Dream Children," *Carroll Studies* 6 (1982): 46–64, Nina Auerbach has described this fall as "a loving parody of Genesis" and linked it to Alice's appetite.

35. Jennifer Wicke, *Advertising Fictions: Literature, Advertisement, and Social Reading* (New York: Columbia University Press, 1988).

36. See Rachel Bowlby, *Just Looking: Consumer Culture in Dreiser, Gissing, and Zola* (New York: Methuen, 1985).

37. In *The Bourgeois and the Bibelot* (New Brunswick: Rutgers University Press, 1984), 42, Rémy G. Saisselin offers a useful encapsulation of the historical forces that made possible this regendering—and thus the restaging—of consumption: "For the first time in history the women of the bourgeoisie found themselves free and with leisure time, whereas formerly they had tended to stay at home and participate in the economic life of the household. The capital accumulation of the nineteenth century made it possible for women of this class to enjoy a certain leisure, leave their interiors, and lead a form of aristocratic life modeled on that of the old nobility. The men worked to assure the women the possibility of conspicuous consumption. This contrast of occupations between men and women was manifest even in their dress: the masculine fashions remained sober, economic, puritan even, while the feminine costume or dress was allowed to be courtly, that is, colorful, luxurious, flowing, impractical, expensive, decorative. Women set the fashion rather than men as had been the case in the old courtly society."

38. As Thomas Richards explains, "the consumer was queen and the queen was a consumer, and festivals like the Jubilees served to dramatize that monarch and commoner alike were equals in the eyes of the market." *The Commodity Culture of Victorian England*, 163.

39. Elaborating the ways in which art collaborated with commercialism to woo the female shopper, Rémy Saisselin declares that "the entire machine of the store—the architecture, special displays, special sales and events—was directed to one end: the seduction of woman. It was the modern devil tempting the modern Eve." *The Bourgeois and the Bibelot*, 39.

40. See Elaine S. Abelson, *When Ladies Go A-Thieving: Middle-Class Shoplifters in the Victorian Department Store* (New York: Oxford University Press, 1989).

41. In *Dangerous Sexualities: Medico-Moral Politics in England since 1830*

(London: Routledge, 1987), Frank Mort argues that a double standard in sexual conduct for men and women shaped the new sexology whereby male continence was desirable but could not be guaranteed because of the strength of the male urge (79). What could be guaranteed was female purity and therefore their impurity as well. Around mid-century, he explains, this "had a profound effect on class-specific forms of male sexuality. . . . Both written and visual pornography represented women for the male gaze across the virtue/vice, innocence/depravity oppositions. The clearest examples were in the early photographic studies of child prostitutes dating from the 1860s and 1870s, where childhood innocence was erotically framed against visible signs of immoral sexuality, such as exposed genitalia or the depraved stare" (84). These and other examples, he continues, "reveal a link between the growing polarization of official definitions of female sexuality and the sexualization of those representations in the fantasies of certain groups of men" (86). Particularly germane to my argument, first, is Mort's description of child pornography as a genre that transplants the features of the other woman (exposed genitalia and a depraved state) onto its very antithesis, the English girl. Second is his use of the double figure of the woman to explain how male desire was historically deflected away from marriageable English women and onto women with whom it was culturally impossible to mate.

42. For a discussion of possible sources for the Duchess illustrations, see Michael Hancher, *The Tenniel Illustrations to the "Alice" Books* (Columbus: Ohio State University Press, 1985), 41–47. I am indebted to Hancher's study for a number of my observations concerning the *Alice* illustrations, especially the contrast between Carroll's sketches for *Alice's Adventures under Ground* and Tenniel's illustrations for *Alice's Adventures in Wonderland*.

43. In *Race and the Education of Desire: Foucault's History of Sexuality and the Colonial Order of Things* (Durham: Duke University Press, 1996), Anne Laura Stoler contends that Foucault established this link at several points in his work: "within Foucault's frame, bourgeois identities in both metropole and colony emerge tacitly and emphatically coded by race. Discourses of sexuality do more than define the distinctions of the bourgeois self; in identifying marginal members of the body politic, they have mapped the moral parameters of European nations. These deeply sedimented discourses on sexual morality could redraw the 'interior frontiers' of national communities, frontiers that were secured through—and sometimes in collision with—the boundaries" (7).

44. Arjun Appadurai, *The Social Life of Things: Commodities in Cultural Perspective* (New York: Cambridge University Press, 1986), 3.

45. Ibid., 45.

46. In *Writing in Parts: Imitation and Exchange in Nineteenth-Century Literature* (Stanford: Stanford University Press, 1995), Kevin McLaughlin offers an ingenious new take on this much-pondered section of *Capital* that resonates

with my reading of Wonderland. Demonstrating that the absolute gap between the commodity's form and its physicality is not consistently present in
"The Fetishism of the Commodity and Its Secret," McLaughlin observes:
"With regard to its exchangers, the commodity is independent and in fact
sovereign: it controls its exchangers. This leads to a very strange situation. As
soon as one's labor product becomes a commodity, as soon as one ceases to
be a producer (or a user) and becomes an exchanger, there is a reversal of
roles. The human producer is no longer in the position of authority or
sovereignty with respect to what used to be his or her product. With the
change to exchanger, it is as though one were transformed from a parent
into a child—a child, in fact, of one's 'own' orphan[ed product]" (11).

47. Appadurai, *The Social Life of Things*, 56.

48. William Minter, *King Solomon's Mines Revisited: Western Interests and
the Burdened History of Southern Africa* (New York: Basic Books, 1986), 3.

49. H. Rider Haggard, *Three Adventure Novels: She, King Solomon's Mines,
Allan Quatermain* (New York: Dover, 1951), 287–288. All citations to *King
Solomon's Mines* are to this edition and are identified by page numbers in the
text.

50. J. Robinson, "The Social Aspects of Colonialism," *Proceedings of the
Royal Colonial Institute* 1 (1870): 135–161.

51. Wayne Koestenbaum has discussed the homosocial erotics of Haggard's writing for the "boy-reader" who was "often a grown man" (151–161).
Koestenbaum suggests that the rise of pure romance by male authors in the
latter half of the nineteenth century offered "a refuge not only from
women's fiction, but from an England that they imagined Queen Victoria
had feminized." *Double Talk: The Erotics of Male Literary Collaboration* (New
York: Routledge, 1986), 155. Such writing obviously served the interests of
empire as it asserted the manliness of men who were attached to each other
by representing the bond between men as that which held the empire together.

52. In her critique of Gareth Stedman Jones's *Languages of Class,* Joan
Scott demonstrates that Chartism was in part defeated by the unconscious
sexism of its rhetoric. Scott writes, "The 'language' of class, as Chartists
spoke it, placed women (and children) in auxiliary and dependent positions. If women mounted speakers' platforms, organized consumer boycotts,
and founded special societies of their own, they did so under the Chartist
aegis to demand male suffrage and thus assert property rights that came to
them through their husbands' and fathers' labor." *Gender and the Politics of
History* (New York: Columbia University Press, 1988), 64–65. The Chartists
acceded to the middle-class concept of gender, in other words, when they
made a deal to remove women from the labor pool and base their political
rights on the fact that ownership of one's labor entitles one to political rights
because it defines one as male. Economic dependency is automatically

feminizing within such a frame of reference—feminizing and politically dis-
enfranchising at once.

53. Eve Sedgwick argues that the kind of anxiety animating late nineteenth-century fiction was a precondition for the kind of bonding that could
maintain an empire. For such anxiety, she says, the "term is 'homophobia.'
In the English Gothic novel, the possibility—the attraction, the danger—of
simply dropping the female middle term becomes an explicit, indeed an
obsessional literary subject. With it comes a much more tightly organized,
openly proscriptive approach to sexuality and homosocial bonding." *Between
Men: English Literature and Male Homosexual Desire* (New York: Columbia University Press, 1985), 82.

6 AUTHENTICITY AFTER PHOTOGRAPHY

1. I borrow this term from the title of Andreas Huyssen's *After the Great
Divide: Modernism, Mass Culture, Postmodernism* (Bloomington: University of
Indiana Press, 1986).

2. Virginia Woolf, "Mr. Bennett and Mrs. Brown," *Approaches to the Novel:
Materials for a Poetics*, ed. Robert Scholes (Scranton, Pa.: Chandler, 1966),
199.

3. Ibid., 190.

4. Ibid.

5. If any one critical work can be credited with establishing this double
antagonism beyond any shadow of a doubt, it would have to be Andreas
Huyssen's "Mass Culture as Woman," in *After the Great Divide*, 22–62.

6. See Thomas Crow, "Modernism and Mass Culture in the Visual Arts,"
in *Modernism and Modernity: The Vancouver Conference Papers*, ed. Benjamin
Buchloch, Serge Guilbaut, and David Solkin (Halifax: Nova Scotia College of
Art and Design, 1981), 215–264.

7. See Suzanne Clark, *Sentimental Modernism: Women Writers and the Revolution of the Word* (Bloomington: University of Indiana Press, 1991). In "Virility and Domination in Early Twentieth-Century Vanguard Painting," Carol
Duncan observes: "In the decade before World War I, a number of European
artists began painting pictures with a similar and distinctive content. In both
imagery and style, these paintings forcefully assert the virile, vigorous and
uninhibited sexual appetite of the artist." *Feminism and Art History*, ed.
Norma Broude and Mary D. Garrad (New York: Harper & Row, 1982), 292.

8. In addition to Andreas Huyssen, see Diana Crane, *The Transformation
of the Avant-Garde* (Chicago: University of Chicago Press, 1987), 11–136;
Sally Price, *Primitive Art in Civilized Places* (Chicago: University of Chicago
Press, 1989); Mariana Torgovnik, *Gone Primitive: Savage Intellects, Modern Lives*
(Chicago: University of Chicago Press, 1990); Douglas Crimp, *On the Mu-
seum's Ruins* (Cambridge: MIT Press, 1993), 13–25.

9. It is worth recalling that an explosion of popular lithographic images preceded the development of photographic technology and the wide dissemination of photographic images. Beatrice Farwell has observed how easily the form and subject matter of lithographic images blended with those of photography during the 1860s. Moreover, she points out how adaptable for high-art purposes lithography also proved to be in the hands of Courbet, Manet, and others. *The Cult of Images: Baudelaire and the 19th-Century Media Explosion* (Santa Barbara: University of California Press, 1977).

10. This point is most eloquently made by Michael Fried's study of the spectacle haunting Thomas Eakins's painting and the graphic element shaping Stephen Crane's prose, in *Realism, Writing, Disfiguration: on Thomas Eakins and Stephen Crane* (Chicago: University of Chicago Press, 1987). Also see *Spectacles of Realism: Body, Gender, Genre*, ed. Margaret Cohen and Christopher Prendergast (Minneapolis: University of Minnesota Press, 1995).

11. In her article on the historically changing ontology of photographic images, Sarah Kember summarizes the foundational assumptions guiding nineteenth-century photographic practice and reception: "Positivism is regarded as photography's originary and formative way of thinking. It appears to transcend historical and disciplinary boundaries and constitute the stable foundation of realist and documentary practices." "The Shadow of the Object: Photography and Realism," *Textual Practice* 10 (1996): 153.

12. In comparing the rival photographers H. P. Robinson and P. H. Emerson, Ellen Handy observes, "Robinson's pictures remained largely the same before, during, and after Emerson's challenge of his photographic position [i.e., the claim he was an artist]. He would not have guessed that he would be all but forgotten so quickly after his death, nor that it would be Emerson whose ideas would be associated with the rise of the American Photo-succession [the avant-garde photographic society, led by Stieglitz], rather than his own." "Pictorial Beauties, Natural Truths, Photographic Practices," in *Pictorial Effect, Naturalistic Vision*, ed. Ellen Handy (Norfolk, Va.: The Chrysler Museum, 1994), 23. Shelley Rice identifies the overlap between Emerson's aesthetic theory and the practices associated with modernism: "With Emerson, art became an internal state, and photography the medium to turn that state inside out." "Parallel Universes," in *Pictorial Effect, Naturalistic Vision*, 65. Abigail Solomon Godeau reminds us that modernist photographers undertook—as part of their project to make photography a recognized art form—the first comprehensive look back at early photography. As part of this effort, Stieglitz reproduced photographs by Julia Margaret Cameron in his magazine *Camera Work, Photography at the Dock: Essays on Photographic History, Institutions, and Practices* (Minneapolis: University of Minnesota Press, 1991), 110.

13. In this respect, the pictorialists did follow Emerson's advice: "Painting alone is our master." Emerson, "Photography, A Pictorial Art," in *Photog-*

raphy: Essays and Images, ed. Beaumont Newhall (New York: The Museum of Modern Art, 1980), 160.

14. Sadakichi Hartmann, "A Plea for Straight Photography," in *Photography: Essays and Images,* 185.

15. Far from accepting contemporary developments in psychology, according to Martin Jay, modernism often found it necessary to set itself in opposition to what philosophers of that period called "psychologism": "Modernism, as Andreas Huyssen has shown, often defended itself against a feminized version of mass culture, which it stigmatized as a debased kitsch. Not surprisingly, one weapon in its battle with these demons was the exorcism of psychologism in the name of a universalism that would, however, be based on non-scientific values." "Modernism and the Specter of Psychologism," *Modernism/Modernity* 3 (1996): 97. Despite their necessarily different oppositional strategies, as I will show, this same objection to psychologism holds true for literary as well as photographic modernism.

16. Hartmann, "A Plea for Straight Photography," 187. Frederick Evans describes photographic styles in overtly gendered terms, when he claims to prefer "the proved charms of Mdlle. Platinotype, rather than flee to the 'uncertain, coy, and hard to please, and most villainously named, Miss Gum Print,'" in honor of the gumming method associated with pictorialism (in *Photography: Essays and Images,* 182).

17. Rosalind Krauss, *The Originality of the Avant-Garde and Other Modernist Myths* (Cambridge: MIT Press, 1991), 109.

18. Ibid., 110.

19. I am of course referring to Laura Mulvey's argument first made in "Visual Pleasure and Narrative Cinema," *Screen* 16, 3 (1975): 6–18.

20. Vicki Goldberg's review of a Stieglitz show supports the view that O'Keeffe was Stieglitz's production, when she pronounces the pair "just about the public's favorite art couple, having the slight advantages of being more beautiful than Lee Krasner and Jackson Pollock and more American than Frida Kahlo and Diego Rivera . . . They created a sensation in 1921 when he showed his portraits of her, some in the nude, while he was still legally married to someone else. These photographs not only catapulted their passion into the newspapers but brought the public flocking to O'Keeffe's next show." *New York Times,* September 17, 1995, 35.

21. Christine Froula, *Modernism's Body: Sex, Culture, Joyce* (New York: Columbia University Press, 1996), undertakes a literary-critical investigation of a similar phenomenon in Joyce.

22. Carol Duncan explains how a second generation of avant-garde painters shifted away from the *femmes fatales* of the symboliste period. Like their predecessors, this generation "believed that authentic art speaks of the central problems of existence, and they, too, defined Life in terms of a male situation—specifically the situation of the middle-class male struggling

against the strictures of modern, bourgeois society." But these artists pushed women all the way over to the nature side of the culture-nature dichotomy, where the painter proved his masculinity by mastering her pictorially. When, near the end of her discussion, Duncan considers why these paintings were sought by collectors, however, she feels compelled to modify the binary terms of her analysis. The collector, she notes, is "acquiring another man's sexual-aesthetic experience. His relationship to the nude is mediated by another man's virility, much to the benefit of his own sense of sexual identity and superiority . . . They are more about power than pleasure." Duncan also makes an interesting attempt at explaining what women got out of having paintings of sexually subjected women hanging on their walls: "no doubt there were women who, proud of their modernity, could value them as emblems of their own progressive attitudes and daring lack of prudery. Finally, we can speculate that some women, frightened by suffragist and emancipation movements, needed to reaffirm—not contest—their situation. The nude on the wall, however uncomfortable it may have been in some respects, could be reassuring to wife as well as the husband." "Virility and Domination," 295, 312–313. My own view is closer to that of Rosalind Krauss. Choosing photography as more central than painting to the conceptual logic of surrealism, she contends, "if there is any question of phallicism here, it is to be found within the whole photographic enterprise of framing and thereby capturing a subject." *Originality of the Avant-Garde*, 90–91. By picturing things that could not possibly exist outside the photographic frame, surrealism gave the photographic image new authority, not over women, I would argue, but over popular images that depend for meaning and value on their subject matter.

23. Barbara Buhler Lynes offers a more nuanced sense of the mutually mystifying relationship that Stieglitz and O'Keeffe conducted through his photographs of her: "In some of these prints, she was dressed in starkly tailored suits and crisp hats, or she posed with a cape wrapped around her body. . . . In other prints, however, she wore a simple dress or a blouse and skirt, looked away from the viewer, and conveyed a passive and demure innocence. . . . From the photographs that presented O'Keeffe as a sexual creature, a third type of woman emerged . . . In these photographs, she became an alluring and provocative female. In others, Stieglitz conveyed the essence of her sexual power at the same time that he overtly declared his compositional skills as a photographer . . . By repeatedly posing her with her work, Stieglitz also made it clear that the woman in his photographs was an artist." In his 1921 show at the Anderson Galleries, almost one-third of the prints exhibited were of O'Keeffe. As the reviewer Henry McBride put it, "Mona Lisa got but one portrait of herself worth talking about. O'Keeffe got a hundred." A few months later, Stieglitz transformed that visibility into something quite new and more sensational: "All at once, someone ran down

Notes to Page 260

Fifth Avenue crying that Alfred Stieglitz had put a price of $5,000 on one of the photographs, a nude, one that was a unique impression with the plate destroyed. Gracious heavens! $5,000 for a mere photograph!" *O'Keeffe, Stieglitz, and the Critics, 1916–1929* (Chicago: University of Chicago Press, 1989), 37–43.

24. Roland Barthes describes such a repertoire of poses as an inextricable part of the modern individual's identity and offers his own experience as a photographic subject as demonstration: "I constitute myself in the process of 'posing,' I instantaneously make another body for myself, I transform myself into an image." *Camera Lucida: Reflections on Photography*, trans. Richard Howard (New York: Hill and Wang, 1981), 10.

25. John Tagg, "The Discontinuous City: Picturing and the Discursive Field," in *Visual Culture: Images and Interpretations*, ed. Norman Bryson, Michael Ann Holly, and Keith Moxey (Hanover, N.H.: Wesleyan University Press, 1994), 83–103.

26. Mary Ann Doane, "Film and Masquerade: Theorizing the Female Spectator," in *The Sexual Subject: A Screen Reader in Sexuality* (New York: Routledge, 1992), 227–243.

27. D. A. Miller, *The Novel and the Police* (Berkeley: University of California Press, 1988).

28. See Anita Levy, "Public Spaces and Private Eyes: Specular Aesthetics in *Villette*," in *Reproductive Urges: Popular Novel-Reading, Sexuality, and the English Nation* (Philadelphia: University of Pennsylvania Press, 1999). I thank the author for allowing me to read this essay in manuscript.

29. Linda Williams, *Hard Core: The Frenzy of the Visible* (Berkeley: University of California Press, 1989), 45–57.

30. Abigail Solomon-Godeau explains the medium-specificity of pornographic photography in terms that suggest it anticipates not only pornographic cinema but modernism as well: "If photography fosters and facilitates a conception of the erotic as a sight, I would suggest that it also constructs an erotics of the fragment, the body part. Indeed, images of the fragmented body—notably, those that isolate the genitals or sexually coded parts of the body—are an important subgenre of pornographic photography." *Photography at the Dock*, 236.

31. D. H. Lawrence, "Pornography and Obscenity," in *Selected Literary Criticism* (London: Heinemann, 1955), 37.

32. D. H. Lawrence, *Lady Chatterley's Lover* (New York: Penguin, 1959), 231–232.

33. While the contributors to a collection of what the editors call "some of the most significant criticism of Joyce to have appeared in French journals over the last twenty years" eschew the term "stream-of-consciousness," their readings of Joyce reproduce much the same brand of formalism in theoretically updated terms. Each regards the Joycean text as an especially labyrin-

thine differential system that contains the outside on the inside. "The text," as Stephen Heath explains, "is never closed and the 'ideal reader' will be the one who accedes to the play of this incompletion placed in 'a situation of writing' [as opposed to reading], ready no longer to master the text but now to become its actor." "Ambiviolences: Notes for Reading Joyce," in *Post-Structuralist Joyce*, ed. Derek Attridge and Daniel Ferrer (Cambridge: Cambridge University Press, 1984), 32.

34. In the wake of feminist theory, many Joyceans feel that Joyce succeeds in this respect. See Richard Pearce, "How Does Molly Bloom Look Through the Male Gaze?" (49), and Kimberly J. Devlin, "Pretending in 'Penelope': Masquerade, Mimicry, and Molly Bloom" (100), both in *Molly Blooms: A Polylogue on "Penelope" and Cultural Studies*, ed. Richard Pearce (Madison: University of Wisconsin Press, 1994).

35. Franco Moretti, *Modern Epic: The World-System from Goethe to Garcia-Marquez*, trans. Quintin Hoare (London: Verso, 1996).

36. James Joyce, *Ulysses* (New York: Vintage, 1934), 780.

37. E. M. Forster, *Maurice; A Novel* (New York: W. W. Norton, 1971), 226. Citations to this novel are to this edition.

38. As late as 1960, Forster lamented that the Wolfenden proposals to decriminalize both pornographic literature and homosexual relations between consenting adults had been rejected by Parliament and the book could not be published. There was little hope, he said, "for the generous recognition of an emotion and for the reintegration of something primitive into the common stock." "Terminal Note," in *Maurice*, 255.

39. Judge John M. Woolsey, "Decision of the United States District Court (December 6, 1933) in the case of the United States of America, Libelant v. One Book called 'Ulysses,' Random House, Inc., Claimant," in Joyce, *Ulysses*, xiii.

40. Ibid., xiii.

41. Ibid., xii.

42. "In respect of the recurrent emergence of the theme of sex in the minds of his characters," Woolsey cautions, "it must always be remembered that his locale was Celtic and his season Spring." Ibid., xii.

43. W. J. T. Mitchell claims that contemporary critical theory's concern with "grammatology," "discourse," and the like echoes "Wittgenstein's iconophobia and the general anxiety of linguistic philosophy about visual representation." He regards this anxiety as "a sure sign that a pictorial turn is taking place." *Picture Theory* (Chicago: University of Chicago Press, 1993), 11–13. Martin Jay's *Downcast Eyes: The Denigration of Vision in Twentieth-Century French Thought* (Berkeley: University of California Press, 1994) documents how and from what sources "an essentially ocularphobic discourse has seeped into the pores of French intellectual life" (15). For a concise description of this paradox, see Chris Jenks, "The Centrality of the Eye in Western

Culture, An Introduction," in *Visual Culture,* ed. Chris Jenks (New York: Routledge, 1995), 1–16.

44. This is Slavoj Žižek's reformulation of Lacan's concept of the symptom, "Rossellini: Woman as Symptom of Man," *October* 54 (1990): 21.

45. Rey Chow, *Writing Diaspora: Tactics of Intervention in Contemporary Cultural Studies* (Bloomington: Indiana University Press, 1993), 30.

46. I have in mind only those feminist theories that uncritically accept Laura Mulvey's premise, as famously proposed in "Visual Pleasure and Narrative Cinema," that being looked at is debilitating and disempowering to women, as well as those postcolonial theories that follow Sander Gilman's lead in regarding the photograph simply as one more blunt instrument of colonial power. Sander L. Gilman, *Difference and Pathology: Stereotypes of Sexuality, Race, and Madness* (Ithaca: Cornell University Press, 1985).

47. Chow, *Writing Diaspora,* 31.

48. To exchange the photograph for the mirror in Lacan's description of the mirror phase would be, as I have argued at several points in this book, to convey a significantly more accurate understanding of how basic such images are to our sense of ourselves as complete and autonomous individuals. See Jacques Lacan, "The Mirror Phase," *Écrits,* trans. Alan Sheridan (New York: W. W. Norton, 1977), 1–7.

❧ INDEX ❧

Index

Index

Index

335

Martin, Paul *(continued)*
Flower Seller, 150; Loading up at Billings-gate Market, 101, 104
Marx, Karl, 1, 28–29, 119–123, 230–231; *Capital,* 119
Masculinity, 107, 109, 112, 161, 217, 235, 241, 246, 259–261, 263–264, 268, 270–273, 275
Mass culture, 2–3, 11, 24, 182, 222, 230–232, 246–248, 250, 263, 273
Mass visuality, 24, 29–30, 123, 155, 274
Maudsley, Henry, 212
Mayhew, Henry, *London Labour and the London Poor,* 319n13
McCauley, Elizabeth Anne, 127
Mediation, 14, 29–30, 45, 73, 84, 159
Middle classes, 7, 96, 102; and photography, 22, 90, 118, 146; aesthetic attitudes, 44, 129, 135; interest in landscapes, 60, 63; and city life, 87, 90, 92, 97–98; and domesticity, 107–109, 111–112, 115; as consumers, 123; Dickens's popularity with, 135, 157; interest in folklore, 181; transmission of diseases by, 210; and gender, 219–220, 235, 240–242, 250, 263. *See also* Class; Working classes
Mill, John Stuart, 208
Miller, D. A., 6, 145, 264
Miller, J. Hillis, 136–137
Mimesis, 4–5, 11, 30, 51, 75, 126, 132, 136
Miniaturization, 193–197
Minter, Walter, 235
Mirror phase, 22–24
Mitchell, Timothy, 82–83, 116
Mitchell, W. J. T., 279n1, 293n43
Modernism, 11, 159, 244, 246–277
Modernization, 6, 19, 28, 30, 85, 87, 89–91, 102, 118, 131, 169, 193, 196, 206
Moir & Halkett, 190
Monetary debates, 47–50, 52–57
Moretti, Franco, 269

Mudimbe, V. Y., 204, 207
Munby, A. J., 108

"Native" women, 212–213, 215–216, 219–221, 225, 229, 237–238, 241, 275
Nerval, Gérard de (Gérard Labrunie), 83
Nordau, Max, 162–163, 272
Nudes, 249, *254,* 255–256, *255, 261,* 263

Observers, 33, 37, 75, 77–78, 81, 92, 97–98, 108–109, 177, 260–261
O'Keeffe, Georgia, 253–258
Orientalism, 84, 199, 237

Panopticon, 25
Panoramas, 87–91, 94
Paris, 16, 82, 88, 90, 98
Parliament, 45, 48
Pastoralism, urban, 116
Phrenology, 17, 27, 125, 130
Physiognomy, 17, 27, 125–126, 130, 138, 140, 151, 155, 158, 162
Pictorialism, 5–6, 8, 28, 51–52, 127, 134, 248–249, 252, 259
Picturesque, 32–34, 36–39, 41–47, 50–70, 72–73, 86, 89, 95–98, 101–102, 106, 108, 112–113, 116, 129, 134–135. *See also* Lower picturesque; Urban picturesque
Pleasure, aesthetic, 33–41, 43–44, 47, 50, 54, 59, 61–62
Poe, Edgar Allan: "The Purloined Letter," 151–153
Polygenesis, 317n1
Pornography, 186, 215, 253, 260, 263, 265–268, 270, 272–274
Poverty, 95–97, 102–104, 106, 116, 148, 168–169
Pratt, Mary Louise, 293n42; "contact zone," 318n5
Pre-Raphaelites, 216
Price, Uvedale, 50–51, 53, 56–58, 60
Primitivism, 84, 96, 173, 176–177, 181–